D1602452

China Learns English

China

Learns

English

Language Teaching

and Social Change

in the People's

Republic

Heidi A. Ross

Yale University Press

New Haven and London

Published with assistance from the
Mary Cady Tew Memorial Fund.

Designed by Sonia L. Scanlon.

Set in Sabon type by Rainsford
Type, Danbury, Connecticut.

Printed in the United States of
America by BookCrafters, Inc.,
Chelsea, Michigan.

Library of Congress Cataloging-in-
Publication Data

Ross, Heidi A., 1954–
    China learns English :
language teaching and
social change in the
People's Republic/Heidi A. Ross.
        p. cm.
    Includes bibliographical
references and index.
    ISBN 0-300-05562-5
(hard : alk. paper)
    1. English language—Study
and teaching—Chinese
speakers—Social aspects—China.
2. English philology—Study
and teaching—China—
History—20th century.
3. China—Social conditions—1949–
    4. Educational sociology—China.
I. Title.
    PE1130.C4R67   1993
    428'.007051—dc20   93-7876
                            CIP

A catalogue record for this book is
available from the British Library.

The paper in this book meets the
guidelines for permanence and
durability of the Committee on
Production Guidelines for Book
Longevity of the Council on Library
Resources.

10 9 8 7 6 5 4 3 2 1

Contents

Contents

Acknowledgments

This book celebrates two distinct cultural conversations about the purposes of education and schooling. It reflects foremost the multivocal world of the American university, which could have no finer orators than the educators acknowledged in these pages.

William Cave has offered invaluable assistance in conceptualizing the school as a locus for cultural continuity and change and has shared his rich experience in portraying distant views with honesty and sympathy. Frederick Goodman has infused this undertaking from its inception with an unfailing wit, as well as a continuous generation of moral and financial support. Harriet Mills has turned her involvement in the major dialogues of contemporary Chinese society to the delineation of the traditional values that continue to inform China's commitment to training young linguists. I am most indebted to Cho-yee To, who has not only facilitated with consummate finesse access to the field setting but also has applied a pragmatic turn of mind to the problematic minutiae that plague ethnographic studies.

I am also grateful to the many scholars who have shared their comments and suggestions on various portions of this book. I wish to thank Valerie Suransky for her direction in pointing ethnographic detail toward its larger social meaning and referent. Martin Whyte has generously applied his sociological understanding to the singular and collective lives of the students and teachers potrayed in this study. Chu-yuan Cheng and Chow Hon Kwong have provided beneficial insights on the concept of modernization in China and the role that nineteenth-century self-strengtheners played in its definition. I am especially grateful to Irving Epstein, Ruth Hayhoe, Stanley Rosen, and Lynn Paine for their careful reading of earlier versions of this book.

The American educational conversation in which all these individuals participate is confronted in this book by a very different dialogue, articulated a hemisphere away in the particular voices of teachers at the Lu Xun Language School. I wish to express my gratitude to these colleagues for their tenacity and patience while upholding the promise of learning, through good times and bad. Their lives and work speak powerfully to the crucial importance and fragility of global communication. Only out of respect for their privacy do they remain anonymous in these pages—for which they share no small authorship. This study would have been impossible without their visions of schooling, as it would have been without their friendship, tolerance, and collegiality.

In addition, I thank my students—bright, impatient, and idealistic—for their committed engagement in communication and their hopes to use it for the betterment of others' lives. The ideals sustained by their persistence and dreams are ones for which any nation would feel proud. I only hope I have done justice in the following pages to their sense of future possibility.

Finally, heartfelt thanks to my family, whose concern and curiosity have sustained this project's dual conversation more than they can know. As always, I owe my greatest debt to my husband, Bill, whose understanding bridged the distance of miles and months that writing this book entailed.

Abbreviations

Achievement:
Zhongguo jiaoyu chengjiu 1949–1983
(Achievement of Education in
China Statistics)

Almanac:
Zhongguo jiaoyu nianjian, 1949–1981
(China Education Almanac)

Chronology:
*Zhonghua renmin gongheguo jiaoyu
dashiji 1949–1983* (A Chronology
of Education)

FBIS:
Foreign Broadcast Information
Service, Daily Report, China

JYB:
Zhongguo jiaoyu bao (China
Education News)

JYYJ:
Jiaoyu yanjiu (Education Research)

GMRB:
Guangming ribao (Guangming Daily)

Recorder:
*The Chinese Recorder and
Missionary Journal*

Records:
Records, China Centenary
Missionary Conference

Repository:
The Chinese Repository

Abbreviations

RMJY:

Renmin jiaoyu (People's Education)

RMRB:

Renmin ribao (People's Daily)

SCMP:

Survey of the China Mainland Press

SHJY:

Shanghai jiaoyu

(Shanghai Education)

WHRB:

Wenhui ribao (Wenhui Daily)

China Learns English

Chapter 1
Introduction

What secondary schooling means to Chinese students and their teachers was my chief concern when I traveled to Shanghai as an English teacher and graduate student more than a decade ago. The ensuing years have brought changes to Chinese schools that were scarcely dreamed of by the teachers and students with whom I studied and taught between 1981 and 1983. Likewise, they have prompted a significant reappraisal of Chinese education, which throughout most of the 1980s was portrayed by and to educators in North America as flat, bleak, and relentlessly reproducing the patterns of a monolithic party-state. We now appreciate a multidimensional portrait of China's 90,000 secondary schools, visible to us as spaces for "competing interest groups" that not only embody state directives but also lead to their deflection or erosion (Samoff, 1991, 4–5).

Although the experiences of 50 million Chinese secondary school pupils and their 3 million teachers are no longer equated with the stylized catechism of Chinese national policy, what students and teachers actually do in their classrooms remains unfocused in our imagination. This book, based upon intensive fieldwork between 1981 and 1983 and 18 weeks of additional research conducted in Shanghai in 1988, 1989, and 1991, attempts to capture some of the richness and unpredictability of Chinese school life for a small number of teachers and students at one privileged urban school.

China, like the United States, has its wags who delight the public with acerbic accounts of the regional variations among Chinese dialects, physical statures, and culinary arts. Shanghai inspires bon mots deriding the cultural authenticity of a city that sprang from mud flats and foreign imperialism. In fact, Shanghai has provided a strategic commercial center linking inland and maritime trade for 800 years. With 12 million inhabitants and as many as 100,000 people per square mile in its central districts, Shanghai is a maze of back alleys and boulevards, looming high rises and universities. Still, the municipality claims few venerable landmarks and lacks imperial scale. Shanghai is instead a "crucible of modern China," joining sojourners together on its shores "above the sea" (Wei, 1987).

The heart of Shanghai is bounded to the north by Suzhou Creek, a barge-clogged thoroughfare that winds through business and shopping districts to drain into the Huangpu River, an estuary of the Yangtze.[1] Suzhou Creek arches downward, like a rainbow, where it flows into the harbor. The municipal district that stretches northward from the point where creek and river conjoin is called Hongkou, the rainbow's mouth.

A major bus and trolley exchange fans out from the district's core, Hongkou Park, the site of the tomb of Lu Xun (1881–1936), China's most celebrated twentieth-century writer. Stark walls skirt roads that radiate out from the park into residential neighborhoods and factory compounds. Such walls surround all 4,300 of Shanghai's primary and secondary schools. They define for students and teachers a sense of space and refuge even as they conceal the daily clutter of school life. In the morning their double gates swing back to reveal a jumble of bicycles, dusty playgrounds, and classrooms humming with students. In the evening, gates firmly locked, schools recede behind walls that stretch endlessly down city streets.

One set of these gates is identified by a vertical sign written in Lu Xun's calligraphic style: "The Lu Xun Language School."[2] Beyond the gatehouse a cluster of four-story buildings emerges from vibrant gardens that most students and teachers in China would eye with envy. The main school entrance is flanked by flowers chosen to complement central China's ever-changing seasons. Immediately inside, a lobby wall greets visitors with a hearty HOW ARE YOU? in five languages. Determined rosy-cheeked youths gaze from a mural. They are China on the move. Rockets and jets ignite behind them in an explosion of technological exuberance that sweeps their hair up and away from their faces. A full-length mirror hangs on the wall adjacent to this picture. Every student who rushes to class past it must ask, "Am I like these model children?"

With impish grins, students respond, "Sure!" Then they shout above the noise from surrounding factories and workers' residences, "But we will try harder!" Glancing up from a textbook, two pupils acknowledge, "No one's like that picture, but it's symbolic—to encourage us, to push us forward. We make fun, but in our hearts we know what it *really* means."

1 Consistent with current practice in the People's Republic of China (PRC), the pinyin romanization system is used throughout this text. Exceptions are made for widely recognized forms, such as Chiang Kai-shek and Yangtze River.

2 Shanghai's secondary schools form a close-knit community, and its educators would immediately realize that this name is fictitious. In the interests of confidentiality, the names of the individuals and institutions under direct examination in this study have been fabricated. National, municipal, and local events, activities, and policies, on the other hand, are reported as accurately as possible.

"Am I like these model children?"

A Place of Privilege

Those who hold that global power and influence emanate from largely "First" World centers to largely "Third" World peripheries frequently identify cities and the elites who dwell within them as the crux of modernity. Such urban settings are pivotal in forging the relative balance between modernity and tradition that secures all the more firmly a nation's peripheral status or supplies it with positive alternatives that offset alienation and dependency.

The city of Shanghai is, in this sense, both global periphery and Chinese center. As a "mediator of the educational open door" (Hayhoe, 1988), the city has highly educated academicians, scientists, and business managers who are influenced by their proximity to global networks and benefit from it. In turn, through their facility with foreign languages, international law, and technology, they help shape the content and exchange of knowledge within China. Shanghai's schools are most certainly judged by the criteria of this urban reality—and they make sense only in its context.

Access to the means of the metropole, however, was limited for the nearly half-million pupils who attended Shanghai's 939 junior and senior secondary schools in 1981. Typically, 11- and 12-year-old students entered junior secondary schools for three years of general academic training. Their placement into a particular school was based largely upon academic success in five or six years of primary schooling and their results in secondary school entrance examinations. The majority of junior secondary school graduates in urban Shanghai enrolled in senior secondary schools that offered full-time academic or technical vocational and teacher training courses in three- or four-year programs. For most of these students formal schooling came to an end upon graduation from high school. Only a small minority have been able to receive the tertiary training that leads to positions of influence in Chinese society. Most of these pupils attended Shanghai's key (*zhongdian*) secondary schools.[3]

The Lu Xun Language School (LXLS) is one of Shanghai's 23 municipal key schools and a prime example of what Chinese leaders and educators believe can be accomplished when optimum conditions of funding and effective teaching are realized. Its teaching staff numbered over 100 during the first half of the 1980s; its student body of 500 adolescents, carefully selected from throughout Shanghai's central municipal districts, boarded at the school.[4] Administered jointly by the State Education Commission, the Shanghai Education Bureau, and the university with which it is affiliated,[5] the LXLS is one of seven foreign language schools nationwide offering specialized training in foreign languages to secondary school pupils.

Despite its privileged status, the LXLS lacks the "comforts of abundance" that characterize elite schooling in North America (Lightfoot, 1983, 221). Its architectural lines and decor are uncompromisingly Spartan, a reminder that the LXLS's considerable reputation rests upon a hard-nosed assessment

3   Between 10 and 15 percent of senior secondary school graduates attended tertiary institutions in 1983, compared to approximately 90 percent of LXLS graduates. Four percent of Chinese secondary schools were key schools. For a detailed dis-discussion of key schools during this period see Rosen, 1983.

4   The LXLS's student population increased from 432 students in 1981 to 543 students in 1982. Sixty percent of these students studied English. There were no English language graduates at the LXLS from 1981–1984, due to a student enrollment pattern that was still adjusting to China's post-Cultural Revolution reestablishment of a six-year secondary school curriculum and the discontinuation of the LXLS's primary school sections. Consequently, the LXLS's enrollment in the early 1980s was significantly smaller than it had been in 1966, when over 1,000 students attended the school.

5   The university to which the LXLS is connected was divided in the early 1980s into three major divisions—adult education (*chengren yeyu jiaoyu*), continuing professional education (*houxiu jiaoyu*), and full-time education (*quanrizhi jiaoyu*). The LXLS was administered under the third division and was structurally equivalent to a department.

of the foreign-language proficiency of its graduates. Prescribed requirements for foreign-language teaching and learning are the school's principal criteria for the selection and evaluation of administrators, teachers, and prospective students. Foreign languages are, in fact, described by school leaders as the "primary channel through which students make their contributions to China's modernization efforts."[6]

The LXLS is an extraordinary school. Far from depicting Chinese education writ small, its portrait is a case study with all of the limitations of research that engages in "procedures for counting to one" (Punch, 1986, 5). Yet, even as the school enjoys enviable material and human resources, it also embodies challenges faced by all Chinese secondary school educators as they approach the twenty-first century. Readers are therefore enjoined to question the generalizations about Chinese schooling contained in this study while considering what might be learned about secondary education in general from one exceptional Chinese school.

Culture and the Contested Terrain of Secondary Schooling

Scholars who envision culture as a continuing conversation about what matters most to members of a particular society frequently use "dialogue" as a metaphor for the process of cultural analysis (Bellah, 1985; Spindler, 1987; Marcus and Fischer, 1986; Clifford and Marcus, 1986). This dialogical conception of cultural studies influences my understanding of the LXLS in three ways.

First, culture as dialogue highlights the central theme of this interpretation of Chinese schooling: the power of language to shape what is most worth knowing and to signal who will benefit from that decision. The LXLS illustrates both how language has been used in China as a tool for social control and stratification, and how fluency in foreign languages has been perceived as both a political liability and a valued economic commodity. This ambiguous legacy of the power of language, more than any other factor, defines and complicates the educational aims of the LXLS, and it places the school's students and teachers in precarious, as well as privileged situations.

6 A large amount of taped or directly transcribed interview material appears in this book. Unless otherwise noted, the materials were collected on a daily, informal basis in staff offices and classrooms at the LXLS.

Next, identifying culture and cultural studies as communicative processes reminds us of how problematic human understanding has become in a post-modern world increasingly experienced as decentered and fragmented. This "predicament of culture" is associated across many disciplines with a "profound uncertainty about what constitutes an adequate depiction of social reality" (Lather, 1991, 21). Such uncertainty, as I note later, is an inevitable consequence of accepting cross-cultural research as "intrinsically shaped by power and the struggle against it" (Clifford, 1988, xvi).

Finally, conceptualizing culture as a dialogue in which meanings are won, lost, and reformulated underscores this book's key assumption about schooling worldwide. As primary social agencies for transmitting and reconstructing values, schools are exceptional places for viewing the inconsistencies and struggles that shape a society's pivotal cultural conversations. Schools rarely realize their potentially subversive position since "education falls low in the hierarchy of academic discourses, and can perform the cultural function of obliquely and harmlessly underlining social truths" (Wexler, 1987, 17). Nevertheless, as a locus for arguments about a culture's past, present, and future, schools are "arenas of conflict over the production of knowledge, ideology, and employment, a place where social movements try to meet their needs and fight for the expansion of the access to resources and citizenship rights" (Carnoy, 1989, 9–10).

Because this is true for schools in China as well as in North America, readers may wonder whether the pedagogical imagination of LXLS educators can be put at the service of their own pedagogical lives. My personal response is cautiously in the affirmative. Good schooling in both countries is equated with the cultivation of literate and numerate students who have the capacity for independent and judicious thinking. Critical indictments of "dead" pedagogy, though aimed at different reference points, are prevalent in both China and the United States, the repugnant modus operandi of "stuffing the Peking duck" in China, of "didactics, practice, and little else" in the United States (Sirotnik, 1983).

Educators, leaders, and parents in neither society are especially able to differentiate school's responsibilities from those of other social institutions or are especially clear about how to establish incentives for its self-examination and renewal (Husen, 1979). So we share the troubling question of whether our definitions of educational goodness, be they shaped by visions of unity in China or caught up in the quest for pluralism in the United States, are attainable if the tandem purpose of public schooling is to serve all pupils well.

Despite our doubts, in both countries we persist in making schools represent a quest for meaning and goodness. Schools become our nations symbolically, epitomizing our achievements as well as our failures. We write about schools in extraordinary ways. "Every morning at 8 A.M. the doors of America's high school are opened," we note, and advise, "Walk inside and look into the future of the nation" (Boyer, 1983, 297). We could say the same about entering our markets, or watching our television screens, or patrolling our streets, but somehow in such locations we do not savor the same rhetorical punch. We pick schools as our "safe bit of transference" when we are disillusioned (Sizer, 1984, 1). Schools can make us feel we are doing right by our children, or they can be the first institution we blame when public and private values no longer seem to correspond.

Confusion and anxiety about schooling are inevitable consequences of the inability of schools to resolve the competing, sometimes mutually exclusive, demands we thrust upon them. Just as schools in the United States seek to balance the interests of participatory democracy with the inequalities upon which capitalism is based, Chinese schools must mediate the demands for socialist equality with the requirements of rapid but efficient modernization through the certification of expertise. As American educators grapple with creating schools that can simultaneously advance individual mobility, construct or renovate community, and respect diversity, Chinese educators struggle to align their curricula and teaching methods with state ideological interests *and* the values of a public whose standards of living and social expectations have become remarkably divergent as a result of market socialism and the open door. Schools in the United States and China must above all else accommodate—political movements, student values, the economy. The language of the market (free or controlled) clashes with the language of morality in schools.

With public institutions in both countries embattled, we share the suspicion and myth that schooling might somehow be the last refuge and defense, and from it we demand nothing other than "it all." Not surprisingly, declining standards provide still more common ground, the commiseration of two nations at risk. In fact, Chinese educators have adapted to their own needs the vocabulary of crisis that has dominated international discourse on secondary schooling. They see themselves tied into a world knowledge network and gauge their success increasingly in international terms. In an ironically international use of nationalist fervor, principals and deans of Chinese secondary schools quote from *A Nation at Risk* to justify their own sense of uncertainty and loss of mission (National Commission on Excellence in Education, 1983).

Throughout the 1980s LXLS educators were engaged in three dialogues on the question of how to define and then achieve educational goodness. These conversations, introduced below, not only suggest the context in which the school's administrative and pedagogical practices were continually being reshaped, but also reveal the seriously unresolved conflicts underlying Deng Xiaoping's admonition to move Chinese education in "three directions" (*sange mianxiang*): toward modernization, the world, and the future. They illustrate how schools in China, like their U.S. counterparts, have become the socially and politically convenient arena for mediating the nation's most deeply rooted social contradictions.

**Foreign-Language
Study for Cultural
Access, Educational
Excellence, and
Creativity**

The socio-cultural implications of foreign languages and knowledge in China provide the point of departure for analysis of teaching and learning at the LXLS. Foreign-language education in China has been linked for well over a century to the quest for modernization, as well as the establishment of an effective system of schooling to facilitate its realization. The persistence of this historical conversation bespeaks the resilience of perceptions about the proper role of foreign knowledge in the Chinese episteme, the appropriate training through which that knowledge is procured, and the political and social reliability of Chinese who have become proficient in foreign studies.

Foreign Languages:
Tools or Frames of
Mind?

Whenever China has opened her doors to foreign influence, foreign languages have been a prerequisite for the smooth passage of technology and diplomacy. Variant political and social values have soon followed, giving rise to a vexing set of questions. If not values, what then makes Chinese culture distinctly Chinese? Is foreign language proficiency to be sought solely for its utility, leaving intact one's axiological landscape? Or is it learned for authentic cultural access and alteration of one's identity?

Administrators and teachers at the LXLS cast these questions in terms of the transformational power of languages. Does access to foreign languages and knowledge significantly alter our students' world outlook? If the world of meanings they are able to discern broadens significantly, must changes in valuation follow? What should we make of our school's close identification with the content of foreign textbooks and the style of foreign teachers? Does this attachment create an institution both more susceptible to political repercussions and more open to innovation?

Educational Excellence
and Equality

Changing definitions of the proper role and purpose of foreign-language instruction in the LXLS's curriculum have been paralleled by continual readjustments in the school's commitment to educational excellence and equality. Chinese leaders charged all secondary schools with two broad responsibilities immediately after the Cultural Revolution. Secondary schools were to prepare both qualified students for college-level training and the next generation of workers for socialist development. All students were to accept either eventuality, in the spirit of "one red heart, two possible paths" (*yi ke hongxin, liang tiao lu*).

As a result of limited college enrollment and higher-level employment opportunities, the path down which most Chinese students were prepared to trod was that of the semiskilled or skilled worker. The LXLS faced the problem of upholding the ideals of equality, public access to knowledge and culture, and service to all Chinese youths while striving to carry out its explicitly mandated mission of preparing all its graduates for tertiary training. The school's high standards, which by definition excluded the vast majority of students who hoped to attend it, were not to negate the ideological and moral concern of providing all students the best possible education.

The perceived and actual path to social mobility in China was in the early 1980s still the formal educational system. Acceptance into schools like the LXLS was crucial to a student's future educational and occupational mobility. The question of how to select students for advanced training has become more complicated during the past five years, but it has been answered by further stratifying secondary schools, with tracks whose structure and training programs are bent definitively by vocational or academic preparation.

Most teachers we meet in this study deny that such stratification seriously compromises the tenets of socialist equality. They affirm that quality, assured for their students, might eventually trickle down to others. They contend that by sharing their experiences with educators in less privileged schools, they justify the LXLS's special status. Yet they also wonder whether teaching strategies that rely on foreign texts, the presence of foreign instructors, expensive equipment, and a protective boarding school environment can be adapted to less ideal learning settings. Do teachers who read *Newsweek* and Shakespeare share a common vocabulary with colleagues trained in six-month intensive language courses? And are their students, reared in a special environment for special futures, prepared for the consequences of possible failure?

Creativity and Innovation

in Teaching

and Learning

The quest for excellence at the LXLS raises among teachers questions not primarily about discipline or "time on task" but rather about whether they can nurture the innovative and independent-minded students officially espoused by their superiors. The goal of cultivating students with "communicative" language skills requires students, teachers, and foreign colleagues to be actively involved in the exchange of opinions in classrooms. Educational settings with the potential for unpredictable interaction are rare in Chinese schools. Teachers wonder how they should respond to such situations when classrooms with restrictive communication are the norm.

More important, demanding that students conform to prescribed state values is the public (moral) obligation of teachers. Does taking this moral stand invalidate a teacher's mandate to train truly independent students? Does independent thinking stand students in good stead or prove a liability? Does innovation carry with it a price tag of unpredictable results, making both educators and pupils vulnerable to criticisms of negligent divergence from officially sanctioned pedagogy?

The Foreign

Teacher's Position

These questions confronted me soon after I began my appointment at the LXLS. At the time my assumptions about schooling were derived from critical ethnography, a loosely defined set of research perspectives that were just being interpreted by comparative educators as significant to the cross-cultural study of schooling (Masemann, 1986). These assumptions included that: all societies are patterned by the unequal distribution of power; schools both reflect and shape these inequities; and educational research, likewise implicated in the distribution of power, has the potential and responsibility for facilitating alternative structures of schooling.

An ethnographic approach to the study of schooling appealed to me, because I believed that a thickly described portrait of the LXLS could provide an antidote to the tendency by scholars to conflate national education policy and local classroom practice. The analytic tools of *critical* ethnography attracted my attention for two additional reasons. First, they helped me consider how the individual experiences of LXLS teachers and students were shaped by the dominant historical, political, and economic patterns of Chinese society. Just as important, they gave me a vocabulary to question whose interests my research served.

Sorting out these interests eventually became my primary research dilemma. Because I was a full-time teacher, I never believed that my account of the LXLS could or should represent an "objective" reproduction of Chinese school life. In fact, I willfully altered the pedagogy I hoped to understand. Yet, my commitment to critical ethnography was challenged daily at the LXLS, and daily I left its gates uncertain about my role as teacher and researcher.

Uncertainty was accompanied by astonishment at how my colleagues, trained in Marxist theory, could accept the role of ideology in education, purposefully deny neutrality in pedagogy, and yet deprive themselves of a critical vocabulary for describing the actual outcomes of teaching. An important function of ideology is "the way in which it turns uncertain and fragile cultural resolutions and outcomes into a pervasive naturalism" (Willis, 1977, 162). The LXLS teachers were explicitly charged to reproduce a particular ideology, and that was precisely, "naturally," what they believed they did. From my point of view, glaring contradictions—between creativity and control, equality and excellence, tolerance and towing the line—distinguished how teachers acted in their classrooms from what their political and professional cultures allowed them to say. My colleagues, however, adamantly rejected my conclusion that unintended consequences of teaching often undermined the LXLS's explicit curriculum.

Our different perceptions intimate the complicated negotiations that influenced this study. My colleagues and students "talked back" because it was their duty as responsible teachers and pupils to do so—to assist a neophyte teacher and newcomer to Chinese society, in the words of one colleague, "get it right." My adopting the role of "acceptable incompetent" so readily made me realize that my assumptions about teaching and research must themselves be critically reevaluated in a school shaped by different definitions of pedagogical authority and action.

That my assumptions about teaching and research were reflected back to me, transformed daily through the eyes of my colleagues generally goes without comment in this study. This is because I am wary of research as a form of "academic consciousness raising." Such a function may indeed point out how ambiguous our positions as researchers really are (Lather, 1991). But it also gives priority to the researcher's personal revelations rather than the subjects of research, in this case the experiences of LXLS teachers and students.

This is not to suggest that the concrete circumstances and uncertainties that shaped my interpretation of the LXLS are unimportant. These emerged as my colleagues and I struggled to make our actions and ourselves mutually sensible. We worked together hour after hour, day after day, within a hierarchy defined, for me, in descending order by foreignness, position, age, and gender. Although caution about my foreignness never waned, it was my status as teacher, then my age, and then my gender and marital status, that structured my daily relationships with colleagues. Being in my twenties and married, I was one of the "youngsters" in the department privy to confidences regarding childbirth, divorce, and the travails of marriage in crowded Shanghai. That my spouse did not accompany me to China was also viewed as cause for solidarity by the many members of the English department who had lived for years apart from husbands and wives who were assigned to posts in cities far from Shanghai.

The generally unsolicited but caring attempts by my colleagues to convince me to conform to their versions of human relationships sometimes troubled me immensely. Of course, this discomfiture influences my analysis. The reader will also note, perhaps with disappointment, that this study is essentially a teacher's narrative, rather than a story by one allowed to roam unattached by status and role through school hallways, forging flexible relationships with administrators, teachers, and students. The LXLS pupils did not see me as the "extraordinary adult" who inhabits the pages of many school ethnographies. As symbol of school authority, I was their teacher, not their confidante or ally against the system, although foreign language classrooms sometimes extended this possibility.

Yet, the inflexibility of being "just teacher" at the LXLS by definition made the business of the students and teachers with whom I worked urgently my own. I interacted with pupils daily, bore their jokes and complaints, held parent-teacher conferences. My failures and successes, my squabbles over teaching assignments, were much the same as those of my colleagues, and my salary, by their standards disproportionately high, came from the same box in the accounting office. At the beginning of each month, on a specified day, teachers and staff hovered about the abacus-lined counter where "monthly envelopes" were distributed. We each slid the cash out of our respective packets and counted it, note by note, certifying the amount was correct. I rushed through this public accounting, embarrassed by the relatively large number of bills I received. The envelopes were then signed and handed back to the head accountant, who kept them as the sole, concise record of our annual pay.

Several months after I had arrived at the LXLS, a colleague, perplexed by my sensitivity to what she termed "this salary thing of yours," decided she would accompany me "for moral support." On the appointed day she linked her arm through mine, and we marched downstairs together to pick up our pay. I thumbed through my stack of 10-*yuan* notes and found her concealing an amused smile when I glanced up. On the way out of the office, she tapped my wallet, into which I was hurriedly stuffing the 560 *yuan* (at the time about U.S.$280), grinned, and said, "Well, it is rather a lot, isn't it?"

The public ritual of counting bills from an envelope eight times as thick as those most of my colleagues received became my signal for the divisions that separated me from my colleagues. Few acts made so obvious the foreign faculty member's guest status and drew so concrete a line between those whose lives depended on unit beneficence and those whose lives ultimately did not.

Not until I left Shanghai did I realize how much research, as a complicated enactment of relationships, continues in the writing process. In the absence of my colleagues, I wondered how I might have thought differently about the possibilities of collaboration and negotiation in constructing this study. Although my analysis incorporates the responses of teachers and students with whom I worked, it does so only implicitly. Those who have generously shared their reactions in private are uncomfortable about doing so for the record. Authorship to them connotes official approval and certitude, a public posture they are wary of assuming for the sake of lending this book credibility. Yet, such credibility is crucial in determining whose interests organize my interpretation of the LXLS, a task that has made amply clear to me whom our free-market conception of knowledge benefits.

Even with my colleagues' commentary, of course, this account would remain partial, since how we made one another foils for our own pedagogical dilemmas influenced its outcome. Numerous ethnographers have commented upon the essentially fictive nature of such an enterprise. As the saying goes, "no one ever finds it convincing—and there are smiles all around" (Clifford, 1988, 79–82). Although this statement may be overly generous when applied to foreigners who travel to China, it is an appropriate reminder that I was an integral part of staff routine one day, a politically or culturally excluded exception another. When all is said and done, that uncertain mooring is the crucial reference point for this study.

Accepting the negotiated uncertainty of cultural studies has altered my perspective on the aims and consequences of studying schools worldwide. I began my fieldwork intent upon sharing with a North American audience what is important in the school lives of a small number of Chinese educators and students. I hoped to make accessible those distant experiences, believing that "to the extent we can succeed in belonging vicariously to other worlds, we become less narrow members of our own" (Geertz, 1985).

I now see that the concept of culture can be a tool for making, as well as explaining, those other worlds (Abu-Lughod, 1991), and that our understanding of Chinese schooling would be enhanced by considering "it as part of our world, rather than as a mirror or alternative to ourselves" (Marcus and Fischer, 1986, 134). In turn, I understand that my "outsider's" position at the LXLS was never just outside but was shaped by multiple and often conflicting relationships with many teachers and students. I am indebted to these individuals for rendering my assumptions about education problematic, and showing me that what I once believed to be the separate conversations of Chinese and American educators in fact inform the same unstable world of schooling.

The Historical
Ethnography

My decision to let history figure so centrally in this analysis of teaching and learning at the LXLS developed gradually as it became clear to me how much the school's official purpose and structure, as well as the dominant culture in which its students and teachers interacted, were influenced by the controversial role of foreign knowledge and languages in China. The history of foreign-language education given in chapter 2 provides a backdrop for the examination in chapter 3 of the cultural, educational, and political tensions that have shaped the development of the LXLS. This analysis focuses primarily upon the 100 years between the founding of China's first state-sponsored foreign-language institution and the establishment of the LXLS. Although this coincidental symmetry pleases me, my decision serves the serious function of cautioning readers away from the tempting assumption that what happened before 1949 in foreign-language teaching must somehow be mightily different from what came after. In fact, the significant impact of the Communist revolution on foreign-language education was its introduction of a new, politically charged vocabulary for the purpose of rearticulating and giving new life to earlier arguments about the structure and organization of knowledge in Chinese education and the place of foreign influence in Chinese development.

Chapters 4 through 7 analyze teaching and learning at the LXLS. Chapter 4 examines how the professional authority of LXLS teachers is prescribed by a hierarchical system of symbolic, ideological, and paternalistic controls. Chapter 5 indicates how these controls shape and are challenged by the pedagogical practices of my English department colleagues. Chapter 6 depicts how the ideal image of LXLS students is constructed within the controlled culture of the boarding school and is intended to parallel the discussion in chapter 4 of the image and authority of teachers. Chapter 7 evaluates the consequences of the school's formal curriculum on the lives of pupils. Although I taught over 200 LXLS students, this chapter focuses upon the experiences of the 20 with whom I interacted daily. Chapter 7 is in this sense a corollary to chapter 5. Both chapters highlight the contradictions that developed between the stated goals of educational policy at the LXLS and the tacit knowledge and practices of a number of English language teachers and their students.

These distinctions between policy and practice are reflected in the two metaphors likening the LXLS to family and theater that animate these chapters. Administrators, teachers, and even students strived to emulate predefined models of excellence in ways that made schooling the enactment of a carefully written script. Yet always behind the scenes of the school's energetically sustained public performance hovered a surprisingly argumentative, boisterous, and sometimes vindictive extended family.

Finally, just when schools seem to remain, where it counts, stalwart, unbending, impervious to fundamental reform, they raise the banner of change. The very nature of a school's yearly renewal of cultural membership and interaction with other social institutions invites this possibility. Chapter 8 examines how the LXLS's task of "making foreign things serve China" has altered in the wake of the social and political upheavals of the late 1980s. These changes both reflect Chinese perceptions about the place of their nation in the world community and provide an illuminating commentary on an international "crisis" in secondary schooling.

Chapter 2
The *Ti-yong*
Dilemma

No matter what arenas we
consider—foreign relations,
domestic economic
development and
management, science and
technology, culture and
education, physical education
and the arts—their
development all depends on
the training of foreign language
manpower. We can do without
foreign languages only if we do
not want . . . to establish
relations with all countries,
train manpower for the
realization of modernization,
and raise the cultural and
scientific levels of the country.
(Report from the National Work
Conference on Secondary
School Foreign Language
Education, 1983)

Foreign-language teachers in China use no word more frequently and with
more ambiguous intent than *modernization*. That modernization provides both direction and justification for their pedagogy is hardly surprising,
since it has become China's most powerful verbal weapon in an impressive
arsenal of social, cultural, and economic reform rhetoric (Henze, 1987). Yet,
unequivocal acceptance that "modernization needs foreign languages
and foreign languages need modernization" (Gui, 1984) belies a long-
standing skepticism about the role of foreign-language training in modernization efforts. In fact, how to "make foreign things serve China" (*yang wei
zhong yong*), the slogan that has guided foreign-language training since
1949, has divided Chinese educators and state officials since the nine-

teenth century, when foreign-language instruction was first used as a vehicle for political, economic, educational, and even individual transformation.

The most divisive controversies surrounding foreign-language education have stemmed from a universally accepted assumption among Chinese scholars that foreign-language expertise can afford access to both the knowledge and the psychology of another culture or nation-state. But radically different conclusions have been reached regarding the social and political consequences of such knowledge. Does familiarity with other cultures allow one greater or lesser control over one's destiny? Does it necessarily alter one's fundamental cultural and political allegiances? Should foreign-language fluency be viewed primarily as a tool or as a significantly transformed vision of the world?

Divergent responses to these questions reflect competing visions of modernity that have complicated the development of foreign-language education. For example, the once common portrayal of Chinese tradition battered down by the forces of modernization only after "conscious, sustained, preserving, dedicated effort against the tide of history" (Gasster, 1983, 4) has recently given way to narratives that dislodge modernity from one geographical and temporal mooring. Any nation in any historical epoch that is "both integrated and receptive, fairly sure of its own identity yet able to join others on equal terms in the quest for new markets, new technologies, new ideas" may now wear the mantle of modernity (Spence, 1990, xx). By this definition, foreign knowledge has had a contradictory relationship with Chinese modernization. Historians are both dismayed by the tremendous cultural costs of its promotion and encouraged that through its judicious use modernity redeemed might provide a model for global educational interchange that is mutually beneficial rather than invasive or oppressive (Borthwick, 1983; Hayhoe and Bastid, 1987).

Despite its conceptual vagueness and problematic political undertones, *modernization* is retained here to introduce the history of foreign-language education in China because it is the English word Chinese leaders and educators have chosen to approximate their desire for economic and social transformation. By tying international communication to modernization, China's foreign-language specialists not only enhance their professional image but also persuade critics wary of cultural contamination that foreign-language proficiency implies neither acceptance of imperialism nor thoughtless Westernization but is actually in China's best interests.

The Initiation of
Foreign-Language
Teaching in China,
1860–1903

Two groups of educators initiated formal English-language instruction in China: English-speaking missionaries, who viewed foreign-language training as the path of least resistance through which to bring the hearts and minds of the Chinese people to God, and nineteenth-century Chinese reformers, who regarded foreign-language competency as necessary for mastering foreign technical expertise and diplomatic procedure. From the outset, English-language instruction was the handmaiden of both imperialism and indigenous reform, an important means to religious salvation, on the one hand, and national salvation, on the other.

Foreign Missionaries:

English and Evangelism

Missionaries introduced formal English-language teaching in China with the deepest, most personal sort of cultural change in mind. English-language proficiency initiated "the native youth" into a "new atmosphere. He will be acted upon by new influences. He will see and feel a thousand new relations. But for a time everything with him will be unsettled—his future destiny will be at stake" (*Repository* 2, 1834, 1–2).

Whatever their proselytizing zeal, China's first English-speaking missionaries were painfully aware of the dangers of ambiguous destinies. The very laws designed to prohibit them from entering China seem to have generated a more genuine, if desperate, concern among the missionaries for initiating cross-cultural exchange than that espoused by many of their successors. Isolated along the southern perimeter of the Chinese mainland, they felt a pressing urgency to engage in any kind of communication with Chinese.[1] Consequently, language study and linguistic research became imperative to their missions. Protestant axiology was as profoundly challenged by Chinese language and culture as the Confucian heritage was confounded by the English language and Judeo-Christian values. The goals of missions like Robert Morrison's Anglo-Chinese College in Malacca were explicitly formulated for "reciprocal cultivation" of Chinese and European literature and science,

---

1 Foreigners were prohibited from residing on the Chinese mainland until after the Opium War.

functions. Foreign languages served quite efficiently to sift students into various academic tracks. Some maintained that an English-speaking congregation was, particularly in treaty ports, a laity with clout. Still others considered English competency a reliable test of a prospective minister's religious commitment and call to preach. Like it or not, missionaries acknowledged that English was the most successful component of their school curriculum, and as there "are many who will study English at the present time, it were better that they study under Christian than non-Christian teachers."

Ironically, the culturally intrusive methods employed by missionary educators in China were denounced in their home country with a zeal that rivaled that of the most fervent antiforeign Qing official. Fearing the erosion of America's cultural heritage by unprecedented levels of immigration, the U.S. National Council of Education issued a statement in 1891 warning that "foreign influence has begun a system of colonization with a purpose of preserving foreign languages and traditions and proportionately of destroying distinctive Americanism" (Tyack, 1976, 371). The predicament in which nativist outcries on the home front placed missionary practices abroad was not lost on some of China's mission educators, who tried in vain to clarify the English question:

"The teaching of English in our schools is like Banquo's ghost: 'it will not down.' The problem meets everyone who opens a new school or who is revising the course of study of an old one.... In our opinion the question whether it ought to be taught or not must be settled upon the same principles which are applied to any branch of study. These principles are two: 1st. What is its value as a training to the mind? 2nd. Of what use is it after it is learned?... Does the teaching of English develope [sic] the powers of discrimination or observation and then truly educate? After it is learned is it put to any good use for the advancement of mankind, either in temporal or intellectual benefits?" (Fryer and Ferguson, 1893, 577–78)

Chinese Self-
Strengtheners: Western
Learning for Practical
Application

Missionary arguments were perceived by Chinese as both presumptuous and futile. Even the most secular foreign curriculum held no legitimacy in the eyes of Chinese and Manchu elites. Acquaintance with foreign languages and science did not guarantee success in imperial examinations and the subsequent procurement of state office. More fundamentally, foreign establishments were perceived as an affront to Chinese sensibility.

Nevertheless, a small but powerful group of Chinese statesmen felt it unwise to ignore the growing presence of foreigners in China because they identified foreign knowledge with a comprehensive military-political system that threatened China's sovereignty (Teng and Fairbank, 1967). The disastrous decades since the Opium War had convinced them that successful resistance to foreign encroachment must come from superior military and technical skills. No revolutionaries, these "self-strengtheners" believed that once access to such skills was obtained, foreign aggression could be met, leaving the spiritual core of Confucian China intact. The solution seemed simple. Military and technical knowledge locked firmly within the hands of foreigners could be wrenched free by loyal students proficient in foreign languages.

The self-strengtheners' assumption that foreign-language training would transmit a body of information that would facilitate acquisition of foreign expertise laid the groundwork for the first efforts at state-sponsored "modern" educational reform in China. "We request Your Majesty to order Canton and Shanghai each to send to Peking two men who understand foreign spoken and written languages to be commissioned and consulted. We note that in any negotiations with foreign nations, the prerequisite is to know their nature and feelings. At present, their speech cannot be understood and their writing can hardly be deciphered. Everything is impeded" (Teng and Fairbank, 1967, 74).

On 13 January 1861, imperial approval of this memorial led to the establishment in Beijing of an interpreters' college, commonly known as the Tongwen Guan. The school was attached to a new office of foreign affairs, the Zongli Yamen, which dealt with foreign ministers to China, who since the Treaties of Tianjin had been allowed to reside in the capital.

The significance of the Tongwen Guan was not its foreign-language curriculum per se. Formal, court-sponsored, and private profit-making foreign-language training had been alternately promoted and banned in China for well over a millennium.[3] The function that such training served within the

3 Successful programs particularly in the Tang and Yuan dynasties led to the establishment in the fifteenth century of the Ming Si Yi Guan, a court-supported institution that trained hundreds of translators and led to such widespread interest in foreign languages that private study uncontrolled by the state was perceived as a threat to national security and stability and banned by the Ming court. In the seventeenth and eighteenth centuries the Qing court relied upon Europeans as

Zongli Yamen set the Tongwen Guan apart from earlier institutions. Prior to the 1860s, knowledge of foreign languages and etiquette was marginal to Chinese statecraft. Foreign emissaries to the emperor were viewed as representatives of tributary states. The Zongli Yamen symbolized a fundamental change in status for foreigners and their languages. As the legitimacy of foreign demands was forced upon China, so in a very real legal sense was the legitimacy of their languages.

British and French treaties stipulated that correspondence between those two countries and the Qing government be written in their respective languages as well as Chinese. Foreign languages thus became much more than polite concessions to vassal states. They became identified with a powerful but mistrusted package that bound together foreign interference and domination with techniques required for China's survival.

The establishment of the Tongwen Guan generated dismay among self-strengtheners about the extent to which Chinese negotiations with foreign powers were dependent upon the only Chinese who were conversant in foreign languages, déclassé merchant-linguists of the treaty ports. Although the Tongwen Guan was originally directed by imperial officers to employ only Chinese foreign-language teachers, none was found who embodied both the gentlemanly disposition of the Confucian generalist and the specialized skill of the foreign-language expert. In 1862 permission to hire foreign teachers was granted with the provision that they agree not to proselytize Christian doctrine.

During its early years, the Tongwen Guan suffered from a largely uncommitted student body as well as a dearth of official support. Chinese Yamen officials and school instructors complained incessantly about the poor quality and apathy of their students, young men who were chosen exclusively from Manchurian Eight Banner families. The Eight Banner description was originally given to Manchu military nobility and later came to refer to Qing nobility in general. Tongwen Guan students in turn deplored their instructors' arrogance and inefficient and irrelevant teaching methods (Martin, 1896).

---

translators until treaty concessions with Russia made Qing officials increasingly skeptical about relying on foreign interpreters. In 1708 the Russian Language School (*E luo si wen guan*) and later a Latin school run by Jesuit priests were established to train Manchu bannermen as interpreters at the Russian Ecclesiastical Mission in Beijing. For a description of the Russian school see Eric Widner, *The Russian Ecclesiastical Mission in Peking During the Eighteenth Century* (Cambridge, Mass.: East Asian Research Center, Harvard University, 1976). For an overview of early foreign-language training initiatives in China see Fu, 1986.

On the one hand, foreign teachers, who thought the Tongwen Guan's living facilities and services luxurious by European standards, did express resentment at pupils they found overindulged and poorly disciplined. On the other hand, Tongwen Guan educators also sympathized with their students' inability to find suitable employment upon graduation (Su, 1985, 53–54). Finally, the Tongwen Guan's operation was severely hampered by the strong opposition it received from antireform officials. Skeptical of the consequences of a "Western" education, they saw to it that students with foreign knowledge, particularly those with previous experience working or studying abroad, were "politically buried in the wilds of Mongolia and in the center of China where it was thought they could do no harm" (Martin in Morse, 1918, 474).

Faced with such obstacles, the school's sponsors despaired that their students were gaining only a smattering of knowledge and were destined to become little more than the treaty port linguists they were supposed to replace. Reasoning that the institution's curriculum might be strengthened by adding basic training in the foundations of "Western knowledge," they proposed to the throne that the Tongwen Guan be expanded to a college with a department of astronomy and mathematics. They sought to make this proposed curriculum more attractive by conferring official rank upon successful students and abandoning the policy of limiting enrollment to scions of banner families. In one of their memorials to the throne, Tongwen Guan backers suggested that "members of the Hanlin Academy shall be required to enter the Tongwen Guan and apply themselves to the study of science."[4]

This attempt to lend the prestige of Hanlin scholars to the school's plans for expansion culminated in a fierce attack against the school, led by Wo-ren (d. 1871), president of the Hanlin Academy. Wo-ren countered the self-strengtheners' revisionist views of what constituted appropriate scholarship and statesmanship by rejecting foreign knowledge and culture as inferior to China's:

"I have heard that the way to establish a state is to respect propriety and righteousness rather than power and scheming. The basic design is in men's minds not in their skills. Now if we pursue one of the secondary arts and also accept foreigners as teachers ... even if the teachers teach with sincerity and the students study with sincerity, the products will be no more than mathematicians. ... If it is necessary to teach astronomy and mathematics, a

4 W. A. P. Martin in Morse, 1918, 475. The Hanlin Academy was China's most prestigious educational institution, whose members were recipients of the highest imperial examination honors. See Liu, 1981.

wide search will necessarily disclose persons versed in these arts. Why should it be foreigners? Why must we learn from foreigners?" (Teng and Fairbank, 1967, 76)

The Zongli Yamen presented the throne with a harsh rebuttal, and eventually the institution acquired collegiate status with a five- and an eight-year curriculum, including courses in physics, anatomy, physiology, chemistry, geology, mineralogy, and metallurgy (Su, 1985; Covell, 1978). However, curricular reform outpaced teacher and student morale (Su, 1985). In 1869, Robert Hart (1835–1911), inspector-general of China's Imperial Maritime Customs and manager of the school's finances, predicted, "The Tung Wen Kuan will, I fear, fall through" (Fairbank, et al., 1975, 43).

Hart's fears proved unfounded, and the Tongwen Guan's expanded curriculum was gradually implemented as support grew among Chinese officials for study of foreign technologies. Hart reversed his initial assessment, declaring that "the Tung Wen Kuan will be a grand success" (Fairbank, et al., 1975, 43). Still, the conception of knowledge and intellectual exchange upon which the school's curriculum was based remained narrowly utilitarian. Tongwen Guan students began studying German in 1871, the same year China received its first Krupp cannon.

Similar institutions in treaty ports along China's coast engendered more enthusiasm. In 1863, the Viceroy of Jiangsu Province, Li Hongzhang (1823–1901), proposed to protect imperial interests from foreign connivance by establishing institutions similar to the Beijing Tongwen Guan in Shanghai and Guangzhou (Fu, 1986; Su, 1985). He envisioned these schools as centers for the cultivation of "men of ability" whose virtuous character, derived from Confucian scholarship, would inform and direct their newly acquired technical know-how. Li averred that foreign-language training was essential for mastery of foreign technique, but he warned that its progressive power was dependent upon the moral rectitude of the language learner.

Shanghai's Foreign Language School (*Waiguo yuyan wenzi xueguan*) opened its doors on 28 March 1864 to 24 Chinese youths from "a better class of society" (Biggerstaff, 1965; Tang, 1983). By August the young men had recited their way through Noah Webster's speller under the tutelage of Young J. Allen (1836–1907), an American Methodist missionary stranded in Shanghai as a result of the confluence of civil wars in China and the United States (Bennett, 1983). The bloody Taiping Rebellion (1851–64) had so unsettled the lower Yangtze River valley that Allen had been unable to leave Shanghai since his arrival in China in 1860. The mission funds with which he was to have supported himself and his family dried up with the outbreak of the American Civil War. Allen sold his mission's printing press to make ends meet and accepted a half-time position as English instructor at the Shanghai institution.

Despite its familiar casting of "Western studies" in Confucian form, several significant characteristics distinguished the Shanghai Foreign Language School from its Beijing counterpart. Its motto, "Seek talented people for China" (*qiu xian hua guo*), reflected a broader conception of who could benefit from foreign study. Never restricted to recruiting its students from Eight Banner Manchu sons ostensibly loyal to the Qing throne, the school offered instruction in Chinese classics, history, literature, and foreign languages to "children from the vicinity below the age of fourteen, of brilliant ability and refined and quiet character." Although the Beijing Tongwen Guan was under the direct supervision of the Qing court, the Shanghai Foreign Language School was a regional undertaking adapted to the needs of a flourishing cosmopolitan metropolis with 150 commercial firms, which accounted for over half of China's trade. The heart of "littoral" rather than "hinterland" China, Shanghai was "more commercial than agricultural in its economic foundation, more modern than traditional in its administrative and social arrangements, more Western [Christian] than Chinese [Confucian] in its intellectual bearing, and more outward than inward-looking in its general global orientation and involvement" (Cohen, 1974, 197). Consequently, the Shanghai Foreign Language School was immediately identified as an institution unusually open to foreign influence, a feeling expressed expansively by Li Hongzhang in a couplet he presented to the school:

Education's influence is felt and flourishes throughout the world;
The learning of the world's languages everywhere facilitates cultural
    exchange.
Such teaching and learning is desirable in all seasons;
From all corners the talented converge to be trained in many fields. (Allen,
    1973, 263)

Within three years the school had developed a reputation for serving the immediate entrepreneurial needs of Shanghai rather than the diplomatic intrigues of the capital. Shanghai students were regarded as the technocratic counterparts of those being trained in diplomacy in Beijing. The institution was renamed the School for Dispersing Languages (*Guang fangyan guan*) and was consolidated with the Jiangnan Arsenal, one of the first centers in

China to train Chinese technicians in modern shipbuilding, armaments, and machinery.

The school's relative success in popularizing scientific and technical knowledge (Bennet and Fryer, 1967; Tang, 1983; Su, 1985) should probably be credited to its predominantly Chinese faculty and leadership. In contrast to the overwhelmingly foreign composition of the Beijing Tongwen Guan's teaching and administrative staff, 24 of Shanghai's 29 teachers were Chinese.[5] They were able to adapt their curriculum to Shanghai's uniquely cosmopolitan character, invoking Confucian tradition for institutional legitimacy and stability, yet meeting the competition they faced for qualified students from a growing number of modern schools established in Shanghai. In 1866 not one person in the entire municipal region sat for a preliminary degree in the imperial examination (Wright, 1966, 84; Levenson, 1968, 53). "Western studies" were attractive to Shanghai youths not just as the second-best vehicle for social mobility but because of the alternatives to tradition they presented.

Unfortunately, the school's energetic response to treaty port interests garnered little official recognition at court. No graduates were recruited by provincial offices, negating the stated purpose for which the school was established. The placard raised over the school's main gates, "Hall for the Investigation of Knowledge" (*ge zhi tang*), symbolized the source of state resistance. To Tongwen Guan supporters, the phrase both connoted scientific and technological knowledge and alluded to a famous passage from the Confucian classic "The Great Learning," which admonishes scholars to "extend to the utmost knowledge by the investigation of things" (*ge wu zhi zhi*).[6] The school's implicit synthesis of foreign and Chinese knowledge threatened traditional interpretations of the latter.

The insistence by state officials on clear distinctions between "Chinese" and "Western" knowledge systems is most brightly illuminated by the work of Zhang Zhidong (1837–1909), a Chinese reformer whose best-known treatise was published just as the Tongwen Guan schools were being transformed (Ayers, 1971). Zhang advocated foreign learning at the turn of the century

5 The Beijing Tongwen Guan's faculty of 3 Chinese teachers was far outnumbered by 60 foreign instructors. There were no Chinese teachers on the 15-member faculty of the Canton school, whose failure is also attributed to following too closely the Manchu Banner school tradition of training sons of the elite in the Confucian classics. See Grams, 1969; Su, 1985.

6 "The Great Learning" was compiled by the second century B.C. and is one of the most well-known chapters of the Confucian classic *The Book of Rites*.

when China's defeat in the Sino-Japanese War (1895) both legitimized the need for reform and gave a new sense of urgency to military and technical expertise. Zhang's interpretation of the nature, purpose, and social implications of this process was embodied in the aphorism "Chinese learning for fundamental principles, Western learning for practical application" (*zhongxue wei ti, xixue wei yong*).

This expression became widely known through the publication of *Exhortation to Study* (*Quan xue pian*), in which Zhang reworked ideas first propounded by Feng Guifen (1809–74), a renowned Chinese statesman who had urged Li Hongzhang to establish the Shanghai Tongwen Guan.[7] Zhang wrote, "In relations between China and the outside world, commercial affairs are the *t'i* [foundation] and armed force is the *yung* [technique]. Understanding regulations embodied in treaties and having a thorough knowledge of various countries' mining production, trade conditions, border defenses, administration orders, schools, military equipment, public laws and statutes are fundamental. The gateway is an understanding of the languages of other nations" (Ayers, 1971, 104).

Zhang believed that the substance (*ti*) of Chinese civilization (Confucian social and political relations) and the functional means (*yong*) of the West (linguistic, military, economic, and scientific technique) could be combined to strengthen the empire. Accepting the Confucian view that societal stability could be achieved through the efforts of just officials, Zhang reasoned that Chinese foreign-language students should be selected from scholars thoroughly versed in the Chinese classics. "To know foreign countries and not know China is to lose one's conscience," Zhang concluded, just as "to know China and not know foreign countries is to be deaf and blind" (Ayers, 1971, 160).

As Zhang was writing his *Exhortation*, the noted reformer Yan Fu (1853–1921) was publishing a translation of Huxley's *Evolution and Ethics* (Schwartz, 1964). Impoverished as a child, Yan Fu was forced to give up training in the Chinese classics for foreign studies at the Fuzhou Shipyard, an institution similar to the Jiangnan Arsenal. Yan concurred with Zhang's impressions that efforts to learn from foreign models yielded feeble results, "like a good orange tree on the bank of the Huai River which, after it was

---

7 Ayers, 1971, 104. Translated as *Learn!*, the book, actually a collection of essays written by students in Shanghai, was published in installments in 1898 and 1899 in the *Recorder*. The Chinese version was given imperial sanction and sold over one million copies.

transplanted, produced thick-skinned oranges. The tree looks as if midway between life and death and we do not get the fruit we sought" (Teng and Fairbank, 1967, 150). However, with as much vehemence as traditionalists such as Wo-ren, Yan Fu rejected Zhang's dichotomy of Chinese-*ti* and Western-*yong*, claiming, "the difference between Chinese and Western knowledge is as great as that between the complexions and the eyes of the two races. We cannot force the two cultures to be the same or similar. Therefore, Chinese knowledge has its foundation and function; Western knowledge has also its foundation and function. If the two are separated, each can be independent; if the two were combined, both would perish" (Teng and Fairbank, 1967, 151).

In the end, Zhang Zhidong's assertions that Confucian values stripped of real-world function would remain meaningful and that foreign knowledge could be narrowly defined as value-free technique proved fatal to gradual reform in China. It was Yan Fu's vision of cultural transformation that was borne out by history. After China's defeat in the Sino-Japanese War and the subsequent failure of the Boxer Rebellion (1900), the Qing court initiated reforms it had long suppressed. A national system of schooling based on a Japanese model was outlined in an imperial edict of 1902, and in 1905 the imperial examination system was abolished by imperial decree.

A brief flurry of interest in the Tongwen Guan system quickly turned to critical scrutiny. Once an affront to traditional learning, the Tongwen Guan by the turn of the century was perceived as an antiquated pioneer. Between 1898 and 1902 a national university established in Beijing absorbed the Beijing Tongwen Guan's science and foreign-language programs. The Shanghai School for Dispersing Languages, administered by the Ministry of War after 1905, became a military-technical school (*Gongye xuetang*) offering courses in mathematics, astronomy, and geography.

Although Chinese historians point to the Tongwen Guan system as the forerunner of modern educational reform in China, they downplay its lasting significance. Scholars from the PRC have described the Tongwen Guan as a "half-colonial, half-feudal institution" whose supporters capitulated to imperialist pressures and whose "diehard" opponents stubbornly resisted inevitable change, as the Gang of Four foiled modernization policies during the 1970s (Zheng, 1979). Scholars from Taiwan are only slightly more sympathetic, crediting the Tongwen Guan system with training China's first generation of foreign affairs experts and scientists (Su, 1985).

Because the Tongwen Guan schools advocated "radical innovation within the old order" (Wright, 1966, 244) they could only be transitional. The attempt by Tongwen Guan advocates to locate a middle ground between conservative efforts to maintain the Confucian order and revolutionary efforts to found a modern republic proved as untenable as the self-strengtheners' endeavor to protect Chinese substance with Western function. Failing "to be modern enough to defend their traditional status, and traditional enough to take the curse off their modernism" (Levenson, 1968, 2:7), the schools were supplanted by an essentially foreign educational system. In the process, foreign-language proficiency became identified with foreign substance as well as function—an explosive connection when Chinese leaders have asserted not "foreign" or "Western" but "Chinese" modernity.

Foreign-Language Training in the Republican Period: 1903–49

The number of mission schools in China grew rapidly after 1903. Expansion was a result not so much of Chinese approval as supply and demand. Missionary institutions had little difficulty attracting pupils as long as government schools failed to accommodate all of the students who wished to study in them, and missionaries took advantage of their new-found popularity, declaring, "The greatest opportunity for Christian education in China now confronts the Church" (Records, 1907).

Modern School Rivals

Missionaries were also acutely aware, however, that they faced a serious rival in their efforts to define modern schooling for China. Between 1895 and 1911 the number of "modern" schools (*xuetang*) in Shanghai District rose from 10 to 218 (Tang, 1983, 136). In addition, thousands of Chinese students were looking to Japan as the emerging modernization model for Asia. Missionary educators perceived the stirring of cultural nationalism as a threat to the continued existence of their schools and lamented "the competition of state schools which are better equipped to offer an ampler preparation for secular occupations than many church schools can afford" (Basford, 1904, 484).

English-language instruction became increasingly important as the viability of mission schools depended more and more upon their ability to provide scarce training. Missionaries turned their attention increasingly from "whether" to "how" to teach English. They developed courses in conversational English, the "basal principle" of which they defined as student interest. Noting the poor quality of mission textbooks, they began to write their own. In an ironic twist, some even applied their experiences in teaching Chinese with a romanized alphabet to standardizing English spelling for second language learners (Wison, 1900; Noyes, 1904; Sites, 1904). Younger missionaries attacked the Confucian legacy with vocabulary drawn from their North American training in progressive pedagogy (Sites, 1904, 251).

Yet, declarations that the "English question" was once and for all settled were premature (Silsby, 1903). Detractors continued to criticize English-language instruction as a grave misdirection of mission funds and energies. A representative critique, entitled "English and Evangelism," was delivered by Reverend Dubose to the Suzhou Missionary Association and later published in two issues of *The Chinese Recorder* (June-July, 1904).

Dubose criticized educators who favored English instruction for its power to "disarm prejudice and break down the great wall of separation between the celestials and the Westerners." He found particularly offensive the argument that since English would be taught in any case, it should be taught by "earnest Christians" rather than "irreligious foreign adventurers." Dubose insisted that English was a costly disincentive both for missionaries to learn Chinese and for Chinese to learn their own written tradition. He concluded that English proficiency lured promising students away from the ministry and into business and commerce, effectively secularizing the very students missionaries were trying to draw into the Christian community.

Although Dubose was described by many of his colleagues as out of touch with the needs of China and unrepresentative of what most missionaries believed (Silsby, 1904), his contention that English proficiency constituted a serious temptation to Chinese students struck a sympathetic chord. The "temptation argument" became a common rationale for excluding English-language instruction from mission schools. A proposal put forward at the 1907 Centenary Conference that would have made training in at least one modern foreign language mandatory for theological and humanities students was defeated by missionaries who were "astonished to hear it stated that if a man could not withstand the temptations which the English language would put before him that he was not the man for the ministry. It is not necessary that we should lead into temptation" (Records, 1907, 459–60).

But "lead into temptation" mission schools continued to do. While government funds that might have been directed toward social programs were used for suppressing regional military disputes, the protection of extraterritoriality and increased funding from mission home boards gave mission schools an institutional stability Chinese educators undoubtedly envied. Increasingly, missionary publications called English a temporal asset perfectly suited to the task of which they were masters (House, 1916).

Missionaries were responding to a growing realization that foreign-language proficiency and the knowledge it could provide would eventually become subsumed by China's indigenous educational system. The time "will surely come," they admitted, "and missionary education is hastening it, when the Chinese language will be able to express, and Chinese scholars furnish, all the ideas or information the nation will require." However, they were quick to add, "until then at least English will be, as the classics or modern European languages have been in England and America, the sign of broad culture and a most useful tool for acquiring and imparting it." Mission educators defended their position by assuming they would "for a somewhat indefinite period" be in charge of Christian education in China. Teaching English had become both a matter of survival and a means to justify "foreign service" to China, a task for which missionaries deemed themselves "naturally equipped" (*Christian Education in China*, 1922, 342–45).

English and Nationalism

As missionary educators debated the "English question," foreign languages became with mathematics and Chinese one of the three essential subjects taught in the secondary school curriculum China adopted from Japan in 1903. From the outset, Chinese educators condemned the pervasive influence of Japanese teachers and texts—a complaint shared by North American and European foreigners who saw their own influence wane with the "Japanization of China" (Bastid, 1987, 45). Nevertheless, during the first decade of the twentieth century, the number of government-supported schools increased over seventy times, surpassing mission schools in both numbers and prominence. The ambitious four-year secondary school curriculum implemented in urban schools from the establishment of the Republic of China in 1912 to 1923 included 1,056 periods of foreign-language instruction (predominantly English), more time than was allotted to any other subject (Fu, 1986, 26–27; Chen, 1961, 509–27).

The justification for this extraordinary commitment was to equip students over the age of 14 with a practical ability to use foreign languages and to provide them with a broader understanding of the world outside China's borders. Although curricular descriptions urged the cultivation of conversational skills, foreign-language teachers relied, by necessity and tradition, on traditional grammar-translation methods, intensive reading, writing from memory or models, and detailed grammatical analysis.

The practical definition of foreign-language education as fundamentally a process of translation not only shaped its structure and purpose in state-sponsored secondary and tertiary institutions but also stratified the educational credentials and cultural experiences of students. The hegemonic insistence that English be the vehicle for constructing knowledge and values in elite mission schools assisted in the creation of what has been called the "alienated academy" of the treaty port bourgeoisie. Foreign languages were employed by students to compose not only their essays but also themselves "in accordance with newly acquired foreign norms" (Yeh, 1990, 15). In contrast, the more circumscribed use of English-language education in state schools required that the acquisition of foreign languages take place "with constant reference to the native language" (Yeh, 1990, 14–15).

Chinese students, many of whom received further training abroad, challenged this dichotomy in foreign-language teaching when they became teachers. Not only did they return to China with extensive personal libraries, enriching the content of foreign-language study, but they also wrote texts and reference books from indigenous perspectives and initiated the study of comparative literature (Fu, 1986). Some became involved in the May Fourth era's attempts to forge a strong, modern nation-state. Inevitably, they brought to their teaching the intense and bitter strife that fueled that movement, and foreign languages became enmeshed in fervent debates over whether cultural or political activism should be the leading impetus for Chinese reform, the merits of traditional Chinese values, the differences between "modernization" and "Westernization," and China's ultimate position in the international community.

The aftermath of World War I revealed to many Chinese reformers that technological expertise could have dark consequences indeed, giving new meaning to Zhang Zhidong's substance-function division. Some concluded that the enduring "spiritual" qualities of Chinese civilization must act as a counterbalance to the utilitarian but destructive power of the "material" West. Others, including Marxists and pragmatists, denied this division and sought to adopt Western scientific and political values wholesale or adapt them in the service of social change. Foreign languages became an indirect vehicle for both the liberal's gradual cultural reformation and the leftist's radical socio-political activism.

In the case of the former, English-language training became associated with the replacement in 1922 of the Japanese educational model with "progressive" reforms borrowed largely from the United States. The hours devoted in the national curriculum to foreign-language training, as well as to other subjects, were reduced, and a direct teaching method (*zhijiefa*) stressing the development of listening and speaking abilities was advocated so that students might learn foreign languages "naturally." Teaching materials and content were redesigned around the interests and motivations of individual students.

Political activists shared with missionary educators an admiration for foreign languages as a tool for human struggle and transformation. In 1920 Communists established a Foreign Language Center (*Shanghai chuang-ban de waiguoyu xueshe*) in Shanghai to train political cadres in Russian and Marxism as well as English, French, German, and Japanese. Although the school enrolled only 56 students, these included such illustrious figures of Chinese communism as Liu Shaoqi and Mao Zedong. The school was absorbed in 1922 into the revolutionary Shanghai University. Although foreign-language programs were ostensibly designed to train Communist linguist-cadres, Shanghai University's emphasis on practice promoted foreign-language training for commercial activities as well (Yeh, 1990). In fact, when the university was violently disbanded as a result of the Northern Expedition in 1927, its English faculty was composed of a widely divergent group of scholars, from renowned writer Mao Dun to Zhou Yueran, chair of the department and graduate of the old Shanghai Tongwen Guan.

The era of eclectic experimentation in politics and education, which could unite such a diverse group of scholars across generation and ideology, lost its vitality as the 1920s drew to a close (Bastid, 1987). Social and economic reforms foundered, and criticism of foreign exploitation of China sharpened. China's mission schools, once tolerated because they offered a scarce commodity, had not only become expendable but also were perceived as a barrier to the instillation of nationalist values in Chinese youth.

As educational policy became more tightly controlled by Nationalist Party efforts to unify China, foreign languages were increasingly criticized as a source of cultural and psychological disunity (Tsang, 1933, 71). Japanese-language education in northeastern China, as well as foreign-language training in state-run schools, came under attack for eroding Chinese nationalism. During the latter half of the 1920s a strong movement to keep English instruction entirely out of elementary schools was based on the argument that English had nothing to do with the "cultivation of a patriotic and efficient citizenship"—the paramount purpose of basic education. The specter of Shanghai, with its vision of utopia embodied in "modernized" girls and boys speaking in foreign tongues (Wakeman, 1990, 28) presented a persuasive case of "inner imperialism" (Saari, 1990) to members of the Central Educational Administration Commission. Its movement for the recovery of educational rights culminated in a series of regulations requiring the registration of all private schools in China. Foreign schools that accepted the terms of registration were required to have a Chinese chief administrator and offer religious instruction as a voluntary subject only at the secondary and post-secondary levels.

This movement was reinforced by a vocal sector of the international community. A 1932 League of Nations Report on education in China concluded that mission schools, "designed not so much for the people as for privileged individuals," created "a governing intelligentsia class."[8] League representatives also directed their charge of excessive North American influence at government schools, which sacrificed preparing Chinese students "for a life of useful work in China" to "the acquisition of familiarity with a foreign culture" (League of Nations, 1932, 113).

At the time the report was disseminated, Chinese secondary school students took five classes of foreign languages a week for six years, for a total of 1,080 classes. Although this number dropped to 972 in 1936, English-language teaching continued to flourish in urban areas, where foreign-language proficiency was perceived as a gateway to social, economic, and geographical mobility, and numerous students were willing to pay for privately run, short-term courses (*Shanghaishi jiaoyu tongji*, 1935).

In addition, both Nationalist and Communist parties continued to support foreign-language training programs for military and political purposes. The Nationalist government ran two specialized schools for translators and foreign affairs officers.[9] Yan'an Foreign Language School, the prototype for foreign-language institutes established after 1949, provided formal language classes for military translators and Communist cadres, as well as informal evening lectures, where speakers such as Mao Zedong advocated the study of foreign languages for the purpose of acquiring a "new voice for the revolution" (Fu, 1986, 101–02).

Immediately after World War II, foreign-language training in both mission and state-sponsored institutions enjoyed a spirited revival. Mission schools in the cities of Shanghai, Fuzhou, Guangzhou, Nanjing, Beijing, and Suzhou trained 40 percent of China's secondary school students, and missionaries

8 League of Nations, 1932. This analysis prompted an angry American rebuttal complaining, in essence, that the League's conclusions reflected not Chinese reality but European sour grapes. See Duggan, 1933.

9 These two institutions were the National Asia Language School (*Guoli dongfang yuwen zhuanke xuexiao*) and the Yunnan English Language School (*Yunnan sheng-li yingyu zhuanke xuexiao*).

began a short-lived effort to consolidate their activities in the name of professionalism.[10] More than 40 of China's 205 institutions of higher learning offered specializations in English, and over 20 offered foreign-language training programs for prospective teachers (Fu, 1986). In 1949 5.5 percent of all college faculty in China were foreign-language teachers, and foreign-language students accounted for 6 percent of all college students.

**Foreign Languages
in the Service of the
Revolution: 1949–83**

China's educational pendulum, which since the late nineteenth century had swung "between traditional knowledge patterns for political control and transformed ones for economic development" (Hayhoe, 1989a, 191) continued its volatile cycle after 1949, reflecting shifting conceptions of modernization designed to achieve an appropriate balance between foreign assistance and self-reliance. Attempts to secure this equilibrium led to heavy reliance upon Soviet assistance throughout much of the 1950s, the xenophobic concern for ideological purity and independence during the Cultural Revolution (1966–76), and the "open door" policies of the 1980s. Although the centrality of foreign influence to each shift has resulted in abrupt disruptions in foreign-language programs in Chinese schools, the assumption that foreign-language proficiency is valuable primarily for utilitarian reasons has since 1949 provided a thread of continuity in foreign-language instruction, embodied in the slogan "making foreign things serve China."

The first attempt to make foreign languages serve China diminished the importance of English-language teaching in China, particularly in primary and secondary schools. By 1951 missionary institutions, viewed as vestiges of cultural and economic imperialism, were disbanded or consolidated with government schools (Schlesinger, Jr., 1974, 336–73). In addition, Chinese who had contact with foreigners came under scathing attack. Ironically, the same concerns "conservative" missionaries had raised about the potentially corruptive influence on Chinese citizens of Western language and culture were now articulated in different terms by their most implacable foes.

In a process begun in liberated areas as early as 1945 (Fu, 1986), Russian

10 In 1946 Shanghai had 124 private secondary schools, including 69 registered and 30 unregistered secondary schools, 2 unregistered senior secondary schools, and 9 registered and 14 unregistered vocational secondary schools. See *Shanghaishi nianjian* [Shanghai Yearbook], 1946.

gradually replaced English as the preferred foreign language of modernization and revolution. The Korean War, the mark of imperialism by which English was branded, and the influx into China of Soviet advisors undermined the social utility and prestige of English. Foreign-language teaching in secondary schools declined as a result of curricular disruption, lack of qualified Russian-language teachers, a widespread feeling that foreign languages were "frills" that could be ill-afforded when basic literacy for much of the Chinese population was at stake, and the discontinuation in 1954 of foreign-language teaching in nearly all junior secondary schools. Implementation of a three-year foreign-language curriculum for senior secondary schools resulted in a decrease in the percentage of class periods devoted to foreign-language instruction, from 12 percent in 1950 to under 6.5 percent four years later (*Chronology*, 1983; *Achievement*, 1984).

Just two years after these measures were promoted, increasing Sino-Soviet tensions called their wisdom into question. Zhou Enlai, the most visible champion of comprehensive foreign-language education reform, urged in his influential "Report on the Question of Intellectuals" that the teaching of foreign languages be extended to include English, French, and German (Zhou, 41). Mao Zedong supported foreign studies, provided that vigilant efforts be made to eliminate their corrosive influences (Fu, 1986). Mao's slightly veiled criticism was soon to become an explicit charge of blind acceptance of the Soviet model. Foreign-language training, especially in English, gained renewed legitimacy, and its presence in national secondary school teaching guidelines rose to over 18.5 percent of total class hours by 1963.

Three years later the Cultural Revolution (1966–76) turned China's global view inward, undercutting the purpose and incentive for foreign-language study. The conservatively presented, locally developed, and highly politicized curricula that resulted were never fully implemented, since they were periodically revised to reflect China's halting rapprochement with the West throughout the first half of the 1970s. The post-Cultural Revolution perception that participation in international affairs was being hampered by a severe shortage of foreign-language expertise led to another spasm of attention to foreign-language education.

English and the "Four Modernizations"

The post-Mao decade became characterized by a redirection of China's vision outward. Chinese in all walks of life were urged to "respect knowledge and respect talent" whatever the source, so long as they strengthened the nation.

Particularly since 1979, self-reliance has been defined in the context of international interdependence. Although the reformative potential of the nation's educational system to direct such change was a perennial topic of debate among Chinese Marxists, most attributed to education a capacity to infuse into the economy skills, training, and technologies that themselves became a potent productive force. All areas of study, including foreign languages, were given new legitimacy as educational reform was targeted as a precondition for the "four modernizations" in Chinese agriculture, industry, national defense, and science and technology. The impression instilled in so many students during the Cultural Revolution that "it doesn't matter if you know your ABCs, you can still take part in revolution" was fading.

Nearly all the circulars regarding foreign-language training issued by the Ministry of Education after 1979 emphasized severe shortfalls in qualified foreign-language personnel, even though the number of English-language instructors in junior and senior secondary schools had increased tenfold from 1965 to 1978. Such spectacular growth was accomplished by adding to the teaching force tens of thousands of young teachers trained in inadequate short-term programs. Even if the majority of these instructors were competent, their numbers added up to only one-sixth of the total number of secondary school Chinese language teachers (see Table 2.1).

In fact, available foreign-language teachers were concentrated in urban college preparatory schools, where entrance examination requirements proved excellent motivation for at least the study of English reading, translation, and grammar. By 1982 nearly 17 percent of the curriculum at key secondary schools was devoted to foreign-language instruction. More significantly, for the first time since 1949, secondary school graduates managed to complete their entire school career without having their English-language curriculum changed in midstream (*Almanac,* 1984, 152). That same year 100 percent of the secondary school students in Shanghai were studying foreign languages.[11]

The sense of urgent expectation that accompanied English teaching reform during the early 1980s can be explained by several factors. First, it reflected general condemnation of the recurrent disruptions of training programs dur-

---

11 Nearly all secondary school pupils in Fuzhou, Suzhou, Tianjin, Xining, Wuhan, and Guiyang were also studying foreign languages. The percentage was much lower in Beijing, where 66.98 percent of junior secondary school pupils and 68.27 percent of senior secondary school students studied foreign languages. See Fu, 1986, 95.

Table 2.1

Number of Full-Time Junior and Senior Secondary School Chinese-, English-, and Russian-Language Teachers

Year	Chinese Junior	Chinese Senior	English Junior	English Senior	Russian Junior	Russian Senior
1957	56,621	8,624	73	770	195	3,991
1958	60,984	11,449	635	1,005	1,932	4,724
1959	85,403	14,899	1,859	1,471	3,976	5,694
1960*	87,500	16,503	—	—	—	—
1961	94,402	19,707	3,384	2,017	11,704	7,523
1962	87,581	19,301	5,822	2,288	13,976	8,052
1963	93,402	18,915	11,704	2,801	18,704	8,295
1964	97,700	18,433	15,608	3,402	20,005	8,007
1965	99,106	17,757	19,751	4,033	19,543	7,727
1978	833,411	189,000	113,866	49,473	5,407	3,439
1979	789,878	158,104	153,802	50,968	3,865	2,669
1980	773,307	123,412	182,150	47,540	2,904	2,151
1981	686,096	99,110	210,937	48,117	2,510	1,641
1982	604,129	88,760	230,327	50,522	2,557	1,398
1983	565,277	84,000	240,989	52,017	2,995	1,465
1987	575,175	96,856	296,914	69,634	2,960	1,716
1989	568,266	95,736	313,369	71,679	2,887	1,524

Adapted from *Achievement* (Beijing: Peoples Education Press, 1984) 192–93; *Zhongguo jiaoyu tongji nianjian, 1987* (Educational Statistics Yearbook of China, 1987) (Beijing: Beijing Technology University Press, 1988); and *Educational Statistics Yearbook of China* (Beijing: Peoples Education Press, 1990).

*Total foreign-language teachers for 1960: 22,415.

ing the Cultural Revolution. Although foreign languages were part of the required secondary school curriculum, teachers characterized foreign-language training as "just slogans." In official educational histories analysis of foreign-language teaching policy simply stopped at the year 1962, resuming, without comment, with post-1977 reforms (*Almanac*, 1984; *Chronology*, 1983).

Furthermore, foreign-language teaching programs benefited from the general optimism in China regarding the progressive potential of education. English proficiency was perceived by urban Chinese as necessary for college entrance, employment, job promotion, and training abroad. English was commonly referred to in academic circles as "the language of international communication and commerce," the sine qua non of scholarly style.

English and the
"Two Civilizations"

The widespread popularity of English-language study also prompted reminders that modernity should be clearly distinguished from foreignness. In an address to the Twelfth Chinese Communist Party Congress in September 1982, Chairman Hu Yaobang announced that China would strive to quadruple the annual gross value of her industrial and agricultural production by the year 2000. Hu identified three areas of development crucial to the success of this extraordinary challenge: agriculture, energy and transport, and education and science (*GMRB*, 8 September 1982) and *China Daily* (3 September 1982). The Chinese educational establishment proclaimed that realization of such high expectations for China's economy was contingent upon human talent. A reformed educational system was the primary social institution upon which modernization would succeed or fail.

Educators took particular notice of the most prominent theme that emerged from Congress proceedings: "that a highly materially developed country, though fundamental for socialism, may not automatically be a socialist society" (*China Daily*, 31 August 1982). China was to become not just another wealthy nation but also a highly cultured, socialist civilization.

The desire to achieve both material and spiritual uplift was captured in the slogan "two civilizations." Foreign-language educators seized upon this message, at once attracted by its familiar logic and repelled by its implied warning. Did the search for spiritual depth represent a new vision for internationalizing China, or did it indicate how troublesome Chinese leaders found the consequences of global interdependence?

In fact, the influx of foreign knowledge triggered by China's open door policies had raised political, economic, and social quandaries as potentially disruptive as those faced by nineteenth-century self-strengtheners. Safeguarding socialist civilization against "capitalist, feudalist and other decadent ideas" made headline news on 4 December 1982, when delegates to the Fifth National People's Congress adopted a new national constitution, which identified education as a moral enterprise. Educational theorists described schools as industries for "creating socialist spiritual wealth," and political study at all levels of Chinese schooling underwent reevaluation (Qian, 1983).

Foreign-language teachers were placed on notice that language study occupied a special place in China's conception of cultural and international literacy. Foreign-language skills promoted self-reliance. At the same time, they could easily result in "spiritual pollution" (An, 1984; Yue, 1983; "Clearing Cultural Contamination," 1983; "Writers Discuss Cultural Pollution," 1983). Unlike mathematics and science, which became "Chinese-modern" as early as 1903, foreign languages remained symbols of nonindigenous modernity. This predicament confused and angered many conscientious educators. "As teachers in a socialist society, we should know why we teach English, how many students we want, what level they should be at, and in the future where these students will be employed. But this is never clear.... After graduation students are rigidly peddled—if a unit doesn't want the student tough.... We have to be clear about the ultimate goals for which we are training. Without that, we can never be clear about our curriculum" (Wang, 1982, 5).

Teachers received little encouragement for such blunt assessments. Instead, they were pressed to read inspirational essays portraying Chairman Mao as continually engaged in English study, despite such obstacles as advanced age and a heavy Hunan accent ("*Mao zhuxi zixue yingyu*," 1981). The inadequacy of official responses to the professional concerns of teachers intimated a rift between the aspirations of foreign-language educators and their leaders' modernization drive. Although policies of the early 1980s had yet to become emblematic of a vision of modernity where efficiency reigned supreme, China was embarking upon a course that emphasized economic development and left reform in political and cultural arenas actively discouraged or obscured by self-serving rhetoric. This erected a formidable barrier to reform proposals linking economic growth to increased political, professional, and personal choices. As we shall see, educators remained hesitant to question too deeply the assumption that the utility of foreign languages could be separated from the cultural traditions that inspired them. Their acceptance, however half-hearted and temporary, that foreign technique must be separated from foreign values made them worthy successors of Zhang Zhidong.

Chapter 3
The Development
of Secondary
Schools

Foreign-language education in China has been presented thus far as a barometer of what China's leaders and population consider appropriate levels of interaction with foreign values and peoples (Ross, 1992). Support for foreign-language training is high when sustained participation in the global community is deemed commensurate with China's political and economic interests and low when it is perceived as threatening to internal political stability and cultural integrity. This fluctuation in attitudes toward foreign-language proficiency has plagued the LXLS since its establishment in 1963.

According to its veteran teachers and leaders, the LXLS, and the university to which it is connected, is a product of the "glory days" of the 1950s when the revolution still inspired heroic acts of personal and professional sacrifice. However, their nostalgia obscures how the imposition and subsequent repudiation of Soviet-inspired educational reforms heightened existing tensions in foreign-language training.

The Development of
China's Foreign-
Language
Institutes: 1949–63

"Learn from the
Soviet Union"

In 1949 Chinese Communists turned to the Soviet Union for assistance in the gargantuan task of restructuring their economy. Training Russian-speaking cadres who would oversee this process was identified as a "strategic educational priority" (Hu, 1962; Hu and Seifman, 1976; Chen, 1981). Just one month after the founding of the PRC, Shanghai Party Committee Vice Secretary Liu Shao recruited the chief editor of a well-known publishing house to act as president of a Russian-language school in Shanghai. Three university administrators, all former liberated area cadres, were appointed as vice president and deans of academic and administrative affairs.

The school was essentially a training ground for political and military specialists. Its daily six-hour curriculum consisted entirely of classes in Russian and politics. Shortly after the school's establishment, its president was taken to task for being too cautious an administrator by Shanghai Mayor Chen Yi, who believed the school should expand its enrollment from 200 to as many as 1,000 students. Though English, Indonesian, Burmese, and Vietnamese were hastily added to the curriculum to achieve this goal, Russian-language training remained the school's priority.

The school's expansion coincided with a Soviet-inspired campaign to make foreign-language education more narrowly specialized. This effort launched the publication of specialized foreign-language teaching journals and secondary school Russian-language texts, the establishment of Russian-language departments in 36 post-secondary institutions, and even a Ministry of Education requirement that made Esperanto, celebrated in China since the 1920s as a vehicle for global solidarity, an elective available to students in foreign-language colleges.

As part of these initiatives the school was upgraded to a college-level institution and the Russian program was expanded to include linguistics, literature, and graduate studies. The college's Southeast Asian language concentrations were moved to a tertiary institution in Beijing, and English-language training was discontinued. China's first five-year plan and the arrival of advisors from the Soviet Union in 1953 spurred interest in Russian studies, and the school's enrollment grew from 1,670 students in 1953 to 2,248 in 1954.

Such rapid growth could not be sustained. Overcrowded classrooms and severe teacher shortages prompted the elimination from post-secondary schools of accelerated "crash courses" originally intended to meet state mandates for massive increases in foreign-language personnel. In response, a 1954 "Target for Russian Language Education Work," widely considered the first influential document on foreign-language education since 1949, prescribed a three-tiered system of institutions to coordinate national foreign-language training programs. The lowest tier consisted of specialized schools to train interpreters, tour guides, diplomats, and practicing teachers. The second tier was comprised of normal colleges, which trained foreign-language teachers for primary and secondary schools, and three-year foreign-language colleges, which trained translators and teachers. Finally, prestigious comprehensive and normal universities offered three-to-four year programs emphasizing literary studies and linguistic research for college-level instructors, editors, and translators.

At least 15 different courses of Russian-language study were being offered by post-secondary schools in 1956. Meanwhile growing hostilities between

China and the Soviet Union, as well as the government's inability to find jobs for the large number of students trained each year in Eastern European languages (*Chronology*, 1983, 199), prompted public criticism that the Ministry of Education had neglected Western European languages. In response, the Shanghai college was again expanded, this time into a four-year institution with programs in English, German, and French as well as Russian. Courses of study were lengthened to keep students out of the job market, a larger percentage of graduates were assigned to teaching positions in secondary schools, and the recruitment of new students into existing departments was suspended.

"Let 100 Flowers Bloom;
Let 100 Schools of
Thought Contend":
English as a Tool for
Political Struggle

The reintroduction of Western European languages in college programs throughout China coincided with the popularization of a classical enjoinder to "let 100 flowers bloom; let 100 schools of thought contend." Though the slogan was ostensibly used to engage China's intellectuals in programs sponsored by the Chinese Communist party (CCP), highly educated Chinese remained skeptical that the movement was a sincere attempt to improve their political and social livelihoods.

Encouragement to engage in political discourse shifted on 27 February 1957 when Mao Zedong delivered his famous address "On the Correct Handling of Contradictions Among the People." Mao distinguished between antagonistic contradictions between the Chinese people and their enemies, and unantagonistic contradictions among different sectors of Chinese society. In Mao's formulation, intellectuals were on the brink of an antagonistic relationship with the people. What would keep them and their students from falling into an adversarial relationship with the people—and the party—was a complete reformation of world outlook through ideological and political study. Mao asserted that "not to have a correct political point of view is like having no soul." He advocated that China's "educational policy must enable everyone who receives an education to develop morally, intellectually and physically and become a worker with both socialist consciousness and culture" (Mao, 1971, 459).

In retrospect, Mao's words intimated the harsh demise of the Hundred Flowers Movement. Yet, not two months after his address, CCP leaders initiated a rectification campaign aimed at eliminating a variety of party abuses. Mao's implicit warning about their ambiguous status notwithstanding, Chinese intellectuals interpreted the party's house cleaning as the gesture of sincerity for which they had been waiting. Their ensuing criticisms exceeded party tolerance, and a month later the Hundred Flowers Movement was supplanted by an antirightist campaign that purged thousands of intellectuals.

Both Mao's image of the well-rounded socialist and the populist vocabulary with which the Great Leap Forward (1958–59) was inscribed were incorporated into foreign-language teaching policy.[1] In 1959 members of the Shanghai Foreign Language Association defined meritorious scholarship as that which "made foreign things serve China." Foreign languages were to be "tools of political struggle in the service of the proletariat." The antirightist campaigns were publicly credited for raising the political consciousness of foreign-language teachers, improving linguistic technique by reducing the "harmful tendency of separating theory from practice," and correcting the reactionary habit of "placing professional interests above politics" (*WHRB*, 26 December 1959).

Today such interpretations are scoffed at by teachers who believe the movement ushered in an era of professional instability, hypocrisy, and self-deception, in which the quest for relevance superseded thorough research, trivialized theory, and began the inversion of authority between teacher and student that would ultimately be crystallized by the Cultural Revolution. Certainly, the antirightist campaign precipitated a loss of jobs and even exile to the countryside of teachers who maintained close foreign connections. Even so, the logic governing self-reliant, grass-roots development paradoxically promoted English-language teaching.

The Great Leap Forward's economic target of "catching up with Great Britain in 15 years" was used to justify renewed interest in English-language study at the official level. Between 1958 and 1960 the Ministries of Education and Foreign Affairs, with the backing of Zhou Enlai, formulated five- and ten-year plans for the "rational" recruitment and training of foreign-language personnel. In the autumn of 1960 Soviet advisors left China en masse, and

1   The Great Leap Forward was characterized by the slogan "walking on two legs," which generally implied the interrelated development of agriculture and industry, local self-reliance as well as foreign assistance, and balanced commitment to theory and practice. Many of the educational policies initiated during this period had their roots in experiments in Yan'an and later became hallmarks of the Cultural Revolution.

the subsequent revision of foreign-language policy far exceeded realistic expectations. For example, the Ministry of Foreign Affairs directed the Beijing Foreign Language Institute to establish five new language specialties each year until in one or two decades 74 of the world's major languages would be represented in the curriculum. Even had there been teachers and materials to support such dramatic expansion, students trained to distrust foreign influence would not have been convinced that the study of foreign languages was worth their time and energy.

In 1961 Chen Yi, now vice premier, delivered a much-publicized pep talk to convince Beijing students of the importance of foreign languages. Chen, like many Chinese leaders of his generation, reminisced about his own unsuccessful attempts to "break through the barrier of foreign languages," which he ironically blamed on "spending too much time on political campaigns." He encouraged students to "temporarily set aside the Chinese way of expression" and learn foreign languages. Echoing Zhang Zhidong, Chen took great care to delineate why wide promotion of foreign-language study implied neither neglect of politics nor loss of Chinese soul. "Please do not misunderstand me by thinking that I am talking against politics," Chen advised. "Foreign languages are prone to have a connection with politics. We want our students to be able to distinguish politically what is right from what is wrong in regard to the major issues" (Chen, 1962, 4).

Chen chided students for imagining that foreign-language study was beneath them, arguing that a tool of such power could only be entrusted to those with great theoretical and political perspicacity, an allegiance to cherished principles, and a correct balance of specialized knowledge and personal commitment. Chen's analysis rested upon a distinction between "individual activism," the right and good efforts of students to study diligently, and "individualism," the self-interest that led to careerism and, in its extreme manifestations, to imperialism, capitalism, and war. In the end, he advised his audience that specialization in foreign languages required constant vigilance in balancing the characteristics of red and expert.

For the next two years this balance tipped away from political rectitude toward technical expertise, culminating in 1963 in an ambitious seven-year plan for foreign-language education. Prestigious "mother institutions" would serve as centers for research and innovation. The 39 language specializations currently taught in colleges were to be expanded to 49 by 1970, and students would be required to study a second foreign language. While Soviet educational hegemony was blamed, as missionary influence once had been, for the preponderance in China of teaching methods and content poorly adapted to the Chinese student, foreign faculty from Western Europe were recruited to teach at 18 of China's most prestigious institutions. Finally, summer English-language camps were designed to bring young students in contact with older scholars whose departments had been decimated by a decade of neglect.

Rapprochement with the West: The Development of the Lu Xun Language School, 1963–83

The development of foreign-language training in tertiary institutions was paralleled by fluctuation in secondary school foreign-language teaching. In 1954 foreign-language education at the junior secondary school level was eliminated from all but the most prestigious urban schools. The policy was not intended as an indictment of foreign-language training. Rather, it was a temporary measure intended to improve student achievement in mathematics and Chinese and to alleviate the extreme shortage of capable language teachers.

The Ministry of Education further advised that English could be taught in senior secondary schools that lacked qualified Russian-language teachers. Second- and third-year senior school students who had already begun English study could continue to do so "unless students were willing to switch to Russian and teachers were available." In such circumstances "proper arrangements" were to be made for displaced English teachers, the most common was their reassignment, after very little training, to a Russian-language teaching position.

Less than two years later, the discontinuation of junior secondary school foreign-language instruction was criticized by the CCP's Central Committee as an example of how basic training in foreign languages, particularly in English, had been seriously eroded, hampering the development of the domestic economy and international relations. The Ministry of Education announced that beginning in the autumn of 1956 English teaching should commence in the first year of all senior secondary schools that could muster a qualified staff. By the fall of 1957, when the first national secondary school English textbook series were published, all secondary schools were to have initiated programs in Russian and English at the junior and senior secondary levels (Fu, 1986).

"Two-thirds English,

One-third Russian"

Secondary school teachers were advised to adopt the direct teaching methods first used in the 1920s as a substitute for the "deaf and dumb" grammar-translation methods that ruled most secondary school Russian-language classrooms. This was no small challenge to teachers who relied upon teaching outlines hastily patterned after Russian models, which emphasized reading, not listening and speaking, and who had access only to English texts published prior to 1949.[2] In recognition of such barriers, the Ministry of Education classified full-day secondary schools into two categories. "A" institutions received more rigorous teaching plans and requirements than schools with "B" classifications. From 1959 to 1960 "A" schools were to begin teaching foreign languages in junior secondary schools; "B" schools were required to do so only in senior secondary schools. Both types of schools were urged to teach two-thirds of their students English and the remaining one-third Russian.

The breathtaking speed with which the Ministry of Education altered foreign-language teaching policy caused consternation among students, as well as Russian-language teachers whose jobs were in jeopardy. Pupils raised on tales of imperialism, the Korean War, and the reactionary deeds of rightists found it difficult to understand that studying English was not antagonistic to the people's interests. In December 1960 *China Youth News* posed the question "Why is English taught in secondary school?" The editors maintained that English, the most commonly used language worldwide, was indispensable for promoting international relations. Its study should not be confused with U.S. imperialism, or the "intention of the reactionary ruling class before the liberation who caused English to be taught in schools to promote education for slaves. If only the ideological contents of the textbooks are made healthy, to study English is not only harmless but even profitable" (*SCMP,* 19 March 1961, 13).

Although 18.5 percent of secondary school pupils' weekly classroom periods by 1963 were foreign-language lessons, few schools were able to meet these guidelines. In fact, 65 percent of junior secondary schools had no foreign-language programs. Despite the "one-third Russian, two-thirds English" target, two-thirds of China's secondary school foreign-language classes in 1964 were Russian.[3]

---

2 In 1957 there were only 73 full-time junior secondary and 770 full-time senior secondary school English teachers in all of China. See *Achievement,* 192–93.

3 Colleges by this time were shifting more rapidly. Of university-level students, 46

Distrust of foreign-language education combined with recurrent policy changes foiled the implementation of a coherent English-language curriculum. Great Leap Forward demands for educational efficiency had led in 1958 to the readjustment of China's school system from a 12- to a 10-year structure. Textbooks just two years old were suddenly outmoded. Preparations for a new junior secondary school English textbook series were well under way when China's primary and secondary schools were abruptly returned to a 12-year system. As the texts went back for revision, the Shanghai Bureau of Education published a provisional set of junior secondary school English texts. This introductory series in turn necessitated revision of the three-volume set already being used in Shanghai's senior secondary schools. Meanwhile, the Ministry of Education issued yet another draft English-teaching outline for full-time secondary schools. This outline mandated six periods of foreign-language study a week and nearly doubled the number of vocabulary items that students were required to learn, making Shanghai's new text series obsolete.

Creating the "Whole Dragon" of Foreign-Language Education

The discontinuity that became the hallmark of secondary school foreign-language teaching reinforced efforts to establish an elite system of foreign-language education for young students. In 1960 the CCP Central Committee Propaganda Department asked the Ministry of Education to establish 10 schools in major metropolitan areas to train high-caliber pupils destined to become China's future diplomats, foreign affairs officers, and translators. The schools would lay the foundation for a carefully coordinated program of linguistic training beginning with 10-year-olds and ending with highly fluent college graduates. Taken together, the whole system would provide the tail, body, and head for a powerful foreign-language teaching "dragon" (yi tiao long).

The complete dragon system was appealing for many reasons. The Soviet Union, whose discredited influence could still serve as a model when necessary, had been developing a similar network of foreign-language schools. Many influential leaders and educators credited their own foreign-language proficiency to the intensive language training they had received in missionary

---

percent studied Russian and 54 percent studied English or another language. See *Chronology*, 1983.

schools, which used immersion techniques. Even the ubiquitous Great Leap Forward "greater, faster, better, with more economical results" challenge was pragmatically reinterpreted to justify the development of elite schools.[4]

Finally, foreign-language instruction in secondary schools had been enhanced by a Ministry of Education decision making foreign languages count fully on examination scores for admission to tertiary institutions. From 1954 to 1957 college entrance examinations did not include a foreign-language component, because even some of China's most prestigious secondary schools lacked foreign-language departments. In addition, until 1957 positions in Chinese tertiary institutions went unfilled for want of qualified candidates. By 1962, however, competition to enter China's tertiary schools had increased dramatically (Pepper, 1984; Henze, 1984). Stringent foreign-language requirements helped post-secondary schools identify academically prepared students. Despite widespread student protest of exclusionary admission procedures, foreign languages became a compulsory subject in China's college matriculation examinations in 1962 (SCMP, 13 July 1962, 8).

The confluence of these factors provided the justification for offering a handful of youngsters advanced training in specialized primary and secondary schools. In April 1961 the Ministry of Education distributed a document entitled "Initial Thoughts Concerning the Establishment of Foreign Language Schools." Once approved, this document was eventually sent to colleges, language institutes, and provincial and municipal educational administrative bodies for informal response. In August 1962 the Ministry of Education distributed a final recommendation that foreign-language schools in six major cities across China be in operation by the fall of 1963.

In May 1963 the ministry convened a conference in Beijing for the purpose of implementing this recommendation. The official circular that summarized conference proceedings, "Concerning Running Foreign Language Schools Well" (see Appendix A), recommended that 10 schools offering instruction in seven languages (English, Russian, French, Spanish, German, Japanese, and Arabic) be established within one year. The primary educational aims of such schools were described as "identical" to those of regular primary and secondary schools, with the exception of upholding "slightly different

4 The CCP Central Committee used the slogan in a similar manner when it announced that the country's twenty national key tertiary institutions could no longer accommodate China's expanding higher education interests. Forty-four additional post-secondary schools, including the Beijing Foreign Language Institute, were designated as national key schools.

expectations and requirements for cultural and scientific knowledge."[5] The schools were explicitly to prepare students for 11 prestigious post-secondary institutions.

By the end of 1963 eight schools were operating in the cities of Beijing, Shanghai, Nanjing, Changchun, Guangzhou, Chongqing, and Xian. After a year of temporary housing in a corner of a nearby secondary school, the LXLS's new campus, situated on five and a half acres near Hongkou Park, was completed in the summer of 1964. The school's chief administrators as well as its core foreign-language faculty had been recruited in part because of the excellent language background they had acquired in missionary schools. Not all teachers appreciated being transferred from Shanghai's best secondary schools into the LXLS's new and unproven experiment, but, as one put it, "the foreign language school had the right to commandeer us." Young graduates of language colleges in Shanghai and Beijing completed the foreign-language teaching staff.

The school's ambitious curriculum (Table 3.1) mandated 2,579 class periods of foreign-language training, 1,217 periods more than the national secondary school outline. By 1966 the school had over 1,000 students studying English, French, German, or Spanish in an intensive boarding school environment. In its three years of operation 10 foreigners were part of the faculty.

The program offered by the LXLS must have appeared exceedingly attractive to Shanghai families. By the early 1960s virtually all young people in urban Shanghai attended junior secondary school. They faced stiff competition when applying to superior key senior secondary schools. The proportion of Shanghai's junior secondary school graduates who went on to academic senior secondary schools (35 percent in 1964) was kept intentionally low to avoid flooding the labor market with unsuccessful college aspirants. However, those who managed to enroll in a prestigious senior secondary school had a fair chance to enter college. While only 9 percent of all secondary school students in China were in senior secondary schools in 1965, the ratio of senior secondary school graduates to university entrants was approximately two to one.

Ideological considerations excluded many gifted pupils from the LXLS. Family background was the first necessary criterion for admission and en-

---

5   In practice this difference amounted to the expectation that students would acquire general fluency in one foreign language by attending no fewer than 2,500 class periods devoted strictly to foreign-language instruction.

Table 3.1
Foreign-Language School Draft Teaching Plan, May 1963. Weekly Class Periods.

| | Primary | | | | | | | Junior Sec. | | | Senior Sec. | | | | Prim. | % All | vs. Reg. |
	1	2	3	4	5	6	Total¹	1	2	3	1	2	3	Total¹	+ Sec.	Classes	Curric.
Assembly	1	1	1	1	1	1	221	0	0	0	0	0	0	0	221	1.5	same
Politics	0	0	0	0	0	0	0	2	2	2	2	2	2	412	412	2.8	same
Chinese	18	18	16	16	13	13	3,475	9	8	8	7	7	8	1,603	5,078	34.5	+11
For. Lang.	0	0	5	5	5	5	725	8	8	8	10	10	10	1,845	2,579	17.5	+1,217
Math	9	9	8	8	8	8	1,844	7	6	6	6	3	3	1,067	2,911	19.8	−504
Physics	0	0	0	0	0	0	0	0	2	3	0	4	4	441	441	3.0	−243
Chemistry	0	0	0	0	0	0	0	0	0	3	2	3	0	274	274	1.7	−167
Biology	0	0	0	0	0	0	0	2	2	0	2	0	0	210	210	1.4	−35
History	0	0	0	0	0	2	70	0	3	3	0	3	0	375	445	3.0	same
Geography	0	0	0	0	2	0	72	0	0	0	3	0	2	276	384	2.3	+66

						Subtotal						Subtotal	Total	%	Change
Nature	0	0	0	2	2	142	0	0	0	0	0	0	142	1.0	same
Phys Ed	2	2	2	2	2	442	2	2	2	2	2	412	854	6.0	same
Music	2	2	1	1	1	371	1	0	0	0	0	70	441	3.0	same
Art	1	1	1	1	1	221	1	0	0	0	0	70	291	2.0	same
Handicrafts	1	0	0	0	0	76	0	0	0	0	0	0	76	0.5	−38
Total Periods	34	34	35	35	35	7,659	35	35	34	34	33	7,074	14,733	100.0	+235

Adapted from Fu, 1986, 249.

¹Number of classes in each subject over six years. The school year may range from 35 to 37 weeks.

tailed a lengthy investigation procedure for each prospective student. Such exclusivity was justified with the explanation that when graduates became interpreters or diplomats they would come into daily contact with foreigners. Class background was equated with trustworthiness and loyalty to the state.

The detailed records that might have clarified the class background of the LXLS's student body during the early 1960s were unavailable for this study, but teachers and students unanimously singled out family background as the paramount qualification for admission. They described the LXLS as "basically a cadre kid school prior to 1977":

"You could say that to be first considered *chushen* [family background] was everything. We used to call the process of looking back through the child's background *yi cha san dai* [literally, investigating three generations]. The student could have no relations with foreigners, which extended, of course, to having close relatives abroad. None of the student's family members could have committed a crime or be of bad class background. In practice, though, this was a school for the sons and daughters of high-level government and military cadres. The school was not a place for the sons and daughters of intellectuals before 1977."

The school's air of selectivity provoked concern at the Ministry of Education, whose officials reminded administrators and teachers that particularly in foreign-language schools political education "must stand as the guiding principle." Selections from the writings of Mao Zedong and translations of important political commentaries were to be incorporated into foreign-language lessons (*Chronology*, 357–58). Productive labor was to be used to dampen the arrogant privilege (*teshuhua*) that was in danger of damaging the attitudes of some students. Class time in all subject areas was to be reduced to conform to regular secondary school teaching guidelines. To compensate for this reduction, the school was urged to work more efficiently, to teach students "more, faster, and with better results than regular secondary schools."

The perennial question of how to cultivate students' fluency in foreign languages without undermining their ideological purity was being raised in foreign-language teaching programs across the country. Reforms initiated at all levels of schooling suggest an increasing tension between innovative reform and correct ideology. By 1964 as little as 56 percent of post-secondary students' class time was devoted to academic pursuits after accounting for increasingly elaborate labor, political, and military activities (Fu, 1986, 128).

In retrospect, English teachers who worked at the LXLS prior to the Cultural

Revolution describe 1965 as the last year they achieved a balance between academic training and moral guidance. This assessment is reflected in broader institutional histories as well, where the decade of 1956 to 1965 is generally depicted as a period of gradual improvement, "despite the 1958 educational revolution's leftist deviations from reality" (Scovel, 1982).

Even the LXLS's "fortnight of learning and labor" in the countryside, which consisted of picking turnips at a commune an hour away from the school grounds, is recalled as "somewhat successful at stopping students from becoming conceited" by "helping everyone identify with the vital labor performed daily by peasants." One teacher remembered, "a general feeling of hope, or optimism.... We did achieve a combination of useful theory and practice, not just empty words. Of course, the latter came soon enough."

By the eve of the Cultural Revolution, the Ministry of Education's goal of implementing foreign-language classes in half of all junior secondary schools and all senior secondary schools by 1970 remained a distant dream. Only 40 to 50 percent of China's secondary schools taught any foreign languages. Specialized foreign-language schools such as the LXLS were perceived as necessary to insure a pool of highly qualified candidates for colleges and were to be expanded within seven years to include 42 institutions with a combined student population of 30,000 students. In the fall of 1965 new foreign-language schools were established in Wuhan, Tianjin, Hangzhou, Haerbin, Tangshan, and Luda, bringing the number of foreign-language schools to 14.

The Mystery of the
Cultural Revolution

Students and teachers at the LXLS returned from their commune stay in the late spring of 1966 to confront the first visible symbols of the Cultural Revolution. Posters blazed across the cafeteria walls cursing "the Peng Zhen black line."[6] Veteran teachers who had received training in missionary institutions or abroad were soon vilified as "loyal ministers to the throne of foreign interests," along with the more common label of "traitorous spy."

Mao Zedong's declaration that every class in every school across China should be temporarily suspended for the purpose of "making revolution" was striking in its timing. The familiar pattern of revision for final examinations was shattered. Mass assemblies attended by the 1,000 members of

---

6 For considerations of Cultural Revolution educational policy and practice see Chen, 1981; Pepper, 1978; Shirk, 1982; and Chan, 1985.

the LXLS community—cooks, gatekeepers, bus drivers, administrators, students, teachers—resounded to slogans stirring to some, vastly disturbing to others. "Defend the Party!" "Long Live Chairman Mao!" "Down with All Enemies!" "Pull Up Poisonous Weeds by the Root!" LXLS leaders told students to "stop writing posters and begin studying." Pupils completed their school year by engaging in "morning manual labor" (end-of-semester cleaning, still practiced in the 1980s) and "afternoon analysis" of newspapers and the writings of Mao Zedong.

During summer holidays the CCP Central Committee approved "the Sixteen Point Decision," which demanded that all those in authority who were "taking the capitalist road" be purged (*Peking Review,* 12 August 1966). Though the decision explicitly criticized only illicit relationships with foreigners, it effectively sealed the fate of foreign-language instruction at the LXLS. Cultural Revolution policies not only discredited elite secondary schooling in China but also sundered connections with the world beyond China's borders. The Cultural Revolution was to eradicate the "four olds"—old ideas, old culture, old customs, old habits of exploitation. The historical connection in China between foreign interests and privilege linked foreign-language proficiency to exploitation. The LXLS was accused of being all things bad—feudal, bourgeois, revisionist, a hothouse for cultivating revisionist sprouts and intellectual aristocrats.

The school lost much of its student body in September. Pupils between the ages of 11 and 15 traveled to cities along the lower Yangtze valley to "exchange revolutionary experiences." Officially, all junior secondary school students were sent to farms and factories. Primary school students attended classes sporadically and even lived at school, but no new pupils were recruited. Eventually the pupils were transferred to their original primary schools. Foreign-language majors from institutes around the country were assigned teaching posts at the LXLS, arriving in time to consider how teaching materials could be rewritten "to capture the correct revolutionary spirit of the times." When the LXLS's last "foreign expert" left China in early 1967, she had not taught for over six months (Knight, 1967).

Veteran teachers associate systematic violence at the LXLS with 16 September 1966, a young foreign-language teacher's wedding day. Caught by Red Guards at school, she was physically abused, her hair shorn, her clothing ripped. She staggered home to meet her wedding party, shaking, barefoot, humiliated, and, as it turned out, professionally destroyed. The school's chief administrator, locked for days on end in the school's makeshift "cow and snake demon shed," was brutally beaten. Sought for a further struggle session, she was hidden by her husband, who confronted the Red Guards himself. He lost the full use of one foot but saved his wife's life.

Teachers who had received harsh treatment refuse to blame their pupils:

"The students were told to make revolution and they did. Many of the students' parents were high-level cadres who had just been severely criticized, so they felt they had to be especially revolutionary. One evening we saw them at the neighbors and we were convinced they were coming for me this time. There were two groups of students. One group wanted to come in, the other group did not. They knew I had just been a teacher from the time I had been very young. They stood outside arguing, and I thought surely they would come in. I finally went out and said, 'Come in and we'll destroy the four olds together, shall we?' Many cried, 'Oh, teacher! We don't really want to!' And I replied, 'Come in anyway and have something to drink. You must be very tired.' So they came in, had something to drink, then left quietly, marching away in two orderly files. I still went to school every day. But after September 16 I told the young teachers with bad backgrounds to stay at home. In those days, many more of us had telephones, so I would call them at night and let them know what was going on at school."

The Cultural Revolution officially ended in 1969. The LXLS, without students, became structurally linked to the university with which it is currently affiliated and administered by a Workers' Propaganda Team.[7] Complaints that misinterpreted policy had devastated foreign-language teaching began to appear in the Chinese media. Mao himself reaffirmed the importance of foreign-language study in 1968, when he declared to a group of skeptical Red Guards at Beijing University, "It's good to learn English. Foreign language study should be started in primary school" (Unger, 1982, 177). On 27 July 1970, a Radio Beijing commentary condemned students who neglected their English studies and pointed out that foreign languages were irrelevant by advising them to recognize that foreign languages were tools for "making revolution."

Students remained uncommitted to foreign-language study not just because it seemed at cross purposes with revolutionary practice but also because they

---

7   The first Mao Zedong Propaganda Team in China entered Qinghua University in July 1968. These teams were composed of workers, selected by their factories, revolutionary cadres, and PLA soldiers. Team members formed the administrative structure at the school, a three-in-one revolutionary committee that included activist teachers as well as workers and cadres.

believed it was deficient in revolutionary pedagogy. Understandably, teachers who proved easy targets for political criticism sought at all costs to maintain control in their classrooms. They cleansed from their teaching materials anything that might be construed as bourgeois. Their texts were made stiff with orthodoxy and their methods "safe" and teacher-directed. Language lessons became sessions for mechanical translation and memorization, hardly achieving the revolutionary aim of promoting egalitarian dialogue between teacher and learner.

The LXLS remained closed for four years. Its documents, books, materials, equipment, and windows were all lost. Its students had vanished into fields and factories. In 1970 the school recruited an experimental group of 49 primary school pupils, followed in 1971 by nearly 300 more. Admitted without examination, these were the children of political officers on the winning side and workers and peasants.

Teachers and administrators credited the LXLS's reinstatement to the efforts of Zhou Enlai. Throughout the Cultural Revolution, Zhou had intervened in the job assignments of thousands of foreign-language college students, assigning many to special positions on designated PLA farms, reinforcing his role as patron and protector of China's foreign-language community (Fu, 1986, 112–13). In five evening lectures delivered to Beijing students and teachers, he reminded his audience that "the rainbow was made up of colors other than red," and that foreign-language specialists must embody "three fundamental abilities": correct political thinking, linguistic skill, and general cultural knowledge (*Chronology*, 1983, 435–36).

Zhou's advocacy of foreign-language education was but one offshoot of China's efforts to reestablish contact with the West and normalize Sino-American relations. The LXLS's recovery coincided with Nixon's visit to China, which prompted Shanghai authorities to reinstate English, which had been eliminated from Shanghai schools in 1969 and 1970, as part of the city's core curriculum.

Foreign-language teaching policy at the newly opened LXLS was left, per-haps intentionally, unarticulated. In an atmosphere where they dared not read or speak foreign languages outside the classroom, teachers questioned the advisability of using the direct teaching methods they had so painstakingly worked to perfect during the early 1960s, because these methods encouraged active student participation. Texts were rewritten and old materials were tracked down for reanalysis. There was virtually no access to new foreign texts, except for the Voice of America series, *English 900,* which had been sent to China by the United Nations in response to Mao Zedong's request

(Scovel, 1982). According to teachers, "Things simply had to start from scratch all over again. We hadn't stopped refining and experimenting in the early sixties, and by the seventies those experiences were obsolete."

The Shanghai Bureau of Education, again committed to foreign-language instruction, attempted to encourage dispirited educators by publicizing model training programs that reflected efforts to "elevate understanding, strengthen leadership, and teach foreign languages well." One highly touted program was developed by leaders at a Jiading County school who concluded that teachers (whose pedagogy was "drab" and "stilted") could not convince students that foreign languages were worthwhile. Rather, members of a local commune were invited to talk with pupils about how foreign languages had helped the commune inform visiting foreign guests of its high standard of living (SCMP, 1 May 1972).

The ironic juxtaposition of foreign languages as tools of struggle and the use of peasant-led foreign guest briefings to inspire students and teachers suggests how bereft of clear purpose foreign-language teaching had become. "Massline" projects continued to receive enthusiastic press coverage, but they were accompanied by increasingly vocal professional criticisms of the decline of the quality of foreign-language teaching. A 1972 national foreign-language conference captured the tension between professionalism and politics, theory and practice. Conferees aired complaints about poor administrative and instructional procedures yet cautiously confined their concerns within a tightly drawn political analysis of the Lin Biao affair (Chronology, 1983, 443).

The LXLS's affiliated college published its attempt to grapple with "politicized professionalism" in a 1972 issue of Red Flag. Although the group described pre-Cultural Revolution texts as bourgeois in nature, they also complained that early Cultural Revolution texts were marred by heavy-handed political content. Students who could say "taking the socialist road" in English had no idea how to ask for a cup of tea. The group concluded that languages themselves were devoid of class character although language learners were not. Effective foreign-language teaching must be predicated upon a correct understanding of three relationships: between ideological and linguistic content ("putting politics in command"), between theory and practice ("putting practice first"), and between criticism and inheritance ("standing with the revolution"). In essence, students were encouraged, much as they had been by Chen Yi 10 years earlier, to acquire basic linguistic skills and general cultural knowledge while remembering that "the correctness or incorrectness of the ideological and political line decides everything." Above all, language learners were to avoid succumbing to "the evil road of restoration," "the worship of things foreign or nihilism."

Concern for educational quality was not limited to foreign languages. In 1973 college administrators throughout China began to reinstate entrance examinations in attempts to raise educational standards. Although negative reaction in the media was swift, traditional methods for screening the academic preparation of college candidates were implemented, particularly in specializations believed vital to national security. Foreign-language majors, as well as students in several scientific and technical fields, began to receive work exemptions and enter tertiary programs directly from secondary schools.

Nevertheless, the work requirement for prospective college students left the LXLS's college preparatory role in doubt. Though the school's leading cadres were gradually "rehabilitated," they did not reassume administrative responsibilities until 1977. The school's recruitment program was dramatically redesigned to insure that only students from working-class, military, or politically reliable backgrounds were admitted. Although teaching materials remained rigidly politicized, LXLS teachers were apparently able to provide their students an impressive, if narrow, foreign-language training. The members of an international linguistics delegation that toured the school in 1974 were struck by pupils' accurate pronunciation and grammar skills and complete ignorance of the world outside China (Lehmann, 1975).

By 1981 LXLS teachers and administrators used the Cultural Revolution to justify any and all personal and professional deficits. Its bitter and violent legacy clung palpably to every school act, the negative reference point against which all practice was evaluated. Yet what actually transpired at the LXLS between 1966 and 1976 remained opaque, dismissed as "irrelevant" or as "gone and good riddance." Teachers resisted rehashing what they considered outmoded pedagogy. When asked to describe how they once taught, they shook their heads sadly or impatiently, denying that such experiences could possibly be worthy of serious attention. Besides, they were apprehensive about sharing such memories with a foreigner. Why should they? Official assessment of the Cultural Revolution's legacy had been published only months before (*Beijing Review,* 6 July 1981), and teachers were just becoming comfortable with the "proper perspective" from which to examine their experiences.

Despite institutional and pedagogical upheavals and appalling personal injury, the composite tale from these reticent teachers was not totally dismal. Some called their year at the LXLS's May Seventh Cadre School in Anhui

Province with nostalgic images of pastoral life.[8] Others merely sighed, "Such a barren, dreary life. That was a long time ago." The most poignant memories were shared by older teachers who had had direct contact with foreigners prior to 1949. Their recollections were laced with the pain of having cherished connections torn asunder. They described piles of smoldering Bibles in an eerie church yard, the slow and deliberate burning of old college photographs by a cheerfully unknowing child. They watched their sons and daughters bend beneath "mental torture." They felt ashamed but justified at sowing in those same children the seeds of distrust at knowing anything at all. "The pity was that I had studied too much. So I did not want my children to learn any more. I thought, if they are labeled an idiot, it's a blessing. It's a blessing."

Younger teachers' accounts were tinged with irony and black humor:

"The Cultural Revolution spoiled two generations. The young and us as well, since we had no opportunity to read English books. At that time, we had just graduated from the university. We took books to the countryside but, for example, I was reported to the Workers' Propaganda Team because I had a copy of *Tale of Two Cities,* and my book was confiscated as a poisonous weed. From then on I brought my knitting. 'The more you read, the more reactionary you will be.' It was nonsense, stupid! And as I think about it, the third generation too is harmed. Middle school students are influenced by all the leftover hostility. That's the hardest to see, isn't it? . . . I became a very good knitter during my countryside stay."

Others attributed their strength of spirit to the Cultural Revolution's violence. For these teachers, the Cultural Revolution provided a time when risk taking and camaraderie gave rise to a moment of empowerment:

"The Cultural Revolution had one good outcome. It liberated people's minds. A thinking generation has emerged. They won't be blind followers. We think by ourselves. . . . We want to improve our living condition, and we know we must improve our economic, cultural, and educational situation to do so. . . . Everything has a good and a bad side. Every cloud has a silver lining. If there was no Cultural Revolution people would not have changed their basic beliefs. We're not wildly idealistic, oh no! You see, we are sometimes fatalistic. But we also believe in present reality. China has one very good aspect—a long-term view, what we need as a nation."

8 These schools, whose name was derived from a directive about educational reform issued by Mao Zedong on 7 May 1966, were for the reeducation of teachers and cadres, upon whose ideological rectitude reform hinged. See Yang, 1982.

All recollections were marked by evasiveness and memory lapses strange in those who could otherwise bring to life so vividly events long past. For them the Cultural Revolution was indeed the "lapse of time" so movingly captured by Shanghai novelist Wang Anyi (1988). It was, in the words of a colleague in her mid-forties, a "fantastic time warp, which defied imagination, nearly as much of a mystery to me as to you."

The extent to which the Cultural Revolution haunted the LXLS came into partial focus for me during a perfectly innocent English lesson involving apparitions. A question in the lesson plan asked students to consider whether their school might be haunted. Pupils found this question hilarious. Although they loved scary stories as much as any North American adolescent, the question appeared incongruous in a classroom setting. In public, they were serious materialists who denied the existence of ghosts. "We don't believe in ghosts," reflected a student, "but, well, perhaps the school has one haunted place—where the student was murdered." The boy's suggestion stunned his classmates into silence. Had they been told to forget this incident that was certainly news to me?

Later a student shared a private account of what she called "the horrible murder." In December 1980 a student was found dead in one of the school's second-floor corridors. She had received a blow to her head late on a Saturday evening when all of her classmates were away from school for the weekend. The girl was a Youth League member and the daughter of a cadre who had apparently made enemies during the Cultural Revolution. "You know," said the student recounting the story, "we were all very scared back then. No one wanted to walk next to where her body was. The doorway was roped off for investigation. It was hard to go to sleep, and we kept a flashlight on in our room all night. It was terrible and confusing. The mother came every day and sat at school and wailed and wailed. Nothing ever came of it."

The student explored several murder scenarios. Perhaps someone was angry at the victim's relationship with foreigners, unavoidable at a language school, or jealous of the girl's success. Highly unlikely. Perhaps she had arranged a late night rendezvous with a lover turned homicidal. More plausible and yet, "We knew her! She was not that kind of girl! It's utterly ridiculous to think of such a thing!" The most credible explanation was that the girl's father might have been the undoing of "someone big" during the Cultural Revolution and her death was a final, mad act of revenge.

With the exception of this one extraordinary moment in a very ordinary English class, the murder went unnoted, despite the fact that school violence in North America was not an uncommon topic in staff lounge conversations. Without the gossip and innuendo that inevitably attended significant events of school life, it was almost unimaginable that this boarding school, so lacking in privacy, could have such a tale to tell.

The LXLS's unsolved murder provides a fitting symbol of how teachers and administrators chose to deal with the Cultural Revolution. The period created a group of educators who were fatalistic revisionists of their own pedagogic histories. "Nothing intentionally carried out has the right to leave such a gaping hole in one's life," concluded an English-language instructor when she gave in to my repeated requests to trace the roots of her own language teaching practice. "But it did. I'm sorry, but for me it just plain wiped the slate clean."

A Crisis of Excellence:
Concentration and
Diversity in Secondary
Schooling

Mao Zedong's death in September 1976 was rapidly followed by the fall of "the Gang of Four," the reversal of the "two estimates,"[9] and a fundamental reinterpretation of secondary schooling. The requirement that senior secondary school graduates work for two years before being recommended for tertiary training was abolished. College entrance examinations were reinstated, and preparation for them in secondary schools became the primary prerequisite for admission into post-secondary institutions.[10] The secondary school curriculum was once again subordinated to the needs of colleges and universities.

---

9   The "two estimates," often referred to by teachers at the LXLS when they discussed the Cultural Revolution, were the fundamental assumptions upon which radical criticism of Chinese educators, intellectuals, and schools rested. The first was that from 1949 to 1966 China's entire educational system was dominated by a revisionist, bourgeois line. The second was that, by extension, the world outlook of most teachers, intellectuals, and students was also bourgeois and that they should be considered potential enemies of socialism.

10 For several years opportunities for attending college were extended to China's "lost generation," those students who had been automatically promoted during the Cultural Revolution years, regardless of school attendance and achievement. Between 1978 and 1980 the entrance examination became increasingly restricted to recent senior secondary school graduates. See Pepper, 1984.

"Run Key Schools
Well"

Reforms favoring lengthened school programs, standardized testing, and "professionalism" as the touchstone for teachers and administrators reflected educational assumptions not unlike those that undergirded China's educational system just prior to the Cultural Revolution. However, despite the Cultural Revolution's antiintellectualism, the expansion of primary and secondary schooling during those years, as well as the dispersion of large numbers of educators to nonacademic posts, permanently altered the landscape of Chinese schooling (Pepper, 1984; Rosen, 1984).

In particular, reform-minded leaders pointed out that scholars trained during the Cultural Revolution were inadequately prepared to take over major responsibility for advanced research and teaching. This lack of intellectual leadership coupled with shortages of middle-level support personnel was seriously compromising China's ability to modernize. The national plan for developing science and technology from 1978 to 1985 charted a course that was supposed to assist China reach "advanced world levels" in scientific endeavor in fifteen years. Such aspirations were recognized as unattainable without drastic reform of China's schools.

Predictions of a crisis in Chinese schooling infused nationwide efforts to create educational contexts in which excellence and expertise could be cultivated and directed toward strengthening the nation. Although concerns about schooling were phrased in a vocabulary quite different from that employed in *A Nation at Risk* (1983), the compelling stridency with which they were articulated was remarkably similar. Educators and CCP officers denounced the "revolutionary" educational policy of the Cultural Revolution as extreme egalitarianism, precipitating mediocrity and far worse.

The post-Cultural Revolution reform having the largest impact on the LXLS—the reintroduction of key schools—was a response to this perceived crisis in educational excellence. The redesignation of such schools nationwide was publicly announced by Deng Xiaoping in 1978. Deng contended that poor Chinese schooling and subsequent shortages of highly trained specialists precluded modernization. By concentrating China's best facilities, faculty, and students in key institutions at all levels of schooling, the training of expertise could be accelerated.

Development through concentration of scarce resources, an economic strategy used by Communist reformers well before 1949, inspired Mao Zedong in 1953 to propose the establishment of key schools to raise educational quality. On 4 September 1953, *Wenhui Daily* announced that four key schools in Shanghai were to carry out new municipal policies in raising the quality of teaching. Over the next decade the number of Shanghai's key secondary schools increased from 10 (5 percent of the city's secondary schools) to 13 (not quite 3.5 percent of the total). Abolished during the Cultural Revolution as elitist "treasure pagodas," key secondary schools were reinstated in January 1978. By 1981 there were 76 district and municipal key schools in Shanghai (over 7.5 percent of the municipality's secondary schools). Twenty-three of these, including the LXLS, were municipal key schools and considered the most prestigious secondary schools in the city (*Almanac,* 1984).

Deng Xiaoping delineated the role of key schools in such a way that he could also advocate in apparent good faith greater access to education for all Chinese citizens. He did so by highlighting the service key schools were to provide Chinese society. In return for their privileged status they were expected to bring a wealth of pedagogical experience to regular institutions, largely through in-service training and applied research. In essence, Deng outlined a trickle-down approach to raising educational quality that concentrated reform "efforts on establishing preferential key universities, middle schools, and primary schools that will act as pivot projects for raising the universal educational standard" (*China News Analysis,* no. 1181, 23 May 1980).

Within a year key secondary schools accounted for 5,200 of China's 112,000 secondary schools. Competition for students, faculty, and funding ensued, as did overzealous attempts by individual schools to push ever-higher percentages of their pupils up an increasingly stratified educational ladder. The media criticized educators who measured merit strictly by test results. Administrators complained that teachers scrambled to protect their own academic turf, disrupted unity in teaching efforts, and produced arrogant, nearsighted students obsessed with grades. Nearly everyone blamed over-ambitious parents for their ruthless educational credentialism.

In 1980 educators and state officials convened China's first National Work Conference on Key Schools to discuss whether the price of excellence was too high. Conference participants concluded that key schools remained crucial to the development of a strong, modern, democratic, and cultured socialist China. At least in the short run, modernization would be impossible without them (Zhang, 1980; *An zhao zhongdian zhongxue gongzuo huiyi jingshen, quanmian guanche dang de jiaoyu fangzhen,* 1980). The Shanghai Municipal Bureau of Education incorporated these findings into a controversial educational campaign called the "two comparisons" (*Shanghaishi zhong xiaoxue jiaoyu gongzuo jingyan xuanbian,* 1980–81). The campaign was designed to evaluate improvements in educational quality measured among institutions and within individual schools. The stated purpose was to honor two types of schools, those of highest quality and those that showed the most improvement relative to their own past performance.

From the beginning of the campaign the bureau was forced to confront the criticism that explicit institutional comparison would lead to increased competition among Shanghai's schools. Schools with poor academic reputations were especially vulnerable to publicity that would further damage their reputation and ability to recruit promising students. Bureau officials countered that outstanding schools were being singled out only as models of successful policy and that such recognition would correct overemphasis on promotion rates, facilitate a more well-rounded curriculum, professionalize administrative styles, and improve teaching efficiency.

As critics had predicted, the comparison campaign generated enormous visibility for schools whose students excelled on college preparatory examinations. To the delight of LXLS teachers, one of their students was featured in local papers for outstanding performance (*WHRB,* 1 August 1980; Liu, 1980). Although such accolades were accompanied by perfunctory reminders of the "dual responsibility" of secondary schools to provide colleges with qualified students and to provide society with competent workers, the latter was of minimal concern at the LXLS. National foreign-language teaching policy, which sought to combine "popularization," the gradual expansion of basic programs to regular primary and secondary schools, with "concentration" of able students and teachers in the key schools, allowed the LXLS a credible justification for directing its energies to the college-bound pupil. Like other key schools, the LXLS would share its "educational harvests" with less-favored establishments, thus increasing the quality of sister schools while avoiding the Cultural Revolution pitfall of enforced uniformity (Zhang Wensong, 1983; Chang, 1983; Chen Pu, 1982). Meanwhile, the LXLS's specialized curriculum became a path to elite college training, assuring nearly all graduates admission into tertiary institutions. Though careful to avoid any appearance of arrogance, members of the LXLS community argued that their entitlement was well deserved. "Key schools like ours are necessary for the training of experts and specialists. Keys can offer more to good students. This doesn't mean that no clever students will come out of regular schools. Our graduates are simply more talented, capable, clever, and knowledgeable. Key schools can provide more *rencai* [talent]. . . . The State attaches great importance to these schools. The idea that ordinary schools are for blue collar workers is not necessarily correct. It only means that key schools offer more opportunities for students to develop their abilities."

"Run Foreign-
Language Schools
Well"

The reinstatement of the LXLS's key school status vindicated not only its commitment to training a college-bound elite but also its specialized foreign-language curriculum. Since the Cultural Revolution, policy concerning foreign-language secondary schools had been a matter of contention between those who argued for continued cultivation of expertise and those who argued that the expansion of foreign-language instruction in urban secondary schools rendered specialized schools unnecessary. Opponents of the schools succeeded in closing several down, but their actions were criticized by college teachers who contended that poor results on English college entrance examinations, ranked lowest of all subject areas since the examination's resumption in 1978, reflected the inadequacies of the secondary school foreign-language curriculum. One disgruntled university instructor complained that the remedial training he had to provide was "like eating all three meals after 6 P.M.; it can't be done" (Wang Zongyan, 1982).

Such concerns prompted the Ministry of Education to sponsor a national conference to evaluate China's secondary school foreign-language teaching policy. The government officials, administrators (including one from the LXLS), and educators from throughout China who attended the 1982 conference acknowledged that the basic problems of secondary school foreign-language programs stemmed from factors over which they had no control. National teaching plans were too ambitious for the limited resources of most schools. Teaching materials were scarce or poorly conceived, and those published abroad were irrelevant to the lives of young Chinese students. The increased importance of English in the college entrance examination (see chapter 5) had forced schools to implement language programs despite the lack of well-trained instructors. This shortage of qualified language teachers was considered the most significant problem facing foreign-language education. Although the number of secondary school English teachers increased tenfold between 1965 and 1982 (see Table 2.1), approximately one-third of these new teachers had been trained since 1978, the majority in short-term programs (Zhu, 1982).

Conference participants concluded that quality in teaching was of paramount importance but advocated that a "correct relationship between quality and quantity" be maintained. Disparities between programs at different schools were not only inevitable but justified by the doctrine of "diversification" (*duoyangxing*). Schools without the facilities to begin foreign-language instruction in junior secondary school were to do so in senior classes. Introductory college courses were to be organized by ability, and exceptional first-year students were to be placed in advanced sections. Most secondary schools were to teach English, although "a certain percentage" could offer Russian or Japanese. Above all, secondary school foreign-language teaching policy was to be pragmatic, "for real, not for show."

The flexible and pragmatic response to secondary school teaching quality implicitly addressed the concerns of rural educators, who questioned mandatory foreign-language study for all Chinese students. They perceived the popularity of English-language study as an urban phenomenon, irrelevant to the lives of most Chinese youths, and as an inefficient use of limited educational resources. This position was articulated by a secondary school English teacher one month after the conference. "Youngsters spend 500 hours or more working at it, but once they leave school, how many will ever have a chance to use it? The majority of our students live and work in rural areas and will have little opportunity to move to coastal cities where English seems so important.... Many of my former students have come to me with the question: 'How are we to use English now that we are working?' I have had to fend them off with some generalities in which I hardly believe" (*China Daily*, 24 June 1982). Rural teachers asked, "Suppose we give ... [rural students] some priority in deciding our school curriculum? ... Suppose we teach them some of the things that can help them immediately after they finish school? Suppose we stop teaching English to those who are not likely to use it?"

The demand for relevancy illustrated how diversification reinforced inequality of educational opportunity and strengthened the official support for privileged foreign-language secondary schools like the LXLS. Proposals to transform the school into a post-secondary institution were denied by a 1982 Ministry of Education pronouncement insisting foreign-language schools should be "run well."

Two ambitious measures for educational excellence defined the LXLS's curriculum by the early 1980s (see Table 3.2). First, the school's general educational program had to equal that offered by any of its 22 municipal key school counterparts. In addition, pupils were to acquire a foreign-language proficiency second to none. An oft-quoted school slogan defined the ideal LXLS pupil as one whose "foreign language ability was better than

Table 3.2

Comparison of Six-Year Key School and Foreign-Language School Curricula, 1981–1983.[1] Weekly Class Periods.

| | Junior Sec. School | | | Senior Sec. School | | | | | Total Annual | |
| | 1 | 2 | 3 | 1 | 2 | | 3 | | hum | sci[2] |
					hum	sci	hum	sci		
politics	2	2	2	2	2	2	2	2	384	384
Chinese	6	6	6	5	7	4	8	4	1,208	1,000
math	5	6	6	5	3	6	3	6	906	1,086
for. lang.	5	5	5	5	5	5	5	4	960	932
for. lgs.[3]	7	6	6	7	9	6	9	6	*1,398*	*1,218*
physics	0	2	3	4	0	4	0	5	292	560
chemistry	0	0	3	3	3	4	0	4	288	432
history	3	2	0	3	0	0	3	0	350	266
geography	3	2	0	0	2	2	3	0	318	234
geography[3]	3	2	0	0	2	0	3	2	*318*	*226*
biology	2	2	0	0	2	0	0	2	200	200
hygiene	0	0	2	0	0	0	0	0	64	64
phys ed.	2	2	2	2	2	2	2	2	384	384
music	1	1	1	0	0	0	0	0	100	100
art	1	1	1	0	0	0	0	0	100	100
key total	30	31	31	29	26	29	26	29	5,554	5,734
LXLS total	32	32	32	31	30	30	29	31	5,964	6,020
labor skills[4]	two weeks			four weeks					576	576

[1]Adapted from Zhang Jian and Zhou Yuliang, eds., *Zhongguo jiaoyu nianjian 1949–1981.* (Beijing: China Encyclopedia Publishing House, 1984), 158, 172.

[2]Second- and third-year senior secondary school students specialize in either humanities or science.

[3]Lu Xun Foreign Language School schedule.

[4]Labor skills are calculated at four periods each day for junior secondary school students, and six periods each day for senior secondary school students.

and whose general knowledge was just as good as" that of Shanghai's best and brightest secondary school students.

We now turn to an examination of the academically rigorous, highly pragmatic, and uniquely cosmopolitan school mission created by this coupling of superior scholarship to outstanding achievement in foreign languages. The attempts by teachers to embody this mission in their daily practice came into conflict with dominant patterns of Chinese teaching and learning. The privileged school climate conducive to foreign-language fluency was a source of great prestige and entitlement. To secure this environment, however, teachers strained acceptable levels of pedagogical innovation and openness to foreign influence to the breaking point. Through their efforts to come to grips with what and how Chinese adolescents should learn as they were groomed for advanced foreign studies, they inevitably challenged one of the most persistent patterns of Chinese secondary schooling: the hierarchical control of knowledge and authority within the LXLS family.

Chapter 4
Teachers in the
School

"You must realize, we are all one big family here. There are no secrets."
This advice was delivered to me during my first hour at the LXLS by a laconic
colleague who lounged against his desk in the staff office. He shared his
experience with an almost avuncular concern, but left no doubt that universal
recognition of unit omniscience would henceforth go without saying.

For months I remained uncertain about the levels of school life from which
foreign teachers were by definition excluded. Numerous inquiries went un-
answered before I realized that "family," the metaphor my colleagues invariably used to describe their workplace, provided the key to understanding
how power and information were distributed at the LXLS. Membership within
the extended school family positioned its 100 teachers in the center of a
decision-making structure that began with one benevolent matriarch and
descended to 500 compliant student children. Though the intensely personal
makeup of this hierarchy minimized the dispassionate application of bureaucratic regulations so infuriating to teachers in North America, it also
insinuated into every teaching act particularistic loyalties and obligations
that placed severe limitations on professional autonomy.

These limitations reflected dominant cultural and political values associated with the Chinese secondary school teacher's social and intellectual roles.
These roles were shaped at the LXLS by the relationships that teachers established with their administrators, by the arrangement of each teacher's
physical space and time within departmentally based collectives, and by the
competing tensions that different generations of teachers attempted to balance in the fulfillment of their school-family and home-family commitments.
Foreign-language teachers confronted the additional challenge of adjusting
their roles to the mission of training exceptionally fluent young linguists. To
this end, their ongoing reevaluation of the teaching process involved the
search for an alternative teaching metaphor that interacted in complex and
often contradictory ways with both the LXLS's familial model of authority
and China's long-standing pattern of state control of the structure and organization of knowledge.

The following discussion of power and teaching at the LXLS rarely strays
from a teacher's perspective on the LXLS's decision-making hierarchy. There

are two reasons for this. First, my understanding of the LXLS derived from that vantage point. Authority and knowledge were given to and withheld from me based upon my positional role as teacher within the school family. Second, teachers all believe, perhaps condescendingly, that they are the robust or failing heart of their institutions. "Know whether teachers are fully and thoughtfully engaged in their work," mused one of my colleagues, "and know the health of a school."

Teachers as Servants of the State

State control of the structure and organization of knowledge in China is often explained as a legacy of the Chinese imperial examination system, which set the ultimate goal of learning as the ethical perfection of state officials (Munroe, 1977). By rewarding scholars with positions of influence, the empire secured the voluntary allegiance of "establishment intellectuals" whose arduous path to power legitimized both their own and the state's "natural right" to govern (Hamrin and Creek, 1986).

During the first decade of the twentieth century the state's involvement in education altered dramatically. Many Confucian patterns of scholarship were challenged by the implementation of a centralized, publicly funded system of mass schooling whose specialized curriculum was designed to promote national development. Education was no longer conceived primarily as a private process of individual learning (*xue*) but a public one of teaching (*jiao*), a "benevolent state activity institutionalized in schools" (Borthwick, 1983, 43).

While the initiation of public schooling cast Chinese educators in the role of professional specialists, it did not fundamentally alter their relationship to the state. Chinese leaders continued to bolster their political power by mandating that knowledge conform to state orthodoxy and that teachers act as state functionaries vested with the intellectual authority of the canon, but without the autonomy that North American educators often associate with intellectual and professional freedom (Hayhoe, 1989b).

The LXLS's familial patterns of authority generally reinforced constraints placed upon the intellectual and moral authority of educators by the centrality in China of state fosterage of knowledge. Yet its leaders and teachers also exercised professional judgment, often with unforeseen consequences. In this sense the LXLS was much more than ideological apparatus of the state, although in its most public performances it appeared more like state theater than extended family. In fact, the interplay of national education policy with the daily interaction of teachers and leaders fostered a school environment similar to the "theater of virtue" that characterized the American high school prior to World War II, an institution whose highly demarcated and neatly prescribed public roles concealed a backstage world of unceasing political maneuvering and family squabbling (Robert Hampel, 1986, 23).

The Ambiguous
Role of the
People's Teacher

Observers of Chinese teaching frequently remark how richly "the language of metaphor reveals the conceptual basis of teaching in China" (Paine, 1990, 50). In fact, LXLS teachers described their own practice with a profusion of figurative expressions. One of their favorite metaphors, by which they likened the teacher to a gardener (*yuanding*), was drawn from long-standing usage and given form in professional journals filled with colorful illustrations of diligent "gardeners" toiling before stacks of exercise books, "cultivating into the middle of the night." Although this earthy metaphor is credited to Stalin, the successful Chinese teacher has traditionally been honored for producing a world of peaches and plums whose far-flung goodness is a mentor's greatest tribute. Like almost all figures of speech popular during the 1980s, the teacher as gardener also evoked disturbing political memories. Even the youngest LXLS teachers witnessed Jiang Qing's attack on the 1972 opera *The Song of the Gardener,* and eventually tasted the bitter fruit it collected.

A metaphor used almost as frequently by my colleagues came less from the heart and described teachers as engineers of the human soul, a phrase adapted from Gorky's comment on the social function of writers. Despite reference to the human being's moral core, the calculating engineer connoted a primarily instrumental role for teachers. Engineers were a respected elite in China whose know-how produced tangible material benefits. The teacher whose ability to make expert knowledge concrete in the lives of students was credited with furthering China's drive toward economic modernization.

The teachers with whom I worked saw their dual role of nurturer and expert as complementary. A teacher combining both qualities was perceived as a guardian of knowledge who intimately understood the moral and affective consequences of knowing. Although knowledge was viewed as entrusted to the teacher by a higher authority, rather than being socially constructed, it is significant that once in possession of knowledge teachers became identified with it. Chinese contend as often as North Americans that

73

quality education "hinges entirely upon the teacher" (*guanjian zai jiaoshi*), and they are likewise ambivalent about and tend to devalue the skills required to teach. Consequently, when expert knowledge is suspect or deemed irrelevant, so are teachers.

On the evening of 26 April 1982, three young female teachers who worked at Auspicious Temple Primary School in Huangkan Commune, a suburban county of Beijing Municipality, were attacked by commune residents. The teachers were rescued after 20 minutes by two colleagues. Near midnight stones and bricks were thrown through the windows of the women's dormitory, and an uneasy faculty refused to go to work the following morning. Auspicious Temple Primary School remained closed for over one month. According to newspaper accounts, two of the three abused teachers had nervous breakdowns. All three were hospitalized. The parents of these young teachers raged against county and municipal cadres. "Our children go to the country to teach and they get beaten up like this!" they protested. "Higher party officials better take care of this [since you won't]!"

A widely publicized investigation into the affair revealed that commune authorities had failed to take action against the primary instigator of the attack, the younger brother of a powerful local cadre (*GMRB*, 24 June 1982). Although it came as no revelation to the Chinese public that primary school teachers, especially young women employed in rural, community-run schools enjoy neither great respect nor security from local bullies, this particular news account drew comment from around the country. The story provided a timely example of failed efforts at raising the status of knowledge and the public school teachers who embodied it. By refusing to recognize the seriousness of the incident, commune leaders not only participated in the systematic harassment of female teachers. They also perpetuated the view that what went on in schools was not worthy of attention.

Discussions about the incident at the LXLS were indicative of a nationwide debate about the status of teaching. Much of the debate centered around a sharp critique of Cultural Revolution efforts to demystify expert knowledge by infusing it with a singular moral-political focus, and around associated policies that exhorted peasants to formalize their practical wits with confidence and warned teachers to apply their theoretical grasp to practical situations with humility. "As a result, some leaders are insensitive to education," a colleague explained. "Everyone talks about China's tradition of respecting teachers, our *xiansheng*.[1] But young teachers in the countryside where the

---

1 This traditional expression signifying that the teacher deserves the respect of one's

kids will be working in the fields, what do you expect? They have no power. At our school, maybe things tell a different story. But there? I'm not surprised. Of course, I'm not saying it's right. This kind of thing hurts the whole profession. But it's not at all surprising. As much as Chinese might cherish children, primary school teachers are not highly regarded."

When another colleague countered, "But, I really believe we *are* respected," a third staff member turned at the office door and settled back against the wall, arching an eyebrow. The second teacher held her ground. "Yes, honestly, I do. I'll be the first to agree that during the Cultural Revolution we were reduced to the lowest status." She launched into what I recognized as the almost obligatory recital of past sins with which teachers prefaced their professional pronouncements. "Then teachers were just the 'stinking ninth category.'[2] But now our status has changed. Lately the government has decided to increase the salary of primary and middle school teachers. Each of us will be promoted one stage."[3]

She paused and added, "you know the traditional aphorism 'all occupations are lowly in status, except the study of books, which is lofty' (*wan ban jie xiapin, wei you dushu gao*)? Well, this is incorrect, feudal thinking. Teachers in China are part of the working class now, just like peasants and workers. It would be ridiculous as well as incorrect to put on airs because we have knowledge. Yet, we are also peoples' teachers. Our work here is mental labor, and it is respected as such."

Her mixed assessment regarding the respect teachers deserved suggests how troubling LXLS teachers found the ubiquitous portrayals of Chinese educators who turn to teaching as a result of failure in more significant

---

elders has now been replaced in China by *laoshi*, literally "respected teacher," sometimes preceded by the teacher's family name. While LXLS students were aware that common English usage made this practice awkward, they persisted in doing so, prefacing a question, "Teacher X, do you think . . . ?"

2　During the Cultural Revolution intellectuals, including public school teachers, ranked at the bottom of a list of nine enemies of the people: landlords, rich peasants, counter-revolutionaries, bad elements, rightists, renegades, enemy agents, capitalist roaders, and intellectuals.

3　After a virtual stagnation of remuneration from 1963 to 1977, teaching salaries prescribed by a national, eight-step pay scale were raised at the end of the 1970s and then again in 1982. Only two individuals at the LXLS in 1982, including the headmistress, held grade-one positions, for which they earned a monthly salary of approximately U.S.$77. Grade four teachers, the highest title held by any teacher in the English department, had monthly salaries of U.S.$45.

pursuits. Familiar images of the ill-educated scholar—the Kong Yijis[4] and bunglers who "can only grow rice on blackboards"—recall George Bernard Shaw's cynical conviction that "those who can't do, teach."

Power and Authority
in the Unit Family

The struggle by LXLS teachers to overcome the images of a diminished profession was hampered by the structure of the LXLS work unit. Next to their own families, it was the most important social group to which they belonged, and they were not voluntary members. "You can choose your friends, but not your family" describes well enough their assignment to the school upon graduation from college. They received from the LXLS salaries and benefits, but also movie tickets and ration coupons, and approval or rejection of applications for getting married or divorced, having children, and joining the CCP.

The assertive permanence of the unit in the lives of my colleagues was marked by the high wall that encircled the entire campus. Its inescapable solidity bound each unit member physically to the collective and extended even beyond the school gates in the form of small enamel badges that students and teachers wore to penetrate them. Pupils who returned to school on Monday morning without their school badges were met by the stern glare of a gatekeeper. "Where's your badge? You are your unit. How can you be here without it?" Teachers, too, were periodically reminded to keep them pinned on. "Actually, I don't think it's such a bad idea to wear them," commented a colleague. "Why not? We should be proud of the school. We are very successful. The students should recognize that there is a time when pride in achievement must be balanced with personal responsibility for acting on that pride. They wear their badges in public, and people know who they are. If they are respectful, mature, well then people will know we are doing a good job at the LXLS."

Even teachers who appreciated the security and prestige their attachment to the LXLS conferred expressed concerns regarding more obvious forms of unit control. Excessive "unitism" was criticized by the media for leading to autocratic irrationality and the squandering of human resources, and teachers agreed that collegial sharing of teaching experiences and the promotion of

4 The name Kong Yiji alludes to Confucius, the first three characters pupils traditionally learned to master in Chinese exercise books, and a drunken and pathetic scholar in a famous short story of the same name by Lu Xun. See Lu Xun, 1980.

their professional interests were often impeded by the possessiveness of unit interests. More seriously, unit attachment had compromised the personal lives of many middle-aged teachers. More than half the female teachers in the English department had been separated from their spouses, some for as many as 11 years. Job assignments in different cities prohibited them from visiting their husbands more than once or twice a year, and alone they struggled to raise children and maintain a semblance of family stability.

By the early 1980s academic and CCP affairs were slowly becoming disentangled at the LXLS. Nevertheless, all of the school's major administrators were party members, and teaching remained extraordinarily taxing for those at odds with the school hierarchy. Private lives were always on the verge of becoming public in the unit setting, and friendships were easily compromised in such a wary environment. Many teachers regretted their strained relationships with colleagues but defended cautious distance in an era when recent political movements had made confidences between friends vulnerable to corruption and betrayal. "The unit requires commitment to the whole good, not just your special friends. With my family and intimate friends, I can ask all kinds of questions that I would never ask at school. But don't misunderstand that we are insincere. It's a question of avoiding clashes of loyalties as much as it is lack of trust or honesty."

Leaders as Parents

The LXLS family was guided by a triumvirate whose most visible officer was the headmistress, the school's primary administrator in charge of academic affairs. The headmistress was the school's face to the public, responsible for justifying its privileged reputation. The school's collective identity was due largely to her forceful leadership. A noted pedagogue in her own right, the headmistress was educated prior to 1949 in two of China's most prestigious private female institutions. She was sometimes accused of intimidating teachers, yet she was physically unimposing, a small, no-nonsense woman in her fifties who dressed unfailingly in simple suits of deep blue or brown. Hers was a moral authority vested in both personality and the position she held in a hierarchical yet personal world. She conveyed to teachers and students that privilege must be paid for with self-sacrifice and control. As the school's "guiding hand," she exercised the final judgment in matters of teaching. Although she criticized as inefficient and unprofessional the autocratic implications of the widespread attitude that "if the hand isn't around, nothing can be done" (*Zhongxue xiaozhang jingyan tan,* 1982), teachers who, for whatever reason, did not gain her favor felt quite powerless. Even so, faculty members who resented what they called her dictatorial handling of school policy admired her resolution. "How can she remain faithful, continue to beat her head against the wall? If nothing else, she's persistent and fights for what she believes. I'll give her that."

The school's second administrative officer, the assistant headmaster, was trained in his youth, like the headmistress, in a private school administered by foreign missionaries. As manager of the LXLS's general affairs, he was in charge of allocating the school's nearly 500,000 *yuan* budget, and served as liaison between both political and academic endeavors within the school and between the school and the college with which it was affiliated. An unflappable, reliable public speaker, the headmaster was responsible for addressing the entire student body during special functions with ideological import.

The school's third chief administrator, the party secretary, had been a college political instructor in the 1960s and was a gaunt, taciturn man. In charge of the school's political and ideological affairs, one teacher described his duties as "making sure education serves proletarian politics." As well as conducting meetings of the 30 CCP members active at the LXLS in the early 1980s, he oversaw the form and content of political study sessions and courses for LXLS staff, faculty, and students, coordinated activities between the school's Young Pioneers and Youth League branch, and provided a link between the LXLS and its college CCP branches.

Although teachers occasionally engaged in direct discussions and even confrontations with each of these leaders, they normally "made their views known" through the school's five deans—of foreign languages, general studies, scheduling, general affairs, and ideological work. Deans served as mediators and assistants to one or more of the school's three chief officers. Occasionally described as the "ears and eyes" of the principal (Li, 1982, 138), academic deans bridged the considerable social distance between teachers and their superiors. The LXLS's dean of foreign languages was extremely effective in this role. A grandmotherly figure admired for her "heart" and ability to empathize, she took on much of the responsibility for regular classroom observations and kept in a spiral notebook a detailed record of her comments about each instructor's teaching style, relationship with students, and facility in motivating students "to think," as she put it, "smartly, quickly, brightly, with curiosity and on their own." She gained the support of teachers even for unpopular decisions "that came down from the main office," thus providing an excellent foil for the headmistress's strict demands and blunt appraisals.

Below deans in the school's chain of command stood faculty section leaders, chosen by colleagues to represent their various academic disciplines. In the case of the English department, two section representatives were appointed each semester, one from each of the junior- and senior-level English offices. Normally, section leaders were selected on the basis of teaching experience and current teaching load. A teacher already burdened with heavy responsibilities would not be asked to take on the additional meetings and paperwork that the section leaders's job demanded.

Finally, foreign teachers had a special representative in the administrative network, the foreign affairs officer. The LXLS's foreign affairs officer was a graduate of a foreign-language institute, and a CCP member who was charged to implement the LXLS's shifting policies toward its five or six foreign instructors,[5] provide living arrangements for their dependents, organize holiday outings, preside over their contract negotiations, and in general discipline those who had overstepped their bounds or overstayed their welcomes.

The foreign affairs officer was relieved of some of these duties by teachers assigned the role of a foreign colleague's "interpreter." Each foreign instructor at the LXLS was paired with a colleague whose responsibility included informing school officers about any and all aspects of the foreigner's life. Interpreters were chosen by the headmistress for political reliability, good sense, and forthrightness. Although close proximity to the foreign instructor was considered a unique opportunity for improving one's language abilities, it did not come without a price. The interpreter, asked to become intimate with the concerns of and yet remain safely distant from the foreigner, was constantly in danger of abusing the school's trust. The complex relationships that developed from this unusual pairing were characterized by tension, admiration, irritability, suspicion, and genuine friendship, reflecting the peculiar fusion of personal and professional life that Chinese colleagues took as much for granted as foreign teachers viewed with consternation.

Some teachers devised ingenious strategies for circumventing the essentially vertical hierarchy just described. One colleague was quite frank about playing two of his superiors against one another to secure a transfer from the LXLS. "I've been trying to get out of here. I want to teach at the college level, but the headmistress won't let me go. She doesn't like me. You've noticed I don't teach any of the main classes. I'll never get any kind of a promotion around here, yet she won't let me go."

---

5 The school employed 23 foreign teachers from 1963 to 1983. Five foreign teachers were at the school from 1981 to 1983—from the United States, New Zealand, France, West Germany, and Japan.

The teacher in question hoped to land a college-level teaching position with flexible hours, which would allow him to take care of his young son. He had been to the party secretary's house several evenings that week, pleading his case:

"Once two years ago when we all got our first raise, I heard that the headmistress was against giving me one. She didn't like my attitude. I told the secretary that I had been teaching 17 years, and had not gotten the raise to 74 *yuan* like the others. I knew that the headmistress had not wanted to give me a raise. I told him, 'Don't think that I don't know about this. It's very clear. She wants to keep me on because of my work. I know the ropes. I'm experienced. But actually, there are no good feelings. It's hypocritical to say otherwise.' I wanted to see if he would admit this. He did. I reminded him he knew the troubles that I have at home. My wife works way out in the suburbs and has to leave home at six and does not return until after dark. So I have to do a lot of chores around the house. I do come to school late sometimes, but I can't help it. I have to go out and buy groceries, and I have to take my kid to school. Next year he'll be in kindergarten, and I will not pay 10 or 12 *yuan* every month for unsuitable day care. Where is he going to eat lunch? And what about after school? Am I supposed to hang a key around his neck and ask him to feed himself? There's no place for him to go."

He continued after a pause. "It's ironic. I'm in my early forties, and just last year I finally got my own flat—20 square meters." He glanced around the office in which we were sitting:

"No bigger than this. Before we lived all crowded together with my parents. My father is crippled, but he could help look after my son. Now the headmistress says I can bring him to the kindergarten in back of our school and then he can stay in the office here during the afternoon. This is no solution, but it's a typical way of diverting the problem. He'll bother everyone in the office. He's a naughty little boy. And it's three buses to the school. By the time he got there he'd be exhausted. He couldn't even learn. It's impossible. So I demanded that the party secretary let me go. I'm working on him first, because he has some influence on the rest. The headmistress would never let me go."

He blamed his frustrated attempts partially upon another teacher who had tried and failed to change units. The teacher to whom he referred had been permitted to divorce her husband but lost custody of her son. She felt isolated from colleagues who made her the subject of continuous gossip and asked the headmistress for a transfer. When the transferral was refused the teacher demanded to be made a foreign instructor's interpreter. She was.

"I'll never get anywhere with that kind of thing going on. But I'll fight. I'll go—and I told him I'd do this—to the party secretary's house every night if I have to. He's the party leader. And now there is a big movement to have the leaders work closely with the people. I told him this, too. Of course, I wouldn't go to his place every night, but the threat is possible. I mean, think about Shanghai. The living conditions are very unsatisfactory. There's simply no place to go. If I go to see him, his wife will get very angry. She'll have to sit while I talk and talk. There's no place else to go. It will put pressure on him."

This teacher's strategy for gaining permission to leave the LXLS, successful only some years later, suggests how the all-encompassing nature of the work unit reinforced a positional system of authority and distribution of power that was both hierarchical and personal. The particular interests of teachers and leaders operated alongside a more formal, vertical decision-making structure. Information was normally given to individuals on a need-to-know basis, and teachers had little direct input into school decisions, even those that profoundly affected their teaching practice. Nevertheless, the LXLS remained a normative rather than coercive collective.

The Teaching and Research Group

The weekly tasks of teaching, political study, and discussion of schoolwide policy were accomplished by teachers in 15 teaching and research groups (*jiaoyanzu*). This organization of teachers into discipline and grade-based collectives began in the 1950s when the *kafedra* system was introduced into China by Soviet advisors to facilitate uniform quality in teaching, as well as the development of collective attitudes about professional responsibilities. "In our teaching group we have been close as a unit, and this is one guarantee for good teaching. Each teacher's work is a part of the whole curriculum. Working together is the only way to plan a six-year program and have it work. High test scores at the end, for instance, are not just the result of the senior teachers. It is everybody's effort."

Of the LXLS's 37 foreign-language teachers, 22 taught English and comprised the school's largest department. Two rooms of blackboards, cupboards, and teachers' desks provided the location of the English teachers' two teaching and research groups, one for junior secondary school teachers, and one for senior-level teachers. Each office had a section head who reported to the dean of foreign languages and the headmistress. In turn, each section was divided into smaller lesson-planning groups that met informally two or three times each week. These groups also had leaders who insured as much continuity as possible in language teaching within and between grade levels.

Since (with the exception of foreign instructors) teachers normally taught no more than eight class periods each week, they spent most of their school day, which began at eight o'clock in the morning and ended at four o'clock in the afternoon, in the close company of colleagues in these two staff offices. Although constant contact functioned primarily to insure conformity in teaching, it also alleviated the problem of teacher isolation, which has been considered one of the major barriers to effective teaching in the United States. While American teachers gain a sense of control and autonomy behind the closed doors of their classrooms, their privacy also discourages professional dialogue. In contrast, Chinese teachers, not students, move from classroom to classroom throughout the school day. As we shall see in greater detail in chapter 5, their teaching and research groups encouraged mentor relationships, especially between veteran teachers and their new "probationary" colleagues, who during their first year of teaching derived considerable support and security from more experienced colleagues.

Political Study and
Party Affairs

In addition to serving as the primary context for teaching activities, the teaching and research group functioned as the LXLS's primary setting for Friday afternoon political study, where state and party mandate found concrete expression in the professional-personal lives of teachers. The content and tone of these political sessions varied considerably, from frank and animated discussion of specific school policies to detached analysis of recent political documents and addresses delivered by prominent Chinese officials. Proper ideological and pedagogical perspectives became a matter of public discourse in these meetings and exerted considerable control over how teachers acted within the unit setting.

The political documents most widely studied during my stay at the LXLS were generated during the Twelfth Party Congress of September 1982. Throughout the autumn, newspapers such as *Guangming Daily* and education journals such as *Peoples Education* exhorted teachers to "Study Twelfth Party Congress documents," and "earnestly carry out the congress

spirit" ("*Renzhen xuexi, qieshi guanche dang di shier da jingshen*," 1982;
WHRB 10 December 1982). Deng Xiaoping's opening address became required reading for teachers. Near the end of December, a single mimeo-
graphed sheet from the college's Propaganda Department was distributed to
LXLS faculty members (see Table 4.1). "Well, look at this," said a colleague
turning to me. "Did you get one? Here, take a look. Could you answer all
of them?"

Several teachers in the staff room suggested that I take the test like everyone
else. "Why not? You can't do any worse than I'll do!" one laughed. "We
teachers don't know anything about politics. You really want to know what
will happen? A group of us will put our heads together and memorize the
correct answers."

"Yes, that's it!" cried another. "You can do it, too. It will show your
spirit!" In the rush of classes, the test covering Twelfth Party Congress documents was momentarily forgotten. As the day wore on, however, I received
sly glances from colleagues in the hallway. "Well, how's it going?" "Got the
answers yet?" "Let's see how modernized you are!"

The humorous resignation with which teachers treated the examination
of their own political understanding typifies their usual response to formal
political activity. They avoided it as much as possible. By relying on respected
leaders to set the course for social change, their political participation in
practice became political discipline. Their decision to withdraw from political
action certainly made their lives easier, a lesson most had learned from brutal
experience during the Cultural Revolution. Yet the ease with which even a
foreign instructor could, with the help of congenial colleagues, slip into a
routine of accepting and transmitting ideals compatible with national goals
should give those critical of the logic of continuing revolution pause. The
pervasive acts of ideological and political socialization, carefully orchestrated
or derived from sheer force of habit, week in and week out, created a sense
of benevolent control teachers simply took in stride.

Only in retrospect and with distance is it clear to me how many concerns
were being privately worked out during those Friday meetings, and how
deeply political devotion and sacrifice touched the life histories of the department's oldest teachers. By the end of the 1980s few educators were willing
to take on the extensive responsibilities direct participation in CCP politics
entailed. However, not a few teachers at the beginning of the decade, when
but one member of the English teaching staff belonged to the CCP, saw party
membership as the only viable position from which to enact social change.

"The way I see it," remarked a teacher, daughter of a family labeled

Table 4.1

Review Questions for the Schoolwide Test
on Important Documents from the Twelfth Party Congress

1. What historical mission did the Twelfth Party Congress fulfill?
2. Why is it said that the Twelfth Party Congress was the most important party meeting since the Seventh Party Congress?
3. Why is it said that since the Eleventh Plenary Session of the [Third] Party Central Committee we have already achieved a great historic transformation?
4. What is the party's chief responsibility in this new era?
5. What are the strategic goals, emphases, and measures for economic construction determined by the Twelfth Party Congress?
6. What principel problems must be solved in order to carry out the 10 policies of economic construction?
7. How should the basic principle of guiding our country's economic work—"food first, construction second" (*yi yao chifan, er yao jianshe*)—be interpreted?
8. Why is it said that a strategic policy problem in constructing socialism is that construction of a high cultural level must be accompanied by diligent construction of a high level of socialist spiritual culture?
9. What is material culture? What is spiritual culture? How does one correctly understand the relationship between material culture and socialist spiritual culture?
10. What are the primary components of socialist spiritual culture, and what is the relationship between spiritual construction and ideological construction?
11. Why is it said that socialist spiritual culture must have communism as its core?
12. What are our duties and responsibilities as teachers, students, staff, and workers in institutions of higher education in constructing a socialist spiritual culture?
13. Why is it said that constructing a high-level socialist democracy is one of our party's basic goals and responsibilities?
14. What are the primary components of the construction of a socialist democracy? What is the basic difference between socialist democracy and capitalist democracy?
15. How does one understand correctly the problem of class struggle today?
16. Why is it said that upholding the guiding principle of self-reliance is the starting point for our country's foreign relations?

Table 4.1 (*Continued*)

---

17. What important problems in the party's construction must be solved in order to make the party's construction the strong core of the business of guiding socialist modernization?
18. What is the guiding thought behind the revision of the party constitution? What have been the primary revisions in content?

---

bourgeois, "working within the system was the only option for changing it." Only as she neared retirement in 1989, a timing she viewed as tragically symbolic of her lifelong quest to become a member of the CCP, was she offered an opportunity to join. Blaming her constant party loyalty for the death of her father, the suicide of her mother, and the inadequate care of a desperately ill, bed-ridden husband, she grappled over and over with a question shared by many of her colleagues. Did she fail the party or did the party fail her?

"I gave up everything to follow the party. I didn't take care of my parents. I opposed them. At the age of 16 I left home to work for the revolution. I was told to criticize my family and I did so. I was so young and naive. I worked hard with no thought of money or reward. And I let my family go. In the 1950s, even when I was still so young, I could not join the party. After going to teach in the 1960s I was getting ready to join when along came the Cultural Revolution. By the 1980s—well, look at my age. If I join or don't join, I will still work hard for my students. All those years, yet the party did not trust me. Because my sister was abroad. All those years I did not write her. I knew nothing about her or my father. I didn't want to know. If I knew, I would have to tell the party everything. If I didn't know, then I wouldn't have to lie. For so many years the party could never see my heart. I had almost given up hope. Finally, my superior asked me what it is I really want, what it is I really think. Well, I said that educational reform for China was essential, but as for the rest, go ask an economist. How can I know? I am told I don't have to worry about all the country's big problems just because I am a party member. I wish party members were like they were in the 1950s. They didn't work for themselves, but for others. Now, it is quite different. The small ones, like at our school, they work from morning to night. They work constantly, thinking little of themselves. But the upper ones. They get involved in all sorts of things. What crimes can we little ones get into? We just work, work, work, teach, teach, teach. My only goal is to help my students. I don't know how to lead. I just know how to teach."

Such tales baffled the school's younger teachers. Frustrated by a monthly salary of about U.S.$23 that "hardly compensated for his daily headaches,"[6] a newly hired English teacher confided that he came to school each morning exhausted by "pent-up dread":

"I seem to be the only one around here willing to talk about how I really feel. I think I'm fairly open-minded. I'm not afraid to speak out. It's not just my teaching, but analyzing my motives for doing things. It's important. Do you think people around here do that? I know they must, but it's all inside. Look at my supervisor, she's such a good teacher, but I never know what she's thinking. Keeping things inside while thinking furiously, this is what it's like. It's a Chinese specialty. We keep so much inside. During political study there really are things we could talk about. Yet we don't analyze. We parrot editorials from the paper, and all the time I sit and look around the table at these people I work with, all more experienced than me, and I know they hold strong personal beliefs but they're tucked away, way down."

Younger teachers admired their older colleagues who could sacrifice with stoic good faith, but teaching to them was no longer a noble cause. Several hoped to be promoted to university positions, which meant to them higher salaries, more flexible working conditions, and a challenging intellectual environment. "Half of my classmates are in the United States studying right now, and look at me," sighed a young colleague. "I don't want to be at this school. It's true, I went to a normal university. I was not surprised that I was assigned to be a secondary school teacher. But I don't want to forget all my own training. Here I always have to deal with baby English. Look at me. This afternoon I will end up playing basketball again here at school, and then listen to evening prep. I am unmarried, a new teacher, so I have night duty. It's not that I dislike the students, but I want to communicate with adults."

Young teachers also embodied the frustration, entitlement, lack of personal freedom, and affinity for cultural and social experimentation that would eventually help ignite the violent protests of the last years of the decade:

"I think Western ideas are important for us. We are educated. We have scales of judgment. We know what is right and wrong and we can still see

6 Probationary teachers with two- and four-year post-secondary degrees received a monthly salary of 43 and 48 1/2 *yuan*, plus a food allowance of 5 *yuan*, respectively. After their first year of teaching, salaries were fixed at 54 and 58 1/2 *yuan* respectively, with an additional 6 *yuan* food allowance.

what others are doing without being influenced adversely. Of course, there are many young people in Shanghai who could not see Western movies, could not read certain books. Just think of it! It's so crowded. When you get on a bus here there's so much pushing and shoving. They don't have the education to be able to handle things from your culture. They'd go crazy. They'd be running wild. But I think for us language students, we've met foreigners, we've been to the university. We are capable of judging things for ourselves. We know how to make our own choices. These things should be allowed for us."

Because teachers rarely shared publicly such deeply held views, the daily activities of teaching were deceptively apolitical. No outward symbols of party authority, no flags, no portraits of Chinese leaders, were displayed in the staff office. Only where school walls remained long unpainted did faded patches indicate a past when teachers paid more visible tribute to the state. Large red characters painted above a blackboard in the south-facing English staff office did exhort onlookers to "study hard to reach the summit." Yet the majority of teachers felt this summit they assisted their students to attain had little connection to the formalized, contained political study they attended weekly. Their separation of pedagogical practice from matters of the state was, of course, just the opposite from the outcome that political study had once been designed to engender

Model Teachers at
Middle Age

In March 1980 *Shanghai Education* reported that the municipal government was "carrying out the target of the Party Central Committee and Chairman Hua Guofeng in raising the political and social positions of people's teachers" by promoting 36 Shanghai educators to "special grade teachers" (*teji jiaoshi*). This title, one of the highest honors bestowed upon Chinese teachers, was awarded to a member of the English department. Two years later another English teacher was honored as a woman of "six merits," which included being a good daughter, wife, mother, and worker and having a correct political orientation and only one child.

Members of the English department faculty were not surprised that these two women were singled out for recognition by the municipal government. The special grade teacher and the six-merit woman were both ambitious, successful, middle-aged educators, and, like most intellectuals in China, they had experienced hardship in their personal and professional lives. Although the special grade teacher had received only a two-year normal college education, she had published numerous articles on teaching, directed a children's foreign-language television program for Shanghai Television, and helped develop the LXLS's "communicative approach" to foreign-language teaching. The six-merit woman was a Chinese supermom, stern, attractive, and politically upright. She lived in a tiny apartment with her husband and one child, a nephew, a niece, and her elderly parents. Neither woman was a party member, although both had attained that status by the end of the decade. In short, the six-merit woman and the special grade teacher were not all that different from the LXLS's 26 other female foreign-language teachers, and their success was attributed by coworkers to this very ordinariness. "In China, there are different kinds of models. An advanced teacher or worker is very often quite common. They are not necessarily some leading comrade. This is because the common model has a special appeal. If leaders do something, well, that's what they're supposed to do. But the common person—it is how she lives that ordinariness. That is significant."

Municipal recognition did bring both women perquisites envied by their colleagues. The special grade teacher received a substantial monthly bonus and was frequently called upon to speak at professional meetings. The six-merit woman was rewarded with a two-week "rest period" at a workers' hostel on the outskirts of Shanghai, where she could interact with other professionals and, in her words, "take a break from cooking, washing, children, and schoolwork for a while." Though colleagues acknowledged that both women were hardworking, they remained skeptical about the motivations for such self-sacrifice. When word spread through the senior staff office that the headmistress was going to a meeting in Beijing, a teacher asked wryly, "Is the ball going to roll along with her?" The "ball" was the special grade teacher, the headmistress's protégée. The six-merit woman was also identified as one of the "headmistress's favorites." Indeed, being a model was a mixed blessing when individual achievement and failure were never separated from a network of intricate social relationships and a legacy of opportunistic political action that had tarnished the motivations for model behavior.

One of these model women explained her mixed feelings about being placed in such a predicament by expressing admiration for (and recommending that I read) the prize-winning short story, later adapted in 1983 into a critically acclaimed film, "At Middle Age." My colleague identified with the story's protagonist, Dr. Lu Wenting, an eye surgeon and "backbone" member of her hospital staff, when she was struck down in the prime of her life by a heart attack. Dr. Lu's touching if melodramatic rendering embodied the struggles of educated Chinese women to define and balance their loyalties to family and country and to personal aspiration and professional integrity. In fact, Dr. Lu's simultaneous frustration with a stagnated career and guilt about not spending enough time with her family aptly summarized the anxieties of many of the LXLS's female teachers.

The following portrait of Wang Wei chronicles a day, which did indeed occur, through the actions of a teacher who in reality is a composite of three of my female colleagues. She, like three-quarters of the LXLS's 28 female foreign-language teachers, was middle-aged by Chinese standards (between the ages of 35 and 55). As a college graduate, she numbered among 230,000 middle-aged intellectuals in Shanghai who were identified by municipal leaders as the "mainstay on all fronts of China's modernization." Both her monthly salary, approximately U.S.$40, and her public recognition were relatively low. A 56-day paid maternity leave, reimbursement of unusually high transportation costs, nearly free minor medical treatment at a school clinic, and a 70-to-75 percent pension upon retirement at age 55 offered her financial stability but no more. To supplement her income, she secured a part-time job as language instructor in a college-level evening school program. Although not prohibited, moonlighting was viewed as a drain on a teacher's time and energies by the school leadership. Consequently, she rarely discussed this job with colleagues and was scrupulous about fulfilling her teaching responsibilities at the LXLS.

Wang Wei at
Semester's End

Wang groaned as her alarm clock clattered across the desk next to her bed. She was moonlighting at an evening school the previous evening and had not drifted to sleep until well past midnight. Wang's elderly mother shuffled through the room, careful not to disturb her sleeping grandchildren. She was on her way to the market to buy the day's groceries.

Wang entered the kitchen her family shared with neighbors, the Lus, screwed up her nose, and cursed. She eyed the Lus' two chickens, which were clucking softly in a crate beneath the table. The Lus remained adamant. They refused to tether the fowl outside. The birds were being fattened for a New Year's feast, and "they'd be damned if they'd put them outside to get stolen."

Wang was still grumbling about the chickens at 7:45 when she arrived at school after a jostling one-hour bus ride. She greeted students on her way to the second-floor office, which she shared with eight colleagues. The school's floors had been swabbed down by a custodian and the damp smell of cement permeated the hallways. The door to the staff office was already unlocked, and the windows were flung open to the winter haze in a singularly ineffective attempt to dissipate the cold air that had become trapped in the office overnight.

Wang found a questionnaire from the cafeteria on her desk. "In order to improve our quality and service, we ask all teachers, workers, and students to circle the foods they most enjoy." A long list of meat, egg, bean, and vegetable dishes followed along with a suggested price for each dish. Wang grimaced and set the paper aside. She opened her satchel and dumped a pile of ungraded compositions on her desk. As she settled in to grade papers she leaned across her desk toward a colleague and launched into her latest installment of "the Wang's valiant efforts at ejecting the Lus' chickens from the kitchen." Her exaggerated tale was rewarded with sympathetic chuckles. The 8:00 warning buzzer rang. The school day had begun.

Wang Wei was a 41-year-old English teacher. Her teaching schedule was enviable by both American and Chinese standards. The average secondary school teacher in China teaches 40 to 80 pupils between ten and twelve 45-minute class periods each week (World Bank, 1985, 9). Wang taught 18 pupils seven periods of English. In addition, she attended an average of five hours of meetings, participated in two hours of in-service training, and was the homeroom teacher for a class of 38 ninth-graders. She had been teaching at the LXLS for nearly two decades. She was recognized as a "veteran" teacher and universally liked by administrators and teachers.

Wang's popularity did not stem from her conscientious performance in the classroom. She was not a model teacher. The department boasted educators of greater virtuosity. She was admired instead for her easygoing personality and penetrating analysis of the flaws in her superiors, fellow teachers, and pupils.

Wang's astute assessments of school life were not, in the view of her colleagues, the product of superior sociological insight. Unlike most LXLS teachers, Wang came from a working-class background. Her most off-handed criticism might very well have earned another teacher a harsh reprimand. Yet Wang's down-to-earth vision was regarded as a touchstone of commonness, a gauge for measuring whether the academic endeavors of the school were straining its socialist commitment. "It's amazing," remarked a colleague, "how she cuts away the crap and gets to the point."

Wang finished grading her stack of compositions at 9:30 and retrieved an enamel bowl and a handful of blue and pink meal tickets from a long drawer in her desk. She walked downstairs, through a tree-lined courtyard, and into the school's huge, drafty cafeteria. The cooks had prepared pork-filled buns for the students' midmorning snack. Wang decided to purchase some to take home to her three children. Another buzzer sounded, and the rumbling of feet echoed through the classroom building. Seconds later a group of boys raced into the cafeteria and received Wang's stern appraisal. "Slow down! What kind of behavior is that?!" she cried. The students grinned at her, but remained disorderly. They shared with Wang an unspoken understanding. "Let students get rid of their energy between classes, and in classes we can all get down to business."

For the next 30 minutes Wang worked on her ninth-graders' final English-language examination. Distracted by a colleague who poked listlessly at the tiny coal burner in the office, she innocently inquired what was wrong. "Nothing! Nothing!" snapped her office mate. The vehemence of this reply was unusual, momentarily interrupting casual conversation in the staff office. Flare-ups among teachers were rare even given the close quarters in which they worked and from which there was no retreat. Her colleague had had a disagreement with the headmistress about the appropriateness of the new, dark red sweater she was wearing. She fumed, "What do you think of this sweater? It's not that bright. Of all the other important things to worry about!"

Nodding in sympathy, Wang picked up her morning lesson plan. The 11:00 buzzer had rung. Wang walked to her students' classroom and stood outside for a moment, watching them. They had already studied lessons in Chinese classical poetry, political law, and geometry. They had arranged their English books on top of their desks, and the high, pulsing whine of the eye exercise tape was playing scratchily over the p.a. system (see chapter 7). Wang entered the classroom and threaded a tape of the day's English lesson into a recorder at the front of the room, keeping one eye fixed on her students. They openly questioned the efficacy of eye exercises and the predictability of their complaints and fidgeting irritated her.

The last strains of the students' eye exercises were still fading when Wang addressed her students crisply, "Good morning." She waited for their reply, "Good morning, Teacher Wang." She continued, "I believe Li Jiang has a report to present?" Wang was a believer in a strictly controlled, rapid-fire classroom. "Don't give them time to think," she advised. "Just get on with it, fast!"

The students knew precisely what Wang demanded and were prepared for her questions. When Li Jiang completed his one-minute "sports brief," Wang announced, "Good. Does anyone have any questions?" "No? Well, today's lesson is new, called 'Dangerous Descent.' What does the title mean to you?" Wang called upon three students to answer her question. The students had reviewed the lesson before coming to class. "The story is about a dangerous flight." "Astronauts are in danger when they leave their spaceships." "I think some astronauts will have trouble landing on the moon."

Wang followed her carefully constructed lesson plan with little deviation, gauging how long each point should be emphasized so she would end precisely with the buzzer at 11:50. "There's some satisfaction in that," she explained. "After a while, it's easy. One simply has a feel for 45 minutes. One knows the problems the students will have. Like clockwork."

Returning to her office, Wang found that a colleague had purchased her lunch for her, "before all the good food was gone." Instead of eating in the cafeteria with students, teachers carried their meals to their staff offices. "You have to get away from those kids sometimes!" Amidst the usual clutter of books, lesson plans, and enamel ware, pale logs of waxy New Year's cake, ordered by the school, had appeared on each teacher's desk. Wang regarded the piles with exasperation. She would have to get them home by bus somehow, along with her pork buns.

This minor aggravation provided the context for one of Wang's fervent discourses on the trials of school life at semester's end. Staff room conversation rose with an impressive crescendo. New Year celebrations, both solar and lunar, were cause for official evaluations of the unit family's progress. At parties sponsored by the school's labor union, teachers and administrators gathered around tables artfully arranged with cakes, fruit, cellophane packets of candy, and tea to be regaled with recapitulations of the school's successes, recitations of classical poetry, and harmonious renditions of "Auld Lang Syne" and Peking Opera. Students expressed formal sentiments and resolutions on classroom blackboards and in poems to their teachers: "In the field of our English study, you are a hard-working gardener, giving us knowledge every day, and letting us grow finer and finer." The media made sweeping proclamations that "Each year is better than the last!" Smiling commuters were polite on buses. Athletes brought home international cups. Newspaper mastheads featured planes like phoenixes and ocean liners like dragons carrying cash-generating exports to foreign ports. Education was grandly defined as a lifelong activity to be supported not only by schools but also by businesses and fledgling private enterprises. Education would provide the crucial bridge between heightened material welfare and spiritual well-being.

Teachers placed these grandiose statements in hilarious juxtaposition with their mundane and generally thankless tasks of writing examinations and grading papers. The hectic rush to tie up the term's loose ends seemed interminable. At 12:30, Wang and her female colleagues shooed three male teachers out of the office. Borrowing an adage familiar throughout China, Wang compared the small north-facing office to the inland Chinese cities of Nanjing and Chongqing, "iceboxes in the winter, furnaces in the summer." Fuel shortages, a fact of life throughout central and southern China, meant the general prohibition of central heating and hot running water outside public bathhouses and better hotels. Yet the teachers had convinced school administrators to purchase a tiny coal-burning stove for the office upon which an aluminum kettle of water was constantly boiling. A teacher whose home was without a bathroom had decided to wash her hair with the scalding water. The men would have to read in the library.

At 1:00 Wang sat down with three other ninth-grade English teachers to finalize their students' examination review procedures. They finished an hour later, in time to attend a faculty meeting regarding a Ministry of Education decision that qualified some teachers in foreign-language secondary schools for the title and salary of college lecturers (*Almanac*, 1984, 745). The meeting was convened to develop criteria for assessing who would receive the promotions, and some teachers complained that the decision had created an uncomfortable division among faculty members.

One had certainly divided members of the English department. A teacher who had studied in England and taught senior level classes for years had gone to a two-year college, which made him ineligible for promotion. He complained that the only way he could qualify for a lectureship was by studying part-time for two or three years. "There's no sense to the system. It's simply irrational!" he fumed. "Aren't we supposed to reward on the basis of contribution around here?!"

Wang sympathized with his feelings but disagreed with his assessment. Her ultimate measure for professional competency was almost always the institution from which a teacher had received training. She argued, "Benefits have to be based on something, and at least how long you've studied is objective. It would be fair."

Throughout most of this debate the oldest member of the English teaching staff, a highly trained educator who was counted on to insure that the school's youngest pupils "learned from the very beginning to speak correctly," sat quietly preoccupied, erasing long lines of writing from a page of newsprint in front of her. She was participating in a short term Fulbright course at the college with which the LXLS was affiliated, and was having trouble completing an assignment on the use of the passive voice in her junior level students' textbook. "I'm so frustrated that I'm beginning to wonder where my head has been for the last 20 years. This talk about salary just reinforces it. It's like I have nothing after so long. This is the first real paper I've ever written in English."

She smiled, apologetic and wistful. "It sounds funny, but this project makes me feel so old and so"—she paused to find the right word—"so resigned. I just don't have the memory I used to. If I could write more papers after this one—build on it—it would be very good for me. But I will come back here where we use such simple English. Is it just a waste of time?"

Wang listened to her colleague quietly, and when the meeting ended walked with her arm in arm toward the school gates. Two teachers discussing the "red sweater affair" joined them. "I sometimes have to question fashion," admitted a colleague who had spent the previous Sunday tracking down a red ski jacket that her daughter wanted for New Year's. Wang was the only member of the English teaching staff who had more than two children. At the mention of the red coat she sighed. "It's a struggle with three kids to get any coat at all." The teachers left the school gates engrossed in a conversation about one of their favorite topics—their children. "My son's not a dull boy, but I don't know how to cope with him. Last night he showed me his Chinese test. Fifty-three! At the bottom of the test paper his teacher had written some comments to admonish him. She was very annoyed at his carelessness. And she wrote a note to me! I'm a teacher and all that and I should be helping him more she said! How can we improve ourselves and our children, too? I go home after school on the bus, then I prepare dinner. After dinner I have to do the housework and help my son with his homework. I have so little time."

The Limits and Possibilities of Professional Autonomy at the LXLS

All of the factors that combined to define the professional roles of LXLS teachers—the tradition of the educator as loyal civil servant, the all-encompassing nature of the work unit, the power of parental superiors to control decisions concerning teaching assignment and promotion, the organization and act of teaching as a collective obligation—were complicated by the school's unusual responsibility to prepare pupils for further training at the college level. The school's formal affiliation with a post-secondary institution not only fostered, from my colleagues' point of view, a detestable "plantation mentality" among their college-level counterparts. It also demanded of LXLS's foreign-language teachers a pedagogy that inspired unorthodox form and content. Not surprisingly, the LXLS's collegiate affiliation provided one of my colleagues' most convenient outlets for criticism. Like most family members, they set aside their internal disputes when attacked from the outside.

A Marriage of
Convenience

The establishment in 1980 of "linked" (*guagou*) relationships between China's best secondary schools and prestigious tertiary institutions was interpreted by foreign educators and many Chinese students and their parents as reflection of the increasingly narrow channel of access to advanced training in China (Pepper, 1982; Rosen, 1983). Students at the LXLS did, of course, obtain an inside track to college training. They, and their teachers, also used the institute's facilities, such as its swimming pool, library, clinic, recording laboratories, all a short walk away. The foreign-language teachers were regularly given one and two semester leaves of absence, normally on a rotating basis, to study applied linguistics and literature with visiting Fulbright scholars. They admitted, grudgingly, that they enjoyed a higher level of public prestige than their counterparts in other secondary schools. "That we are an indirect part of a college community rubs off on us. So people might say, 'Oh, you work at the foreign-language school. Well, you have nothing to complain about do you? You are lucky.' To be fair, I must say this is true to an extent."

My colleagues were by no means unequivocal about the benefits they received by being affiliated with a post-secondary institution. In fact, they reacted with uncharacteristic fury to complaints that their students who entered the college became lazy, willful, and eventually quite mediocre students, and certainly refused to accept the blame if it were true:

"If our students pass their exams with flying colors, what happens to them afterward is hardly within our jurisdiction! I can't believe it. We split our guts turning out the best students, the best test-takers, students who speak fluently. We've done a great job. They get the same students and blame us because they can't help them advance. They couldn't conceive of the idea that it might be their problem. Oh no! I'll tell you what the problem is. It's their outmoded teaching. They're too challenged by our students. Our students are a threat. The students receive the same materials from the institute that they studied with us when they were just junior high students. If they can't face it over there, they should ask *themselves* why. Not us!"

The bitter regard with which LXLS teachers held institute teachers can be partially attributed to the common absence of mutual respect among secondary school and college educators in China (Wang Peidong, 1981; Zhang Heru, 1983). However, what also troubled my colleagues, who were fully qualified by Chinese standards to teach at the college level, was their disqualification from the benefits enjoyed by their institute counterparts. Teachers at the LXLS were often last to receive new housing assignments, were eligible for fewer square feet of housing when they got them, had less hope of going abroad for advanced study, and worked longer hours:

"It burns me when I hear what they grumble about over there. I went to college just like they did. I had the same professors, the same courses, the same training. We're assigned here because we're good, because we have good accents. We're excellent models for children, that's why we're assigned to work here. The leadership demands that we are at work everyday from 8:30 in the morning until 4:30 in the afternoon. We can't just show up for several hours of class a week and then run off and do our shopping. We have to be responsible for the ideological well-being of our students. At the institute, they don't have to worry about any of that. They simply have no idea what we do. When I'm with them, I can only shrug. I was speaking with the English department's chairman the other day, and he told me about two scholarships from Hong Kong. I said, "Well, it's better to work at the institute after all. I suppose you haven't arranged for us to have one of the positions.' He had no reply. They're so protective of their chances. We're supposed to get chances too, we pass all the right tests, but we still don't get any consideration."

Another teacher reminded her that the dean and headmistress understood these frustrations. "Yes, yes," retorted her colleague. "But what can they really *do* about it, that's the question. It's just a *baozi* [stuffed bun] with no filling."

The angry cynicism expressed by my colleagues was even more evident at one of the LXLS's sister schools. Its veteran teachers openly accused their institute superiors of betraying their trust. Many veteran teachers had volunteered to work for three to five years at the secondary school level with the guarantee that after that period they would be promoted to a college teaching position. "But," explained a teacher, "the institute reneged on its promise, and here we all are, after 15 years, still at the high school, still with no promotion. Of course we're bitter. So we just come to teach, and put our energies elsewhere. Most of us have outside jobs. How are we supposed to have spirit here? It's ridiculous."

When I recounted this conversation, my colleagues were surprised that teachers from another unit would make such criticisms openly to a stranger, but they added their own sentiments:

"Because we're all part of the same unit the institute can get more money and housing allotments from the government. Also the union can get more money, since each teacher pays one percent of his salary to the union each month. That's what keeps it going. But the problem is that when it comes time to return some of the money and housing, the institute says, 'But you're just the secondary school, and you can't have the same kind of treatment.' This is what people mean when they say what we have here is a marriage of convenience. The school and the institute are married when it is convenient for the institute, and divorced when it suits the institute."

"Explorers of the Human Soul"

The LXLS's marriage of convenience had the paradoxical outcome of limiting the professional choices of English-language teachers while serving as their greatest potential source of professional autonomy. Although my colleagues resented the condescension and (from their point of view) unfounded accusations of their university colleagues, their responsibility to train many of its future students encouraged them to seek an alternative metaphor with which to envision their pedagogical practice. They collaborated with foreign educators, attended meetings on teaching reform, and began to speak of themselves as "artists with creative intuition" whose vocation required enhanced "autonomy." "We must have the natural sense of direction of an explorer," explained a colleague. "That's what it's all about, you know. The teacher is an explorer of the world of the child's soul."

In fact, the opportunities for exploration available to LXLS English teachers were envied by their colleagues who taught French, German, and Japanese. Though first-year LXLS pupils were as often as possible assigned to language specialization by preference, the vast majority of entering students hoped to study English. English teachers maintained that their high visibility brought added teaching pressures and administrative constraints. The English department not only served as "trend setter" for the LXLS's special teaching style, but both the headmistress and the dean of foreign languages were trained in English and could directly assess each teacher's English competency. "The headmistress has very definite ideas about how to teach foreign languages properly," explained a colleague. She paused and made a tight fist. "Because she understands English we are tightly in her grasp. She watches what we do, and if she likes it, of course, she tries to force it on the other language groups."

The German-, French-, and Japanese-language teachers faced different challenges, ones that negated any advantage they might have garnered from program autonomy. Few Chinese secondary schools taught these languages, and effective materials and textbooks were limited. In addition, the English department placed a larger percentage of its students into China's best universities. While English-language graduates were recruited by tertiary institutions on the basis of their scores on the English language portion of the national college entrance examination, students of French, German, and Japanese were obliged to take specially designed tests that were commonly recognized as more difficult. Most important, students assigned to study alternative languages, especially Japanese, were little consoled by Zhou En-lai's oft-quoted rationalization, "You train soldiers for a thousand days to be able to use them for one hour." Pupils supposedly among the brightest in Shanghai did not relish the prospect of studying like mad for just one hour in the sun.

Sensitive to such complaints, the headmistress temporarily succeeded in ousting Japanese from the LXLS curriculum. To her dismay Russian was introduced instead. Her arguments that the introduction of yet another language would "spoil the LXLS's academic symmetry" did not persuade the president of the college to which the LXLS was affiliated. A renowned Russian specialist, he insisted that his was the only tertiary institution in China that awarded a doctorate in Russian. His program was in need of high-caliber Russian-language students, and the feeder school would indeed provide them.

Though English-language teachers remained cautiously hopeful in their efforts to secure room for professional exploration, they often settled for the "small victories" that have come to characterize the profession of teaching worldwide:

"I know you must think we complain, but you see our lives. I've heard how many hours teachers work in the United States. It's hard for me to comprehend, but I have a real feeling life is harder here. Surely, you see, it's a question of motivation. We make jokes that we don't all eat out of the big pot anymore (*chi da wan fan*) but actually there's a serious side. Really people should get more for working hard. Before, well you weren't working for money, except small raises. Maybe you were working for a chance for something else, a back door, your children. Or you are working where you are assigned and you have no choice. You've weighed your alternatives and mustered up all the good PR you can and that's it. That much is harder here, isn't it? I don't know. Sometimes, well, I just want to go home and collapse. Really, I work to the point of exhaustion, and find the bus is crowded, the meal's still got to be cooked, and the lines for shopping, and the prices, and the wash, and the compositions, and my child's been naughty at school. I just sit and wonder if we'll all make it, and whether what I'm trying to do is appreciated in the least little bit. But then just when I think I'm at the end of my rope, I get to school and there are the student compositions for the week neatly stacked; the students are brilliant in class. And I think to myself, What do I get myself so worked up about, anyway? Every day is a challenge, I'm alive and working, and my family is growing. I can say, yes, I have improved my English work in the last five years."

As we turn to a detailed discussion of teaching practice at the LXLS, we see how the teachers' position within the unit family, and concomitant lack of influence on the content and purposes of learning, limited their abilities to respond critically even to those pedagogical challenges openly considered problematic. Teachers gained security as collective extensions of explicitly guided educational mandate but lacked intellectual authority and the possibility of dissent, without which the promise of their alternative teaching metaphor remained unfulfilled. This contradiction placed teachers in an especially awkward situation, since the quest for perfect performance through which they struggled to balance their roles of state functionary and exploratory professional not only furthered the interests of the state but also contradicted its logic.

Chapter 5
A Quest for Perfect
Performance

In October 1982 the LXLS hosted a National Foreign Language Conference, the first gathering of representatives from China's foreign-language secondary schools since their establishment in 1963. The conference's principal activities were meticulously constructed "demonstration lessons" presented by LXLS faculty for the school's 54 visitors. Moments before my model lesson began, 15 teachers carrying small bamboo stools crowded into the classroom, forming a low, hushed ring around 20 pupils, who were wedged together at their desks. The students put on an outstanding performance, although they were visibly distracted by so many note-taking adults. When the period ended, the onlookers nodded hastily to the students, grabbed up their stools, and without comment rushed on to their next observation.

On the fifth day of the conference, I asked a colleague how the school's visitors were reacting to our demonstration classes. I was puzzled by the absence of free-wheeling exchange among professionals that the frenetic planning preceding the conference had led me to anticipate. She responded, "Oh, we've had no meeting about this yet. Next week there will be a meeting, and then we'll decide what the outcome is. The headmistress will have something to say."

My colleague resisted venturing a personal opinion, apologizing that she really hadn't had time to talk with representatives from other schools. She had been too busy preparing her own demonstration class. It was only after our conversation that I realized how badly I had misinterpreted the purpose of this "working conference." Hardly the time and place for risky pedagogy or open debate about the purpose and method of foreign-language teaching, the meeting was designed to showcase the accomplishments of foreign-language schools in perfectly orchestrated model lessons and formal presentations.

The English-language teaching staff did not discuss the conference until several weeks after it had ended. Ironically, our conversation focused upon the school's least politically charged and most frequently discussed topic. "The LXLS's cafeteria was voted first-class, hands down!" joked a colleague. She simply assumed that stellar performances had been achieved in other arenas. "Well, after all, school leaders *have* agreed to hold annual conferences."

The structure and process of the conference underscores the definition of successful education at the LXLS, as well as the appropriate role of teachers and students in achieving that success. Successful teaching and learning stemmed from predictable, detailed planning for which precise expectations were clearly understood in advance. "Mistakes" might be intentionally crafted into lessons by teachers who knew so well the vocabulary items or grammatical points understood by their students that they could unfailingly predict "the students won't get that. We'll have to devise another strategy." However, an unanticipated error or deviation that caused a rupture in the formalized educational scheme was viewed as an unfortunate, even dangerous, carelessness.

The Ambiguous Goals of Foreign-Language Instruction

The outward unity displayed by Chinese teachers when they discuss their teaching can be astonishing to North American educators, who generally find articulating a "philosophy of education" a painstaking and confusing process of self-reflection. When asked about the primary purposes of education, Chinese teachers, in sharp contrast, provide immediate, unanimous replies, often commencing with Mao Zedong's well-known admonition that "all students must be developed morally, intellectually, and physically, and become workers with a socialist conscience and culture" (Mao, 1971, 459).

Mao's formulation of the well-educated Chinese citizen provided the preamble for nearly all statements regarding education in China during the early 1980s. When encouraged to expand upon their teaching aims, LXLS teachers continued easily:

"The foreign-language curriculum at the primary and secondary level, like instruction in all other subject areas, is designed to provide students with basic and essential knowledge and skills. The language teacher's primary responsibility is to lay for each student a firm foundation; students are to be proficient in listening, speaking, reading, and writing, developed all-round morally, physically, intellectually. We believe that education must serve proletarian politics and be combined with productive labor so that those who receive it must develop in those three ways. In a word, our goal is for socialist construction, to turn out qualified, both red and expert, students with a good grasp of vocational specialization and to adhere to the socialist road, love the motherland. Of course, the primary task of school is to enable children to learn, to help them master all their subjects. That's why we want them to master foreign languages. We want them to be good language workers. Students are asked to plunge into the revolutionary movement, but if there's no sound knowledge, it's no use just having a high political consciousness.

Virtually identical summaries of educational purpose appeared in scholarly journals and the educational sections of major newspapers, and were repeated by officers at the Shanghai Bureau of Education. Teachers who had come of professional age during the Cultural Revolution were accustomed to clarifying publicly the political dimensions of teaching. Before discussing specific pedagogical tasks at formal meetings, they placed their palms squarely down on their desks, as if stabilizing themselves for the well-known phrases about the political ramifications of teaching with which they were about to banish ambiguity from their own practice.

When pressed to describe the purposes of English teaching in detail, my colleagues quoted from the "Six-Year Key Secondary School English-Teaching Outline" (see Appendix C). They were genuinely bewildered when further prodded to clarify. They assumed they were being asked to describe, yet again, the specific teaching methods they used to implement these goals. They cried in exasperation, "But, surely *you* know about that! You're with us every day, week in, week out, discussing and writing the lesson plan." When I pressed, "Yes, but we never talk about what a firm foundation is, or why we want it, do we?" "*Why* we want it?!" they cried. My colleagues were mystified that I could be so dense.

Controlling the Language-Learning Environment

Teachers at the LXLS believed being able to articulate the official goal upon which educational practice was based implied that it was understood, that it was being implemented, and that it would lead to the consequences for which it was intended. Great time and energy and argument were devoted to how to bring these goals to fruition, but almost never as to "why."

It is paradoxical, then, that in the face of such consistency, education at the LXLS was characterized by a lack of clarity about how these purposes were ultimately linked to the outcomes of teaching. Or is it? By necessity, LXLS teachers had become adept at justifying their pedagogical practice in politically acceptable terms. As a result, they used past and discredited discontinuities in the purposes of foreign-language education to both explain and justify their current dilemmas. When referring to the Cultural Revolution, teachers insisted, "Well, those days are all over now." Yet they blamed the slow process of innovation and reform precisely on the legacy of those days. Consequently, present problems, firmly rooted in past mistakes, remained insoluble.

Eclecticism and the
Communicative
Approach to Foreign-
Language Teaching

Because the political, social, and pedagogical goals for language teaching were inviolable in theory, LXLS teachers became masters at the art of eclecticism in practice. They were encouraged to experiment with teaching methods, which in turn led them to initiate reforms that they then had to justify by bending official views to fit their own actions. This pedagogical legerdemain was rarely discouraged, since teachers found creative ways, derived from contemporary practice and long tradition, for bringing their teaching practice into harmony with educational policy. "Adapting policy to the actual conditions of the LXLS" became the teachers' common justification for innovation.

This eclectic teaching style encouraged teachers to employ a hearty, contradictory mix of teaching and learning metaphors. Though teachers rejected the definition of learning as the passive absorption of knowledge, a perception they roundly disdained as "stuffing the Beijing duck," they nevertheless asserted that language was a discrete body of information that could be jointly transmitted and tested. At the same time, they hoped to conceptualize language learning as a creative and synthetic process whose success lay in the interaction between what the teacher and individual students were doing. English teachers described this dialogical process as communicative (*jiaojixing*) teaching and learning, where language was primarily a tool of communication. Yet, they also adamantly maintained, as do most foreign-language teachers in China, that foreign-language proficiency must be achieved through formal, teacher-centered lessons. They believed that only controlled environments allowed the sound foundation from which students could go on to understand the difference between "real" and "false" communication. "There must be harmony between form and content. This means form should be secondary to communicative purposes. This is the difference between a dead and living language knowledge. Your knowledge of the rules of the language are important, but so is your feeling for the language. We want our students to think, to communicate."

Teachers at the LXLS proudly contrasted their communicative method with "outmoded" or "pragmatic" approaches they felt were used by their colleagues in other foreign-language secondary schools:

"In our opinion Beijing uses what we call the old method. We disagree with their approach. Teachers talk a great deal in class, and, like teachers in our own institute, emphasize an extraordinary amount of vocabulary work. They work on the belief that this word density is an efficient way to get students to learn the language. Our question to them is, 'Who is doing most of the talking?' Maybe the students have more words at their disposal, maybe they have words that more accurately fit a particular situation, but no attention is paid to developing the students' creative abilities. What about the students' intellectual development if it's always the teachers in the lead? Now, Chongqing and Hangzhou use what we call the 'practical method.' This is a matter of necessity for them. These schools have no foreign instructors or elaborate equipment. In the evenings they may have no electricity. They must concentrate on the national standard texts. Their aim, quite unabashedly I might add, is to get their students into foreign-language institutes. Well, can you blame them? They have to do this. So they focus on lots of written exercises, memorization of vocabulary. The speaking and listening abilities of their students, well, leaves something to be desired."

The teacher most closely identified with this "LXLS approach" described teaching as, "a process of communicating with students, where the students learn new words through understanding the context in which the communication is taking place. Mechanical drills do not allow or encourage students to think. . . . Language must be a habit, of course, something you don't think about, as natural as breathing. But time in class given over to anything other than real language is wasted. Meticulous explanations of the text wastes time. What we need to do is stop talking and start teaching."

Her efforts to stop talking and start teaching made her a local celebrity and a victim of success. Her students were extraordinary communicators but not always enthusiastic grammarians. In addition to aggravating the conflict between facilitating "real" communication and producing outstanding test results, the shift to a more student-centered classroom that her communicative approach demanded also complicated the teacher's responsibility for maintaining control of the learning environment. Confusion resulted in classrooms where the teacher both led and interacted, and the students both reacted passively and were spontaneous. Language was called a "vehicle of meaning" by the same teachers who found safe harbor in formal grammatical explanations.

Finally, teachers felt they must maintain a coherent academic task structure that was as free as possible from mistakes and unrehearsed remarks. They were distressed when open-ended discussions in one classroom were not repeated in the classrooms of all teachers who constructed joint lesson plans. "How do we assess, if everything's different?" they wondered. In their struggle to balance the consequences of spontaneous language use with the longstanding educative role of properly transmitting and evaluating discrete, predefined knowledge, eclecticism (by incorporating numerous assumptions about language learning) did allow teachers flexibility. However, it also created an environment in which it was neither necessary nor easy for teachers to question their ultimate goals, or understand why results did not always match teachers' intentions to produce creative, natural language users.

Preparing the Collective
Lesson Plan

We have seen in chapter 4 that LXLS teachers constructed their teaching plans in discipline and grade-based teaching and research groups. These collective units placed strict controls upon what individual teachers could do in their classrooms. However, they also minimized the dangers of professional isolation by providing an atmosphere in which professional contact was frequent and the sharing of professional experience and knowledge was essential.

The primary academic function of teaching and research groups was the construction of weekly lesson plans that articulated, sentence by sentence, what teachers responsible for the same texts would be doing in their classrooms. The meetings in which these testimonies to the power of the collective were prepared were informal and based upon a mutual and implicit understanding of each member's strengths and weaknesses. Heads nodded as new text passages were evaluated. "Yes, I'll take care of those exercises," offered one member. "Who wants to look up some material on the Tower of London?" asked another. The grammarian in the group devised clever exercises. One teacher was responsible for typing the final copy of the lesson plan and distributing it to each teacher. The most fluent teacher, a foreign instructor if the group had one, wrote vocabulary exercises, discussion questions, and quizzes incorporating the vocabulary items and grammatical patterns introduced in the students' lessons.

Though the construction of lesson plans rested upon an endless stream of hasty meetings of teachers whose individual differences were clearly recognized, such differences were intentionally downplayed in the teaching act. Individual competence and creativity were necessary but could never become a substitute for collective effort. Rather than feel confined by this demand for conformity, teachers maintained that their "differences have to be subsumed so that we all teach the same." They accepted the lesson plan as a reliable and consistent guide for each group member that would thereby provide all students, "not just the students of the best teacher," with the best possible education:

"It's really a good system, you see, since everyone's good ideas and experience are here, and we all are clear about what we can and cannot expect all students to know. Of course, the lesson plan does not guarantee good teaching, and some teachers just can't inspire students quite as much as others. We realize this. But the opposite situation would be worse. Mixing students with obviously bad lesson plans—it's like trying to steam dumplings in a tea pot. When the dumplings are done, you can't pour them out. If the students haven't been well prepared, then whose fault is that?"

Foreign teachers new to Chinese schooling learned quickly just how scrupulously such lesson plans were to be followed. My turn came when in the middle of my first model lesson I invited a group of visiting observers to participate. The reluctant teachers were astonished that I had breached the lesson plan by interacting with them. Didn't I realize the lesson plan was a script to which both teachers and students unswervingly adhered? In fact, some teachers at the LXLS referred to themselves as Beijing opera stars who must spend three years in the wings to perfect three minutes on stage. They regarded the learning process within classrooms as an act of transmitting preconceived knowledge efficiently and eloquently, and their fulfillment as educators came from moments when their carefully rehearsed lessons were masterfully delivered.

The Teacher as Moral Authority

A copy of *Peoples Education* was lying on my desk one morning, opened to a series of six papercuts that illustrated the Chinese fable "Zeng Zi Slaughters the Pig." Zeng Zi, a famous scholar of the Spring and Autumn Period (770–476 B.C.), was about to leave on a journey when his young son demanded he be allowed to accompany his father. Zeng Zi's son was dissuaded only after his mother promised that when his father returned they would slaughter a pig for a feast. Delighted at this unexpected treat the child was mollified, and his mother promptly forgot her rash proposal. When Zeng Zi returned, he began to sharpen his butchering knife. Despite his wife's pleading that he stop, Zeng Zi refused. To do otherwise would teach their son duplicity.

The colleague who had placed the journal on my desk commented, "As a teacher of course our first obligation is to teach, I mean to pass on our professional knowledge to students in some manner. This is what we call our expert role, in passing on one kind of culture. But we can't merely 'teach things but not people' (*jiao shi bujiao ren*). We also have our red role, our responsibility to help students understand what is right and wrong, to become cultured spiritually as well as knowledgeable about certain subjects. The students must respect us for how we act, you see. This is what we mean when we say we must be models for students to follow."

Teachers at the LXLS maintained that one factor more than any other was essential to student achievement: the teacher's ability to instill in pupils the willpower and self-discipline to learn. The development of these qualities was a gradual process that occurred through imitation of appropriate moral and intellectual examples. No matter how gifted or motivated, all students needed to be shown appropriate behavior. "Teachers," advised a colleague, "must infuse their lessons with the force of personal example":

"Teachers must exhibit in every action and every word the virtues of diligence, rigor, meticulousness, and love. Teachers must be diligent in their thinking, in preparing their lessons, in understanding their students' difficulties. Teachers must be rigorous, make strict demands on themselves, hold high expectations for their students. Teachers must be meticulous in their outlook. They should know precisely what each of their students' strong and weak points are. And they must love their students. When students are valued they will trust the teacher enough to regard him as a model. I'm not saying I always do this all, but if you ask, it's really the only way. It's why teaching can be so damned frustrating. You always know any less is not enough."

She paused, then added that being a model also required humility:

"One of our favorite traditional sayings, and I really think it is true, is from Confucius. 'Among three people, I will find one who is surely my teacher' (*san ren xing, bi you wo shi yan*). It means that you should learn from others, you shouldn't be too proud of yourself. We continually have to learn in our jobs. You know we are all college graduates here. The students respect us for our knowledge, thus we gain their respect. But we have extremely clever students. It is important to be well prepared and on our toes all the time. But we have to admit it when we're wrong. 'Real knowledge is to recognize both what you know and what you do not know' (*zhi zhi wei zhi zhi, buzhi wei buzhi, shi zhi ye*). Admitting our limitations is essential."

This teacher's sympathetic if essentially conservative pedagogy of telling has been compared by analysts of Chinese pedagogy to Philip Jackson's distinction between mimetic and transformative teaching (Paine, 1990; Gardner, 1989). Indeed, the LXLS's discourse of answers suggests an image of schooling not so different from that found in U.S. classrooms, where barely 5 percent of instructional time is devoted to questioning. While the custodial and bureaucratic structure of formalized schooling shapes such similarities worldwide, the source of the LXLS's teacher-directed pedagogy also resided in how and why "teaching as a virtuoso performance" is rewarded in Chinese schools (Paine, 1990).

The Text as Knowledge

The teacher's obligation to embody model behavior, to stand in not as the creator but as the transmitter of received knowledge, helps us understand why the act of learning English for millions of Chinese teachers and students is primarily the detailed study of texts. Just as the goals of Chinese schooling are codified in national teaching outlines, the knowledge that teachers are to transmit to their students is embodied in state-approved textbooks. The central importance of these texts in foreign-language study is reinforced by the disavowal that knowledge transmitted by a competent teacher might be reconstructed by different learners in different ways with unanticipated consequences. Furthermore, the foreign-language classroom also provides the sole contact most Chinese teachers and students have with the target language. Hesitant teachers see the text as their most reliable model for correct language use. Such a position is defensible primarily because their role is to reproduce in their students the knowledge in which they themselves have been grounded. "You know the old saying," a colleague explained, "if you thoroughly study the Tang poems you may not be able to compose the poetry yourself, but you can still recite them."

Foreign-language training at the LXLS was centered around textbooks that were purchased by students and studied literally to shreds. The 150 to 300 words in a typical text passage (see Appendixes D and E) were often treated not as the springboard to productive language activity but as its end. Students assessed as exceptional readers were those who could recite their lessons flawlessly. Even though the teaching outline suggested that only 60 percent of a text's vocabulary be available in a student's active repertoire, distinctions between performance and competence were rarely made. Students were encouraged to know everything, and rewarded when they did.

English: The
Textbook Published
in China

From 1981 to 1983 the vast majority of secondary schools in Shanghai based their English curriculum upon a national unified textbook series entitled *English* (1979). The six-year English teaching outline for key secondary schools (see Appendix C) was organized around this series.

The series begins with brightly colored pages depicting several of the lexical and syntactic items introduced in the text: the English names for various colors, numbers, locative prepositions, familiar objects, animals, and people, and appropriate articles and plural forms. Two casts of characters that figure prominently in the first three volumes are vividly drawn. A Chinese couple named the Lis have a son, Li Ping, and a daughter, Li Ying. The second family is British. The central character (Li Ping's counterpart) is Mike, a boy whose parents are known throughout the text as simply "Mike's father and mother." Mike has an older sister named Rose and a younger brother named Jack. The two families never meet. Chinese and British live worlds apart.

Presumably, Shanghai students feel at home the moment they pick up this text. On the first page a red accordion winds down a tree-lined boulevard, past a high-rise, and into an intersection where a young woman on a black bicycle vies for position with a military jeep and a blue sedan. In the background a passenger plane soars over a harbor that is immediately identifiable as Shanghai's Bund. Surely, this is a place where English will be useful. Turn the page and there are idyllic pastoral scenes, one dog, two cows, three horses, and so on up to 10 eggs. In this rural context students might not be so sure where English-language proficiency leads.

The foreign-language curriculum for Chinese primary and secondary pupils of the early 1980s was theoretically based upon a direct or modified audio-lingual approach often described as emphasizing the "priority of listening and speaking in all-round development of the four skills" (*English Teacher's*

Book I, 1979). That this approach to language learning was difficult for teachers to implement in their classrooms was not surprising. Through their *English* primer students were introduced to the dominant pattern for learning English in China, which remained relatively consistent even in many colleges. Students completed five chapters of *English* before they were introduced to the complete English alphabet, its pronunciation, and the *wh* question: "What's this?" The letters *a–g, h–n, o–t,* and *u–z* were accompanied in successive chapters by ruled spaces for students to trace faint uppercase and lowercase letters four times. A smattering of sound-symbol pronunciation exercises were based on 22 common nouns chosen to illustrate one or two letters of the alphabet. A picture accompanied each new lexical item. Each chapter was concluded with a three- or four-sentence exchange called "everyday English": "Good morning (afternoon)." "What's your name? Are you Li Ping?" Instructions, headings, and explanations were printed in English followed by a Chinese translation in parenthesis.

New Concept English: The Text Published Abroad

The English curriculum at the LXLS was quite different from the one just described, although no less reliant upon a textbook series. The textbook used at the LXLS, *New Concept English* (NCE), was compiled by a British applied linguist, L. G. Alexander, and is widely used in Hong Kong and mainland Chinese tertiary institutions (Alexander, 1967). This four-volume English series has been so popular it is available in a pirated edition that includes Chinese translations of each text passage.

New Concept English fits extraordinarily well what Chinese teachers perceive as an "efficient balance of linguistic knowledge and skill." Each volume is sequential, consistent, and accompanied with precise directions. The book provides a sense of security for teachers who are not entirely sure of their own fluency. Alexander explains that he has attempted "to provide the teacher with well-coordinated and graded material which will enable him to conduct each lesson with a minimum of preparation. As many of the exercises are 'self-correcting,' the teacher will, incidentally, be relieved of the arduous task of correcting a great many written exercises" (Alexander, 1967, xii).

The NCE syllabus is also organized by general principles of language learning with which Chinese teachers are familiar. Alexander sets forth the following axioms: "Nothing should be spoken before it has been heard. Nothing should be read before it has been spoken. Nothing should be written before it has been read" (Alexander, 1967, viii).

Alexander's approach provides a model of how students can use the language actively while simultaneously learning systematic grammatical and lexical knowledge. Patterns and sentences or phrases are used as the unit of study and continually reinforce new information and skills. Mistakes are minimized; English is learned efficiently and actively. And this "lively efficiency" is exactly what LXLS teachers hope to achieve in their classrooms.

Necessary Lessons
for Junior Students:
Bridging the Gap

Raising the quality of junior secondary schools captured the attention of Chinese parents, teachers, and the educational press during the early 1980s. Junior secondary schools were perceived to be suffering under "the tyranny of the college entrance examination," their best teachers transferred to senior levels in efforts to increase college promotion rates. In addition, a policy of tracking senior secondary school students into academic and vocational programs placed responsibility for an effective school program squarely on junior secondary schools. These concerns were shared by junior secondary school English teachers who insisted "to build a tall building it is necessary to begin with a firm foundation." "If the purpose of secondary school English is to lay a foundation, then junior secondary school English is the foundation of the foundation" (Huang Zhiqiang, 1983, 62–63; Zhang Jianzhong et al., 1982, 6–10).

One of the most common measures educators advocated to insure such learning was to "bring all first-year students up to one level of achievement." Differences in student ability were to be viewed primarily as differences in prior educational environment. If teachers placed the same demands on all their students, they could eventually "lessen the gaps" between individual academic performance. Teachers were to address individual needs only as a means to this end (Xu, 1983).

Teachers at the LXLS took this policy seriously but found its implementation difficult. Even though their first-year students were carefully recruited and had all received at least two years of English training in primary school, their language abilities varied markedly. The task of reducing these variations frustrated teachers so much that they came to view their students' previous English training as a dubious advantage at best. A colleague, paraphrasing

Mao Zedong, complained, "On a piece of clean white paper it is easy to draw whatever picture you want. But on one with all kinds of lines, strewn here and there, you must rub out all those useless lines first."

This teacher of beginning English had a true gift for impersonation and frequently had the entire staff in convulsive laughter over her devilish imitations of first-year pupils' pronunciation. "You should see the kinds of kids we get!" she exclaimed, getting up from her desk. Gesturing hilariously, she cried, "Their pronunciation is soooo BAD! Cold, col-da, col-DA!" Wiping tears of laughter from her cheeks, another colleague sighed, "Sometimes, I really wish we could just put them into a machine that would induce complete ignorance on their parts. Then we could teach them properly from the very beginning."

"Talent Stems from
Diligence, Knowledge
from Accumulation"

Despite the jaded eye my colleagues turned on their young pupils, they rarely questioned that "all students could be brought up to one standard and maintained there." Although they knew that students would arrive at the LXLS with different levels of ability, they also believed that their students were all capable. Whatever a student's native ability (*tiancai*), it must be channeled toward socially useful purposes with the help of a teacher. Only through this process could initial gifts, no matter how great, become developed into mature talent (*rencai*). A teacher explained that "nurture is more important than nature. Of course, among kids, some are more clever than others. Perhaps their brains are simply better. Before they were born, their brains were better developed. This may be true, but what's the use of schools and teachers? After all, all kids receive education. They can all be very good students. The way we help them develop is the paramount concern."

Precisely because teachers believed that students "were basically the same," they were anything but reticent about their pupils' academic performance. They rarely worried that their impressions might unfairly label students and hinder their future performance; instead, they discussed students' "weak points," "slowness," and "exceptional abilities" with frank and unsparing directness with both parents and colleagues.

Such candor was not grounded on a perception of complete understanding of the sources of individual talent. Variance in school performance was recognized by teachers as the result of complex social, biological, and personality factors. Nevertheless, teachers felt it was their responsibility to assess student potential "as it came to them." While they acknowledged that investigation "of the reasons for differences was important for research," they "could not bother with" or "ignored" sociological or biological factors in their assessment of educational achievement. Instead, they resolved, "once kids are here, our job is to get on with the business of teaching everyone as well as possible."

Teachers felt this could best be accomplished by instilling in pupils a firm will and perseverance. Classrooms were viewed primarily as places to encourage hard work. In addition to raw talent, the acceptance of the necessity for hard work was what separated the "best" students from their less successful classmates. Diligence figured prominently in the aphorisms most favored by students and teachers when discussing achievement, and homilies promoting its importance were often featured on classroom blackboards: "Talent stems from diligence, knowledge from accumulation"; "Study is like a boat sailing against the current that must forge ahead or it will be driven back"; "The beauty of a bird is in its feathers, the beauty of a human being is in diligent labor."

Not surprisingly, teachers seldom used the word intelligence (*zhili, lijieli*) when discussing a child who seemed exceptionally resourceful or academically successful. Their explanation for excellence pivoted around two interrelated factors—talent and persistence:

"What the successful student has is perseverance in the face of difficulties and the self-control and will to keep going. One part talent, one part hard work (*yifen cai, yifen xinglao*). That's what leads to success. Talent is not enough. It must be coupled with diligence and willingness to help others, to sacrifice. Students have to understand what they're about. They have to be resolute even when they are having problems. . . . Of course, we teachers can't just pounce on students with every criticism about something we are worried about or not satisfied with. Even a good student can behave strangely sometimes. Sometimes the best students have problems. We have to know what they are thinking. Different students have different problems. Weak ones are nervous, afraid of being criticized, or making a poor show in front of other members of the class. So slower students get easy questions in class for encouragement, the best students get more difficult ones to urge them forward, maybe they'll be afraid and study more, not grow complacent. I place high demands on all of them."

The pressure upon schools to train students who are successful in the college entrance examination had given rise to teaching practices that ran counter to the policy of bringing all students "up to standard." In fact, a number of secondary schools were assigning first-year students to homeroom classrooms on the basis of ability. At the end of 1981, a flurry of newspaper and journal articles warned of the negative repercussions of separating students into "fast" and "slow" sections. These were discussed with keen interest at the LXLS, where students had been assigned since the 1960s to homerooms and foreign-language teaching sections on the basis of student record, test scores, and "study attitude." Most teachers expressed ambivalence about the practice:

"Separating quick students and relatively dull students is done to step up teaching. In some ways, it could be taken as an insult to the dull students. They might feel, 'Formerly, I didn't know I was dull. Now, I realize I'm not as good as the others.' Before, they had no inferiority complex, but they developed one after they had been separated. People are still talking about this process. In our school we have ability grouping, and there really has been no conclusion. Both sides hold their ground. Some people say it will encourage everyone to learn more. Others say it will slow everyone, or at least the dull students, down. Personally, I'm not sure what to think. All I know is that I definitely do not want to discourage any of my students."

Regardless of this uncertainty about the efficacy of ability grouping, teachers remained convinced that all of their students could exhibit mastery. All class groups studied the same curriculum with the same lesson plans. "When a student is behind," a teacher said, "he may be slow or he may be having family problems. But the student could never be too slow for the material. "After all, he made it into this school, didn't he? And there was nothing mysterious about subjects required at the school. Really, with the proper handling, any student can do it as long as he works hard."

The Episodic English
Class: "Lively Efficiency"

Junior secondary school foreign-language teachers were remarkably adept at at bringing their students up to standard. First-year students began their studies with the first volume in the NCE textbook series, *First Things First*. Their lessons were constructed almost entirely around textbook passages that consisted of dialogues and descriptive or narrative accounts accompanied by picture sequences. These illustrations were reproduced in filmstrips for students to react to and talk about in class.

Teachers believed these basic lessons provided students with "two foundations." The first was basic linguistic knowledge, meaningless without the second, the ability to apply knowledge in communicative contexts. To facilitate the establishment of both foundations, teachers forbid beginning students to study a new text passage on their own. Rather, under the teacher's expert guidance they learned to retell the new passage and have it virtually memorized during one 45-minute class period. The lesson was completed the following day when their teacher demanded perfect duplication of text materials.

Pronunciation was especially emphasized because teachers pointed to correct pronunciation as the "basic foundation, the antecedent," for listening and speaking abilities. The first weeks of English classes were devoted to helping students perfect their pronunciation while becoming comfortable with the phrases of classroom discourse basic to the monolingual classroom. "We'll begin with lesson two. Repeat the name of the lesson?" "Twoooo!" "That's it. Liyue, please move that desk here. Where class?" "Here!" "That's it. Oh! I need the eraser. Where is it?" "There!" "Repeat! Where is it?" "There!" "Good! What do I need?" "The eraser." "Where is it?" "There!"

English language teachers were adamant that grounding in "essentials" through "repetition and modeling" led to eventual creative performance. "It is like writing with the Chinese brush. Once you master several styles you have a feeling for what will lead you to something we can all admire. It's hard work, like any other skill. Confucius once said, 'There are those who innovate without knowledge, but that is not a fault I have.' "

Regardless of their emphasis on developing communicative abilities, English teachers generally used the neo-audiolingual approach that was nationally advocated for Chinese secondary schooling. They considered listening skills "the foundation of the foundation" of language learning and maintained repeated listening would enable students to speak (*ting de duole, jiu hui shuole*).

Care was taken that the pace and activity organizing the classroom shifted every 5 or 10 minutes. The division of lessons into distinct episodes combined a Herbartian approach to teaching introduced in China in the late nineteenth century with the Soviet teaching program adapted in Chinese schools in the 1950s, which advised teachers "to review old material, orient new material, explain new material, consolidate new material, and set the next assignment." Although students were encouraged to talk as much as possible in class, it was the teacher's primary responsibility to orchestrate how this talk would flow and to decide what heuristic purpose it would serve. The teacher was expected to be in complete control of classroom events, developing and utilizing effective audiovisual aids, gestures, simple explanations, and timing to create a carefully confined context into which student output must fit.

Two bells punctuated class breaks at the LXLS, a warning bell two minutes before a period began, and a final buzzer, which indicated to students they must be in their seats with books at hand. Classes did not begin formally until a teacher entered a room. Classroom configuration directed the focus of student attention forward, toward a teacher who stood on a slightly raised platform behind a lectern or high desk. Students rose in unison to greet their teachers, although this procedure was carried out cheerfully, without military precision, and was not always followed. Nevertheless, the teacher was quite literally raised above students on a stage, reinforcing expectations that teaching was a performance for which students must provide an informed and cooperative audience.

The first classroom episode commenced immediately and predictably, like clockwork, with "warming up" exercises. Normally these discussions or prepared presentations took no longer than two or three minutes. Teachers felt strongly that a direct teaching approach was crucial for beginning students, and throughout the 45-minute lesson used only English. In all of my classroom observations this was never violated, although English use was associated with classroom work. Quick exchanges in hallways or serious discussions about misbehavior or personal problems always took place in Shanghai dialect or *putonghua* (national dialect). These conversations were often punctuated with English exclamations. "OK!" "That's wonderful!" "My god!" "Bye-bye!"

The second classroom episode, an aural-oral presentation about 10 minutes long, introduced pupils to their new text passage. A black-and-white filmstrip illustrating text content was shown, accompanied by a tape recording of the text. The students "looked and listened" carefully, with their books shut in front of them. The film and recording were played a second time, with pauses between every one or two sentences. Students repeated the tape recording in unison. Occasionally, students were called upon to repeat a segment. Students in foreign-language classes were not required to stand when they answered questions, nor were pupils who could not respond left standing while another classmate attempted to answer. This was not done to protect students from public exposure, which happened often and was viewed as crucial for motivating students. Rather, it was a recognition that constant standing up and sitting down interrupted the fast pace of the foreign-language lesson.

The third episode comprised five minutes of pattern drills or vocabulary practice. All new vocabulary words were written on the board by the teacher, sometimes as cues to help students repeat the text passage they were learning. Students repeated new words individually and in unison, perfecting their pronunciation. During pattern practice, students opened their texts for the first time. All drills in the text were accompanied by pictures that the students worked from orally.

During the fourth episode, oral reconstruction, books were closed and students listened again to the taped passage. "All right, students. Close your books now and listen carefully to the tape." Students repeated sections of the text or the whole passage from memory. No students were allowed to remain unengaged. Teachers called upon all students, and errors in pronunciation or syntax were corrected immediately and often repeated by the whole class. By the end of the class period students might have seen the filmstrip five times.

After viewing a particularly energetic display of repetition and reconstruction of a text passage, I commented to a colleague that I was surprised that not one student seemed bored by such constant attention to the text. She replied, "Oh, no! Not if it's done well. See how engaged they are? They want to learn the new lesson. They have so much energy. You know, we have a saying, 'It's wonderful to repeat what we are learning again and again.' The students delight in it. It gives them confidence and a feeling of learning."

Teachers had two favorite methods to encourage these feelings. The first was requiring students to read text passages aloud, a method adopted from the Chinese language classroom. In addition to increasing fluency, reading aloud was considered a basic skill, the perfection of which would facilitate retention of vocabulary and grammatical patterns that formed the foundation of the student's linguistic ability. It was also considered a teacher's quick measure, along with recitation from memory, of whether a student had prepared and understood a lesson thoroughly.

The second method, memorizing text passages quickly through repetition and reproducing them confidently on demand, was thought to be the single most important strategy for learning a foreign language. Most teachers at the LXLS could still call upon a large repertoire of English phrases and passages they had committed to memory as secondary school pupils. "Sometimes my English could be considered bookish, but you see, at least I have something to say in a new situation. Without that I may be completely stumped. Memorizing and reciting text passages are important methods for students to consolidate material they might need later."

Each lesson was concluded with a "wrap-up," which integrated newly studied vocabulary items, student dialogue, and the setting of homework.

With the exception of spelling and simple fill-in-the-blank exercises, junior one homework was completely aural-oral. Because speaking at the beginner's level was identified with rote recitation of models, homework assignments consisted largely of learning the text by heart. This was done during "evening prep," an hour of study after supper when homeroom class groups of about 40 students listened to tape recordings.

In their second year of language study students began the second volume of NCE, *Practice and Progress*. The text was completed by the end of junior secondary school. Example passages (see Appendix E) clearly indicate the increasing complexity of the text. Passages were written for the first time in paragraph form. Students were required to arrange sentences into short summaries of the text passage. Grammar was much more formally explained.

Although classroom episodes for second-year students were organized in the sequence described above, more emphasis was placed upon active student dialogue. One teacher was fond of dividing her class of 16 pupils into two groups for this activity. "All right, now I want you, yes, those of you on my right to take the part of the boy. You, the rest of you, you are his father. Jianghua, ask Yiren whether you can go to the movie."

The students turned in their seats and faced one another. They raised their hands for recognition (a nod from the teacher) each time a turn was taken, yet the dialogue and questions moved along at extraordinary speed. The teacher moved about the front of the room, arms crossed or pointing to various students. After each student had a chance to ask a question or reply, the teacher drew the session to a close by asking two students to summarize the entire exchange. Students were rarely interrupted when they asked one another questions unless there was a complete breakdown in communication. Only after the students finished were corrections made. "Very good. But I noticed some of you are mispronouncing the word *bargain*. Please, everyone, say after me 'bargain.' Again. Meizhen, please? Yes, good. Again. Yes, that's it. All of you, that's much better."

For passages that did not lend themselves to excited dialogue, the teacher chose one or two students to be "teachers." The selected students came to stand in the front of the classroom and asked their classmates questions about the text. Sometimes the teacher employed a "20 questions" exercise in which five students left the room after they had heard the taped recording of a new lesson. While their classmates opened their books and discussed the new passage, the five students in the hallway talked about what they had heard in the recording and prepared questions. When they returned to the classroom four or five minutes later they asked their classmates questions about the text. In all of these exercises emphasis was placed on accuracy and speed.

No matter how much active participation these exercises engendered, they were carefully structured to promote understanding of the text. Spontaneous or uncontrolled language use was neatly confined in five minutes of discussion at the end of a class period or shunted off to a rare aside when the teacher could incorporate an unforeseen question from a student smoothly into the predicted flow of the lesson plan. Teachers were uncomfortable with an unguarded flow of questions, because they worried that students would veer too far from the lesson, that too many errors would go uncorrected, and that classroom efficiency would decline. "Uncontrolled output" in class would interfere with the teacher's responsibility to implement the slogan "less is more," implying a clear, concise lesson plan of high quality, and ultimately compromise the teacher's charge to "make full use of the 45-minute class period."

In truth, a teacher's inability to answer an unexpectedly challenging question also implied negligence. By asking a question to which no answer was immediately forthcoming, not only did a student "challenge" the teacher's authority, but the teacher also failed both student and her duty to have everything in order. Such a failure reflected upon the teacher and the entire class. The best class was the class that made the fewest mistakes. Thus, total preparation was the primary criterion for teaching effectiveness. Despite their recognition of the importance of humility in teaching and learning, a question taken as a mark of honest teaching in the United States—"I don't know, I'm asking you" (Lightfoot, 1983, 232)—would be met with gentle disapproval by LXLS teachers.

This demarcation between teacher and student talk promoted a classroom atmosphere of great mutual interdependence. In fact, it was not unusual for teachers and students publicly to minimize one another's failings. If students did poorly on a test, there were two common explanations. Either the test was poorly constructed by the entire teaching and research group, or the individual teacher failed to teach her students. Individual success was so tied to group achievement that on bad days teachers glared at one another in frustration. "What did I do to deserve you for a teaching partner?" "Why don't you discipline your students more?" Student monitors reacted by scolding their classmates. "You didn't hand in your workbooks." "The teachers are upset."

What is remarkable about these classes, which made such rapid, heavy, and public demands upon pupils, is that students rarely seemed anxious.

Their teachers' expectations were clear and predictable. Pupils were supported by classmates with whom they worked closely and felt tight bonds. In the hundreds of hours I taught at the LXLS, not once was a lesson disrupted by an announcement over the public address system. Classrooms were protected from arbitrary interruption, varied enough to engage the attention of students, and predictable enough to give them a sense of daily continuity. In fact, teachers were frankly dubious about their pupils' attention spans and felt that the language classroom must be "rapid, lively, and constantly shifting" in order to direct student motivation and concentration.

If an ideal learning environment is a safe and stable place of "unanxious expectation" (Sizer, 1984, 174), LXLS teachers came close to achieving it for their junior secondary school pupils. Teachers monitored student progress toward instructional objectives, built an optimum amount of redundancy into their lessons so as not to bore or frustrate pupils, gave regular feedback on student performance, held high expectations, and demanded mastery. Their uncompromising equation of strict and disciplined coaching with student success helped produce students who were exceptionally adept performers. Such skills were reinforced by the school's model stature. Visitors poured through its gate in a brisk stream, and students learned to perform for them upon demand with astonishing aplomb.

Most important, teachers regarded their pupils with the "fearless and empathetic regard" so highly valued by those seeking good teaching in the United States (Sara Lawrence Lightfoot, 1983, 342). That teachers did so, of course, was due in large part to the LXLS's elite status. Students recognized that their school was providing them a scarce and valuable opportunity. The growing popularity of English-language training also confirmed what teachers hoped to be true about their professional worth. Though LXLS teachers were by no means unanimously content as secondary school teachers, their hard work was at least rewarded by the value it held in the eyes of students and their parents.

Necessary Lessons for Senior Students: The Constraints on Sponsoring Independence and Creativity

The central pedagogical dilemma facing LXLS teachers was how to transform this pattern of rewarding predictable classroom discourse into the "independence," "critical thinking," and "creativity" they desired in older students. Despite sincere attempts on the part of teachers to follow a schoolwide injunction that "whatever the students can do by themselves, don't do for them," older students faltered in the transition from precise reproduction of carefully constructed models to creative performance. My colleagues wondered why students who had shown so much promise in junior secondary school became passive and hard to engage as they grew older. Was it merely a function of age? Had the Cultural Revolution's devaluation of study and knowledge affected the school's oldest pupils so much that their scholarship would always suffer? "How can we get students to go deeper into the texts they study and the books they read? They have no problem answering surface questions but beyond a rather superficial approach to a story or lesson they hesitate, they have nothing to say. Why?"

The Text:

Developing Skills

Like their younger schoolmates, senior secondary pupils at the LXLS were exposed to the state-approved *English* series only enough to insure their success on state-sponsored examinations. Although they met in its pages predictable portrayals of class-based poverty, racial discrimination, and lack of authentic freedom in the United States and Great Britain, more typical passages summarized the achievements of famous male foreigners such as Nathan Hale, Thomas Edison, and Galileo or examined the construction of the Egyptian pyramids, the physical properties of water, the life of a cell, or provided simplified selections of well-known stories such as "The Emperor's New Clothes" and "Gift of the Magi." The dominant lessons students learned from this text were not overtly ideological. Instead, the book provided a curious mixture of ideas and literature that have been introduced in China and have come to leave their mark on how millions of schoolchildren experience "Western culture."

Developing Skills, the third volume in Alexander's NCE series, was the senior secondary pupil's major text and was identified as one of the primary sources of what teachers called the "creativity problem." Students began studying the text during their first semester of senior secondary school. Text passages served to illustrate abstract concepts or cultural traits that students often found vague or strange or boring. They included explanations of the British legal system, the subtleties of modern art and black humor, freedom of the press, and the joys of pastoral living (see Appendix E).

Because these selections did not lend themselves to the rapidly paced classroom exercises to which teachers and students were accustomed, teachers were forced to alter their teaching style. Students, frustrated and even threatened by having to deal in class with difficult passages without advanced preparation, were no longer introduced to text passages for the first time by the teacher in class. Instead, they listened to a recording and prepared the written text in advance. As they read they were required to make certain they understood the passage, to look up the definitions of unfamiliar vocabulary items, and mark any problems for discussion in class.

Although teachers introduced students to independent reading strategies such as guessing the meaning of new vocabulary items from context, they continued to design lesson plans around intensive and exacting study of each text passage. Reading, writing, and translation in both oral and written form became increasingly emphasized in classroom work. Translation exercises were used regularly to force students to a precise understanding of vocabulary and complex language structure. "Vague feelings about what this or that word or sentence means is not enough," insisted a teacher. "If they can take a lesson and translate it into good Chinese, or vice versa, well then, we know they have grasped the true meaning of the text."

Teachers regarded incorporating extensive reading into the English curriculum as the most viable option for extending the range of their students' contact with and enthusiasm for English. The distinction between extensive and intensive reading skills and goals had been widely debated since the early 1960s (Wu, 1962; Zhang Weijun, 1983). "If we incorporate real reading into our work it would all become meaningful—reading for meaning and natural learning. The students will see the use in foreign languages, because they will be learning from their reading; they will be able to see their own achievement and progress, and their interest will rise. They will begin to love the subject, and that's the best teacher of all."

While LXLS teachers and leaders accepted in theory the value of "exposing" students to larger amounts of English material, in practice teachers were concerned about the consequences. If materials were not taught intensively then what was to take up class time? Conversation? Discussion? Teachers had little experience in working in such an interpretive mode and wondered whether more controlled patterns of teaching wouldn't serve students just as well.

Students were assigned the same materials to read extensively, one selection each month and during summer and winter holidays. Teachers expressed concerns about whether students learned much from these reading assignments or, given their hectic schedules, whether they would take the time to read them seriously. Consequently, teachers felt compelled to turn every extensive reading activity into an intensive project to give the assignment legitimacy in the eyes of their pupils, and to reassure themselves that they were responsible teachers.

In the end, no practical distinction was made by LXLS teachers between linguistic competence and performance. As in the moral realm where student behavior signified correct thinking, in the linguistic realm student performance signified correct learning. What remained dominant in the English classroom was meeting prescribed performance demands. Extensive reading did little to alter either the way teachers perceived learning or the passivity with which older students approached their English studies.

The College Entrance Examination

So intractable did the patterns of teaching outlined above seem that teachers sought in factors beyond their immediate control explanations for their inability to reform their pedagogy. They unanimously identified their chief barrier as China's college entrance examination system. Although changes have taken place in Shanghai's examination system since the early 1980s, the entrance examination remains a powerful determinant of China's social elite, an instrument for allocating scarce post-secondary training, an intriguing shadow of China's imperial legacy, a touchstone for academic achievement and pedagogical success, and one of the most controversial aspects of China's educational system. Like its counterpart in Japan, the examination provides a counterbalance to a system of power and authority based upon personal relationships and obligations (Rohlen, 1983, 62) and has become central to debates about who should and does have access to prestigious knowledge and training.

From the setting of its questions to its evaluation, the examination was in the early 1980s a mammoth and surprisingly public undertaking with direct impact on the daily work and lives of both students and teachers. Justifications for changes in examination form and content, the relative importance in total score of different subject areas, the grading sites and formal procedure for scoring different sections of the examination, were all published in education journals and discussed in detail by senior level teachers whose responsibility was to review examination materials with their pupils.

The examination created a subculture of college and secondary school teachers who participated in its evaluation year after year. Short stories describing this culture frequently appeared in newspapers and magazines.

Before the introduction of computer grading simplified the process, the onset of "black July" (Chen, 1986) brought to mind images of hot, stuffy classrooms filled with the scratching sounds of grading pens, the drowsy quiet broken by loudspeaker announcements reminding teachers to "Be impartial!" "Abide by the rules!" "Maintain strict standards!" (Tu, 1982)

Foreign-language teachers at the LXLS were active participants in this subculture. Their membership was one of the reasons parents wanted to have their children enter the LXLS. What better way to insure your children's successful examination results than to have them guided by teachers who graded and even occasionally wrote portions of the exam?

Like these parents, LXLS teachers believed that no other factor so shaped the definition of excellent secondary school education than the college entrance examination. Of course, they criticized this definition, claiming the exam not only denied the importance of the authentic communicative skills possessed by their students, but also stifled creativity and individual development of special talents. And they were not alone in these assessments. The examination stood almost universally accused for encouraging narrowly focused, dependent students who could not adjust to college life. Newspaper accounts and education journals were filled with disparaging commentary. "Break schools out of the chains of the entrance examination." "Constant test taking makes a nervous wreck of our children!" "We are cultivating the future of China, not Peking ducks!" (Ye Chaoyang, 1983, 25–26)

Nevertheless, my colleagues maintained that the examination placed secondary school practitioners in a particularly intolerable situation. College-level educators criticized them for overemphasizing test scores and training passive graduates who "seemed to be cut from the same mould," graduates who were, in the favorite expression of teachers throughout China, "high in score, but low in ability." Teachers also faulted the media for hypocritically asserting in one column that schools denied China's children their childhood while reinforcing in the next that very denial by sensationalizing prodigies, infants of four to six months old distinguishing between Chinese characters. Parents, thus predisposed toward fostering early academic success, fought to have their toddlers placed into the best kindergartens. "If the children pass, they are dragons. If they fail, they are nothing but insects," exclaimed one teacher:

"Teachers feel that in reality they have no choice. So they just make sure students can do exercises, without putting any emphasis on whether they truly understand and can use the material. We all agree schools should teach, really *teach* basic knowledge, not just get kids to pass tests. Good students are really tested in society, not in tests. If a person is productive in 10 or 20 years, that is when we'll really know we've done a good job. The entrance exams reflect a certain level of achievement, but by steering our teaching solely in that direction we are not necessarily helping our students. Teachers can't be short-sighted."

"What you mean," interrupted a colleague, "is that society can't be short-sighted. No matter what we do, if the test remains the same, if jobs remain the same, the pressure will be there. Because the students have little notion where they will be working after graduation there's little motivation. We may be against the view that all we should emphasize is promotion to college, but that's not enough!"

Most teachers were, in fact, resigned to the entrance examination's powerful hold on their pedagogy. On the one hand, they sincerely supported attempts by the Shanghai Bureau of Education to reduce student workloads by banning excessive examinations, by stipulating the number of hours secondary school pupils must sleep each night, by restricting homework during winter holidays, and by preventing special perquisites for instructors who taught solely "to the top" (*yousheng zhongxinhua*) students destined to pass the examination. On the other hand, they made certain that their students experienced many a "practice run" on crucial examinations. The average score of LXLS *junior* secondary school pupils who were given the English portion of the 1982 entrance examination (see Appendix F) was 87. "Not bad," commented one teacher. "It will give some students confidence. But it also presses them on. They've got to know it's not all roses out there."

The Troubling Quest
for Creativity

Because teachers believed the real solution to their creativity problem lay in fundamental alterations of China's educational system, which was beyond their control, they directed their reform efforts at the one thing they felt they could influence—traditional teaching methods. "Well, after all," said a colleague, "we can't do anything about the entrance exam, can we? So we've got to focus on things we can change. Our methods. Our attitudes."

The methods and attitudes that LXLS teachers identified as in need of reform have been summarized in Chinese critiques of foreign-language education as the "three-centeredness" of classrooms: "teacher-centeredness, textbook-centeredness, and grammar-centeredness" (Yen, 1987, 53). As we have seen, eclecticism provided teachers with one concept for thinking about dislodging the authoritarian hold of teacher, text, and grammar-translation methods, especially because it allowed them simultaneously to minimize the tensions and justify the experimentation that shaped their pedagogy.

Many teachers, however, were skeptical about attempting much more than this. Accepting that they were first and foremost transmitters of knowledge, these instructors concerned themselves with content, not process, and bridled at the prospect of one more discussion about creativity. "All this continued going on about this method or that method drives me crazy! After all, what are we doing? What's important is teaching the language! Period! I can't always be worrying about every kid's psyche. I'm here to teach, damn it! I do it, and I prepare. I lay out the information for them as coherently as possible. That's all I can do!"

When I suggested that the creativity problem might stem from an implicit curriculum that rewarded intellectual passivity and conformity on the part of both teachers and students, teachers were adamant that I was absolutely wrong. My suggestion was unfounded not because there was no student conformity and passivity, which, as we have seen, teachers openly admitted. Rather, my suggestion implied the existence of a category that rested upon the assumption that things of great importance in a school *could* go unseen and unexamined. My colleagues simply did not agree that there could be more to their lesson plans than met the eye. For some crucial part of the teaching process to so escape their notice implied fantastic neglect, a lack of understanding of the "principles of education," and an inability to define properly the purpose of schooling or, more specifically, language learning. "Things so important cannot possibly go undetected," concluded a colleague. "Our goals are specific; everyone is clear about what they are. If there are problems we address them. And that's that!"

By accepting predefined educational goals at face value and demanding perfect performance in the classroom to achieve them, my colleagues did not accept that their actions might lead, even unwittingly, to an erosion of the very aims they wished to achieve. From my point of view, however, they decried "passive," "dependent" students, as well as their own lack of profes-sional autonomy, though their actions confirmed an asymmetrical student-teacher relationship and protected the individual teacher from censure through collectively interpreted pedagogical prescriptions. I believed that by not recognizing these contradictions, my colleagues bypassed an entire con-stellation of questions whose answers might have alleviated some of their gravest practical concerns. They, in turn, were convinced that I misinterpreted the outcomes of good teaching.

My colleagues' certitude that it was possible to achieve both conformity to model behavior and creative independence was a point upon which we would never agree. The students' prodigious abilities to memorize huge portions of their English texts were impressive. Yet, as I often asked my colleagues, "What was lost in the process?" "What do you mean, lost?" they retorted. I replied, "The students know one way of thinking and acting and learning very well. But these have been presented as the only acceptable ways to behave. Perhaps this gives the students a certainty, a security—" "That's right!" a teacher interrupted. "And it also teaches them what is right and wrong."

I continued, "It smooths the waters. I've heard some of you say most people just want a smooth life. Don't rock the boat. Don't you think it's a little unrealistic to expect to get questioning, mature, absorbed students, with the ability to be independent, to choose for themselves, if you don't give them the option of rocking the boat? How can you expect students to ask questions, yet always come up with the same answers? Isn't that what you're really hoping for, even demanding?" "No! No! No, it's not! Why do you assume that thinking always has to lead to disagreement with our system?"

An especially diplomatic colleague tried to deflect these arguments that had no other outcome but to lead us onto sensitive political ground, a space to be avoided at all costs in the public arena of the staff office. "It's not just a question of what's right and wrong. The students are caged up in a boarding school and pressed with homework. They get a lot of book learning but not much in the way of life experience. Perhaps, well, we overprotect them. This is in part a reaction to the Cultural Revolution. We all felt that so strongly, and now we want to keep these kids from harm, and at the same time give them more. We don't want to spoon-feed, to hold their hands, yet we do. I'm not sure we can win."

Another teacher interrupted:

"No, I think we do win, maybe even quite often. Teaching is an art. It's not as simple as we might imagine. Creativity and freedom are both very important. Of course students depend on us as teachers. Our task is to help them find their own support. I don't think creativity is problematic. Far from it. It makes the job easier. This doesn't mean that I'm not strict with them, that I don't have a very firm plan in mind. A teacher is like the director of a film. You have to give guidance, to know how to draw the best from students, but also know when they can do it. When they've got a good idea, let them go with it. By teaching step-by-step, knowing when to do what, one leads the students from a state of ignorance to a state of beginning to acquire knowledge. This doesn't mean they just follow. They also learn how to judge. They accumulate knowledge like a pyramid. Confucius meant this. 'Through reviewing the old one can learn the new' (*wen gu er zhi xin*). What I'm trying to say is that creativity and correctness shouldn't conflict."

The efforts by Chinese educators to strike a harmonious balance between perfect performance and creative production has recently been championed as offering "clues to the dilemma of contemporary education" (Gardner, 1989). The challenge presented by Chinese educators does indeed prompt teachers schooled and trained in North America to reevaluate their assumptions about the optimal intersection of basic skills and spontaneous expression. Yet, crucial to this reevaluation must be the acknowledgment that Chinese teachers ground their assumptions about creativity in different notions regarding the sources of knowledge, human talent, and the individual's relationship to and responsibility for others.

In spite of their sincere belief that control and creativity can coexist in the classroom, the centralized management of the structure and organization of knowledge in China, as well as the public image of teachers, supports the former very much more than the latter. There is little room for risk taking in foreign-language classrooms where teachers are not native speakers, where the material to be covered is mandated by teaching outlines and eventually tested by the college entrance examination, and where positive evaluation is tied to perfect performance. Teachers are expected to present a jewel of a lesson, precisely cutting up their 45 minutes into neat episodes. Students are rewarded much more for exact reproduction than creative but awkward attempts. A remarkable essay can be judged "filled with mistakes" while a dutifully guided précis is assessed as "perfect down to the last punctuation mark."

Most important, creativity is ultimately bound by moral purposes, and measured by support of one official worldview, not its alteration. Consequently, teachers who spoke interminably about developing a communicative teaching style simultaneously avoided many of the fundamental issues of the value of talking. The more spontaneously LXLS students communicated in their second tongues, the more their conversations sounded unorthodox. Although teachers rarely said so explicitly, they understood that free expression could be found "attractive as a tool of modernization but feared as a threat to the communist social order" (Tobin, Wu, and Davidson, 1989, 198).

Interpreting the role of the foreign-language teacher in this context raises questions central to the issue of professional autonomy discussed in chapter 4. Teachers at the LXLS were certainly not naive about the role of formal education in linking knowledge and power. However, they defined their responsibilities in such a way as to undercut the possibility of developing what educators in North America might call a critical pedagogy. While "modernizing" foreign-language teaching was supposed to engender greater professional autonomy, teachers were themselves not unlike empty vessels, accepting and then effectively transmitting knowledge defined, certified, and organized by state authorities.

Relinquishing the empty vessel model of teaching and learning challenged LXLS teachers to consider the learning process as an unpredictable, socially constructed activity. Forced by definition to reject this possibility, they turned to eclecticism as the pragmatic solution to foreign-language education reform during the era of the open door. Eclecticism accommodated educational efforts to diversify school programs. It encouraged teachers to experiment with a wide range of teaching methods while relieving them from having to ally with any one particular approach.

This detached flexibility, however, did not merely protect teachers from straying into unapproved territory. It also concealed from them the contradictions inherent in their two-foundations language policy. Classrooms that engendered active involvement, exchange of opinion, and spontaneous language use ran counter to common Chinese educational settings, where restrictive communication designed to foster socially shared values was the norm. On the one hand, foreign-language knowledge was called upon to "bring to the daily lives of students and teachers an international perspective," to give access to a marketplace of "modernized thinking," the cultivation in citizens of a creative consciousness (Qian, 1988, 14–15). On the other hand, foreign languages and knowledge gained approval for their ability to support, not alter, the Chinese worldview.

In this sense, eclecticism had the potential of being both enriching and explosive, a quality increasingly evident as the decade progressed (Bastid, 1987). Teachers who advocated communicative language use for an "internationalized" curriculum found themselves struggling to mediate economic imperatives, which required foreign knowledge, and cultural-political imperatives, which attempted to limit its impact. Their attempts to make the first foundation of pronunciation, vocabulary, and grammar not the end of language study but the means to the second foundation of communicative ability began to loosen the linchpin of the three-centered classroom, as well as alter the teacher's traditional role as moral and intellectual example. Consequently, foreign-language instructors, the institutions in which they taught, and finally their students, to whom we now turn, were squarely placed in the century-old and ambiguous position of being unusually open to both innovation and political scrutiny.

Chapter 6
Students in the
School

"English Lesson One: The New School Year

It's September, and we're back at school. It's good to see all my teachers and friends again. They all look fine.

We're going to have some new subjects this year—history, physics and physiology. I'm going to work hard at maths. I'm not very good at it. And I'm afraid physics is going to be difficult for me, too. Wei Fang says she's going to help me. I think I'll do better than last year.

I like English very much. I always work hard at it. This year I'm going to speak much more English. I'm going to help Zhang Hong with her English, too.

My classmates want me to work for the wall newspaper. They say I draw well, and my handwriting is good. It's interesting work, and I must do my best." (*English*, 1979, 6–7)

The school year began as predictably at the LXLS as the one described in its youngest pupils' English primer. A faint smell of whitewash clung to the cement steps of the school's main entrance. A blackboard placed among vibrant azaleas proclaimed the opening of the Twelfth Party Congress in Beijing. Display cases in the lobby featured brush paintings executed the previous spring during a school outing at Southern Lake, the picturesque site of the founding of the CCP. A group of senior pupils clustered in intense discussion around black and white photographs taken by members of the school's photography club. Their jostling, animated activity ceased momentarily, and they cocked their heads to the strains of classical music, which erupted over the public address system.

Newly arrived pupils, lugging bags stuffed with clothing and bedding, paused in the lobby to glance at the 10 "Secondary School Student Regulations" posted there in large black characters:

1. Love the motherland. Love the people. Support the Chinese Communist Party. Study diligently. Prepare to contribute your efforts to socialist modernization.
2. Come to school on time. Don't leave early. Don't skip class.

3. Concentrate on lessons. Think hard. Complete all assignments conscientiously.
4. Be persistent in physical exercise. Actively participate in beneficial recreational activities.
5. Actively participate in labor. Cherish the products of labor.
6. Be frugal. Practice good hygiene. Don't smoke. Don't drink alcohol. Don't spit.
7. Maintain school discipline and public order. Obey the country's laws.
8. Respect teachers and elders. Unite with classmates. Be polite. Don't curse. Don't fight.
9. Love the collective. Protect public property. Don't engage in activities harmful to the people.
10. Be modest, honest, and correct mistakes.

Gradually students dispersed in groups of two or three to the playing fields, the courtyard, the dormitories. A pair of girls who were designing their homeroom's rear blackboard mused, "We want to be back, and yet we don't. We already have so much *work* to do." They spread their arms wide to indicate the dusty emptiness of the classroom. The room seemed lifeless and oppressive after six weeks of gritty summer heat.

As they decorated, symbols of National Day, still a month away, emerged in a profusion of colorful chalk. The girls created a swirling, exaggerated portrait of nationalism and socialist development. Snapping red flags and silver rockets flanked silhouettes of famous national personages. A luminous moon hung over a cornucopia spilling forth the autumn bounty of central China. I noticed the girls were leaving a large space in the middle of the blackboard for classmates to add their own "Welcome back!" wishes. They stood back to appraise their work, then returned to the board and added over its blank center "reflections on being a good student during the coming semester." This tiny negotiation between the publicly accepted image of the LXLS student and its personal core struck me as significant. One of the students turned from the intricate mural and complained, "meetings and homework. It's unfair! All I want to do is gossip with my friends. Being at home was *sooooo* boring. There was nothing, nothing I tell you, to do! Just talk on the phone or watch TV—which usually stunk!"

She stopped, considering how much to share with the foreign teacher. I realized I was also in the process of being negotiated. I imagined her thinking, Teacher first, can't forget that. But foreign, what does that mean? "I bet you don't know this," she said finally, and began to chant:

Spring's not for school, everyone knows,
Summer's scorching, go to sleep,
Autumn mosquitoes, winter snows,
Wait 'til next year, your books will keep.

Her classmate pointed to the blackboard moon. "We don't even get a break until Mid-Autumn Festival." She had apparently decided to take me on as a cultural project and explained that this year Mid-Autumn Festival, celebrated on the 15th day of the eighth month of the lunar calendar, fell fortuitously on 1 October, the anniversary of the founding of the PRC. The girls called it their double holiday. "In Shanghai, you'll see, the moon never comes out. Yet my family sits and waits anyway. And every year my father will say the moon is mocking us. He says for a real moon festival we should go back to the countryside where my grandparents live. The moon shines there."

The Collective Management of Adolescence: Children of the Boarding School

The LXLS's manifest design provided the central direction for these two students and their classmates for the next 10 months. The unit family became their temporary household, its omnipotent regimen (see Table 6.1) every bit as much a "total institution" as private American boarding schools (Cookson and Persell, 1985). With the blare of a buzzer or flick of a master light switch, student use of time and space was monitored in classroom and dormitory. During free periods teachers and school leaders channeled their pupils' energies into "productive engagement" in sport teams and clubs. While these activities, which included mathematics, track and field athletics, singing, stamp collecting, chess, photography, and astronomy, were popular among students, they left little room for individual initiative or relaxation from group control.

Pupils were required to remain on campus except for the hours between Saturday afternoon and Monday morning. On weekends the demanding and highly visible image of the LXLS accompanied them in the small red and white enamel school badges they were required to pin to their shirts or jackets. The badges, as we have seen, were meant to instill school pride and mutual responsibility, obliging each student to announce publicly, "This is my formal attachment. If you find fault with my behavior, you find fault with this group."

Even the student newspaper, *The Star,* conformed to the formal representation by which LXLS leaders hoped their school would be known. Although pupils were responsible for writing, editing, and publishing the paper, it included no gossip columns, no mild protest of school policy or swipes at adult members of the school community. Aside from a somewhat sensational "Believe it or not!" column, it contained no discussion that would not be appropriate in a formal classroom setting. *The Star* was symbolic of student life at the LXLS. Behavior displayed in classrooms, meetings, and school outings was carefully managed to convey a highly idealized portrait of schooling.

In truth, student action that modified this portrait was remarkably restricted. Much of the ingenious repertoire of negotiation, compromise, and resistance strategies evident among students in North American schools was neither culturally appropriate nor materially possible at the LXLS. The school's privileged pupils were intensely social, yet they had little unsupervised time or material culture—music, posters, apparel—in which to construct what North American educators take for granted will be a youth culture containing oppositional elements. Dormitory rooms were spartan and self-patrolled. A room for 10 students consisted of bunk beds pushed up against gray concrete walls, a small wardrobe, four desks, several chairs, and two benches wedged into a corner on which to keep duffle bags. While Chinese educators currently grapple with the power of the marketplace to redistribute authority, in the early 1980s there simply was not yet the paraphernalia young people worldwide are encouraged to consume and then use to distance themselves from the incessant lessons of formal schooling. In addition, the moral and cultural order of the LXLS was mandated by CCP policy. Though this reality was obscured, sometimes even dismantled, by the daily rhythms of boarding school life, its dynamic kept school ritual firmly in the hands of scrutinizing adults.

Like the girls in charge of the classroom blackboard, students expressed vague, contradictory feelings about their confined vulnerability. While they appreciated their good fortune in studying at a school that seemed to guarantee academic advancement, they also reported feeling cheated out of experiences they were certain their non-boarding school counterparts must be having. "At first we were very happy here. We didn't have to take an examination. You see, we were in the third grade and that was still during the Gang of Four. I remember it was so sudden. Most of us hadn't even heard

Table 6.1
Lu Xun Language School 1982 Fall Semester Daily Schedule

Morning	
get up	5:50
wash	5:50– 6:10
morning exercises	6:10– 6:40
breakfast	6:40
morning prep	7:20– 7:55
first period	8:00– 8:45
second period	8:55– 9:40
broadcast exercises	9:45– 9:50
third period	10:05–10:50
eye exercises	11:00–11:05
fourth period	11:05–11:50
lunch	11:50

Afternoon	
Saturday:	
fifth period	12:45– 1:30
sixth period	1:40– 2:25
Tuesday, Thursday:	
assembly	1:15– 1:30
fifth period	1:30– 2:15
eye exercises	2:25– 2:30
sixth period	2:30– 3:15
seventh period	3:25– 4:10
eighth period	4:15– 5:00
dinner	5:00

Evening	
daily chores	5:40– 6:30
evening prep:	
first period	6:30– 7:20
eye exercises	7:30– 7:35
second period	7:35– 8:30
prepare for bed	8:50
lights out	9:00

of this school or even the Foreign Language Institute. We didn't choose English, either. The school also taught French and Spanish then, but we were told to study English. Why not? But some bad boys say our school is like a prison. We're locked in so we can't enjoy any occasion to go out."

Senior secondary school students chafed at "being patronized," "being treated like babies." "We are not free in this school. That became clear after we were here for a while," said a boy with a firm shake of his head. "Even our sense of time is not our own. See this watch? I keep it way up here under my shirt. We're not supposed to worry about the time here, just study. The teachers will tell us when class is over. The bells will ring. Well, I want to know the time. So I wear this watch way up under my shirt. We have a TV, but we can't watch it. When we first came, we were very young. Some of us cried at night. One classmate even climbed over the wall and escaped home."

Because of such incidents school leaders deemed independence and self-sufficiency critical to student success at the LXLS, so much so that "independent living skills" was part of the school's formal curriculum for its youngest students. However, independence was defined as being able to cope with laundry, homesickness, heavy homework demands. It did not include encouraging students to think of themselves as adults. Pupils accepted that they "were in the end still children" with resignation, as "the way things are." A 15-year-old girl explained the behavior of the student who had run away from school by declaring emphatically, "Well, of course, the student who did that was a *boy*! We girls like the boarding school more than the boys. They are too young, too immature. The boarding school is a good idea, because if we were at home we would be infected by the rest of society. We would see others playing and not do our homework, and it would be a waste of time."

Teachers were sympathetic with student complaints about lack of freedom but also maintained that the positive consequences of the boarding school's imposition of discipline warranted intrusion into their lives. They, like the girl just mentioned, viewed the LXLS as a calmly ordered shelter in which students could strive academically without being distracted by Shanghai's increasingly rich and varied popular culture. "It's true that the students are very busy, every minute of the day. But we don't want to waste time. Education is a very precious thing. Not very many students in China can go to a school like this. They have to make the most of their opportunity. Teachers must provide students with a sense of security, a conviction that all their work is valuable and meaningful. I guess you could say it is like a family working together toward the same goals. The students can concentrate their minds on their studies here. They won't associate with bad ideas coming from society."

The LXLS was successful at obtaining student compliance with its protective collective ideology precisely because teachers and leaders conceived of that ideology as a social process. They understood that if students were to respect and internalize the formal messages of the school they must be actively and continuously engaged in their construction. As we turn to how LXLS students were recruited for this mission, it becomes evident how much their own values assisted the school's success. Their parents' universal desire to have their offspring receive a higher education lent even rote school tasks powerful social, if not pedagogical, significance. Students were willing to bend to school rules because they believed these rules were, as they often put it, "for their own good."

This acknowledgment ultimately allowed the LXLS to encompass, both in rhetoric and in practice, the social agencies of family, school, and political organization, and in the words of a colleague, "make them work harmoniously. Here, education becomes important on three fronts—on the school front, the family front, and the societal front. All of these must work together. We're lucky, because the boarding school combines the best of all these fronts. We have greater control to bring them together, since this is not just the students' place of study. It is also their place of play and their home."

The sense of achievement and purpose that provided LXLS students with a common aim was reinforced by school rituals, assemblies, field trips, and ceremonies designed to inspire loyalty and commitment. This collective identity, sustained by the school's recruitment of students designed to fit it, was acted upon daily and given meaning by the students' three most important reference points: their families, their homeroom classrooms, and the Young Pioneers or Communist Youth League.

Recruiting Students

Most Likely to Succeed

"An examination of who goes to boarding schools reveals a great deal about the schools and their perception of their place within the larger educational and social system. If people can be known by the company they keep, cannot schools be known by the students they admit?" (Cookson and Persell, 1985, 57).

The LXLS's most powerful method for sustaining its school ethos was its ability to shape its student body with precision through an elaborate procedure for recruiting students. In the spring of 1982 the Shanghai Municipal

Bureau of Education provided the LXLS with a list of hundreds of potential new students who had been chosen from the best central (*zhongxin*) elementary schools in Shanghai's 10 central districts.[1] From this large pool of pupils, prospective candidates were selected on the basis of teacher recommendation, parental approval, and health. According to a teacher,

"health is at the outset quite important, more so than mental or moral qualifications. If a child is nearsighted or in poor health, he would not be selected for an interview, no matter how gifted. Each candidate is required to have 'three-merit' status. They must have scored at least 90 points on the junior middle school entrance examinations in Chinese, mathematics, and English. This gives us a sense of the student's real all-round ability, which is essential. Actually though, to get into the best key schools in Shanghai students need a combined score of about 280, and for the LXLS 290 is the ideal. Parents are frantic about this score, because if their kids get into a good middle school the teaching will be good, and their chances to enter the university are already better. For our students, it's true, the door to the university is already opened a crack."

One experienced foreign-language teacher was assigned the duty of selecting students from two of the city's ten central districts. The teacher visited several preselected schools, which served as interview sites, and talked with the principals who had prepared the lists of potential candidates. She or he reviewed each student's record, which consisted of average marks, family background and occupation, and an assessment of moral and physical well-being. Students were then divided into groups of 20. After interviewing each student, the faculty member chose four or five children from each group, to make a total of 60 applicants from each municipal district.

Interviewing procedures were similar to those used to admit pupils into Shanghai's most prestigious elementary schools. Each interview was comprised of three components to determine the child's alertness (*guancha*) and mathematical (*suanshu*) and communicative (*jianghua*) abilities. During the first portion of the interview the teacher asked each student to describe his or her life in primary school. The child's ability to present him or herself favorably was crucial. While the child talked, the teacher assessed his or her

1 In October 1981, Shanghai municipality replaced controversial key primary schools with a "central" school system. The city's 635 urban elementary schools were divided into 71 districts of no more than 10 primary schools each, with one central school to act as model and resource center for its counterparts in the district.

poise, ability to communicate, physical composure and attractiveness, voice quality, ability to get along with others, and "quickness." Next, the teacher asked the students to work out simple calculations "in their heads. If the students were bright and fast, that is a plus. If they were obviously slow, they could be rejected on these grounds."

Finally, each child was asked to imitate English, French, and German phrases and sentences. As students repeated each phrase, teachers assessed the students' "ear, their ability to pronounce carefully. If they cannot pronounce well, if there is some difficulty with particular sound groups, then we certainly won't choose those students." Some teachers found this process extremely worrisome. "Actually, I was very scared. I wondered, how can I do right by these children I don't even know? It really is rather subjective, although we try hard to choose the best candidates. When we finally teach some of them, will we waste their talent? It's such a big responsibility. I was in many ways deciding a good portion of their young lives. I have to admit that I felt very badly for those students I rejected. I even felt depressed at home about it."

Other staff members, however, brushed aside such concerns. "Well, we really know best how to decide. Who could do it better? For example, if children are too quiet, too shy, I rejected them from the group. If they fidgeted, were restless or always moving about or talking to other children in the group, I simply did not select them."

The 60 students from each city district, making a total of 600 students who could apply for admittance, were given further physical examinations, from which they were exempted if they were an active member of a primary school athletics team. Family background was also reevaluated. One of the teachers who had taught at the LXLS since before the Cultural Revolution described how family background considerations had changed:

"Some of our students come from PLA officers' homes, and a small percentage from intellectual families, but most are from working class backgrounds. Before the Cultural Revolution we enrolled kids from the countryside as well. Now the students just come from the city. This is because it takes so long to get to school. Up to five hours to get in to school for some children. There was a period of time, before and during the Cultural Revolution, when students were selected strictly according to family background. The group you are teaching is the very last selected that way. Their parents are workers or party and military leaders. We know that selection according to family background is not rational or productive today, so we have examinations and criteria regarding health and attitude, not just who your family is. However, our school differs from other schools in its investigation of the family. We can't have students of criminal background. These students may become diplomats or interpreters for foreigners someday, and they have to be trusted."

Each teacher involved in admitting students had a tale to tell about telephone calls from parents anxious to have their child attend the LXLS. "The parents call night and day, you wouldn't believe it! Some parents have even come in crying, saying how all sorts of things have happened in the family. Sometimes I just don't know what to tell them. I want to be polite and sympathetic but fair, too. I've even had to refuse gifts from people. My husband counts them. He says there's been a dozen."

Parents wanted to have their children attend the LXLS for two reasons:

"First, it is a kind of honor. Only the best are accepted. By coming here students already have a foot in the Institute's door. So parents don't have to spend nights worrying about their children's futures. A fairly good one is already secured. In addition, since this is a boarding school, parental responsibility for looking after the child is minimized. Parents give the child to the school, can save up energy and time for the weekend, and it is really not that much more expensive.[2] The children have to eat at home, too. The children's lives are looked after carefully, and they are not running out on the street."

When the approximately 600 applicants had finally been selected, they were given written examinations in English, Chinese, and mathematics. The English-language examination assessed the students' knowledge of pronouns, present, past, and present continuous verb tenses, measure words, and prepositions. Students were required to correct the order of jumbled sentences, transform statements into questions, distinguish count from noncount nouns, read a short passage and answer questions in English, complete a dialogue between two speakers, and answer a number of multiple-choice questions. Much to the dismay of English teachers, this test proved too easy for most pupils in 1982, and only Chinese and mathematics examination results were used to rank them.

Finally, the 300 students with the highest scores were given oral tests and

2 Tuition at the LXLS was six *yuan* (then, about three U.S. dollars). Students paid an additional sixteen *yuan* each month for room and board.

one more physical examination. Of these, 120 students were finally accepted. Eighty were assigned to two English-language homeroom groups, and the remaining 40 formed a single homeroom group of students who would study German and French.

School and Family
in Accord

The LXLS collective gained considerable support from the remarkable continuity its recruitment process assured between the values and aims of the school and those of its students' parents. Parent-teacher conferences, held twice each semester, were considered an essential conduit through which to consolidate family and school values. Although intense family involvement in the students' school careers insured high participation in these meetings, the school nevertheless sent to each family a formal letter of invitation, which allowed one parent to take a half-day off work to visit the LXLS.

Conferences began in the afternoon with a welcome address delivered by the headmaster over the public address system. Parents gathered in their children's homeroom classrooms, sitting awkwardly at the narrow desks of their daughters and sons. After the assistant headmaster had concluded his review of the term's significant events, homeroom teachers summarized the successes and failures of their students. Finally, parents talked individually with their children's homeroom and foreign-language teachers. Normally, parents discussed their children's progress with other teachers only if they were having difficulties in particular subject areas. Homeroom teachers handled these discussions by referring to detailed performance records they had been provided by each of the student's subject area teachers. Foreign-language teachers were singled out for special consultation, since language proficiency was considered the school's paramount academic goal. Between conferences parents wandered about school hallways, examined classroom blackboards and student displays, and were provided with refreshments from the cafeteria. During my first conference I noticed that fathers rarely attended meetings unless a child was having an especially difficult semester. When I asked a student why her father had never visited the school, she shrugged. "I don't know why exactly. It's not really that our fathers don't care." "Hah! You can say that again!" interrupted a classmate. "But our mothers understand these things better. They know how to talk with us. Maybe they see it as more their responsibility."

The comments of the mothers with whom I spoke were surprisingly similar. They also suggested that they took responsibility for talking with their children's teachers because it was more convenient for them to leave their work units. They uniformly denied that their children were studying as hard as they could and urged teachers to be "as strict as possible." "Make them work hard, that's the important thing," one mother told me firmly. "They must be made to understand how important their schoolwork is." During one of my meetings a mother especially apologetic about her son's poor grades shared her concern that he receive extra attention at school, "because there is really so little I can do for him at home." She was working two factory shifts and looked exhausted. Her husband was ill and could not work.

A colleague who listened to her story with me remarked afterward:

"I feel sorry for her. We must work together. When a student goes bad, it's often because there is a gap between education at home and at school. The child stands somewhere in the empty place between the two: parents who don't raise their children, teachers who don't teach strictly. Parents and teachers at our school have a very harmonious relationship. We have a common goal—to train the younger generation to be both red and expert. "You are studying for the four modernizations, not yourself," we tell them. Each term we talk about the students' behavior and progress, and what we want the parents to do at home to complement our work at school. Parents educate their children by saying they should listen to the teacher in class. Parents pay attention to us, because they respect what we are doing for their children."

The Homeroom

Collective

The winds turned sharply out of the North in November. Dense fog and rain obscured the windows of the classroom in which I was teaching. As if on cue, the 25 girls and 15 boys in the homeroom classroom had donned their layered long underwear. Spidery crabs, symbol of autumn in Shanghai, crept along the border of the long blackboard on the rear wall. The crabs were interspersed with chrysanthemums, known in China as a feisty flower that defies the cold with "hues brilliant as the scales of the Chinese unicorn." Dust pans and brooms were propped next to a small table where a bucket of water was kept filled by the student on daily cleaning duty. A Garden of 100 Grasses partially covered the room's inside wall, featuring a selection of the students' Chinese compositions. Another section of the wall was entitled *The English Garden* and displayed the pupils' best English essays.

The room's two doors were stamped with the red seals of a sanitation inspection. A large tape recorder sat on a table in a front corner of the room. A teacher's lectern opened toward the front blackboard, where teachers invariably stood on their raised platforms. The lectern contained three shelves for the students' enamel soup bowls, chopsticks, and aluminum spoons. Many utensils were covered with cotton drawstring bags to protect them from chalk dust. Four large characters, "study your Chinese promptly," were scrawled across half of the front blackboard, an admonition left by the Chinese-language teacher. The students had been awarded the school's "roving red banner" for keeping their homeroom neat and clean. It hung in the front of the room above the blackboard. At the beginning of the following month each homeroom's daily tallies for diligence and precision in broadcast exercises, and homeroom, dorm room, and cafeteria tidiness would be added up again, and the banner would rotate among the school's 16 homeroom classrooms.

The pupils, who were completing a quiz about a short story written by Mark Twain, sat with partners of the same sex at double desks, which were aligned in four columns of five rows, a pattern duplicated throughout the school. The columns formed the homeroom classroom's smallest division of students, the homeroom section, which moved every other week from right to left, "so seating in the class is always fair," explained the class monitor. "We don't change from front to back along the row, that's too confusing. Anyway, some of the naughtier boys are in front so the teachers can keep their eyes on them and make them work harder."

The students occasionally glanced up from the quiz they were completing and turned their heads to windows that were flung open to the winter chill and deafening traffic, watching the streams of vapor from their own light breathing dissipate. One student had wrapped his palms around a small plastic flask of hot water to warm his chillblained fingers. Several girls wore white and blue scrivener sleeves to protect their brightly colored padded jackets from dust and ink. Each student had a pencil box opened and placed at the top of the desk.

Homeroom classrooms such as this one were the principal social, peda-gogical, and administrative units for students at the LXLS. They were the primary setting in which academic and ideological goals and discipline were transmitted and maintained. Approximately 40 students were assigned to each homeroom classroom, and there they remained surrounded by their own compositions, schoolbooks, bulletin boards, and, most important, each other. Teachers were the ones who scurried from classroom to classroom at the sound of the buzzer; students had all of their lessons, with the exception of small group work, laboratory sciences, art, music, and physical education, in their homeroom classroom. It became their territory.

The students' homeroom groupings were further solidified by the common practice of assigning one homeroom teacher to a group of students for two or three or even four years. This system of cyclic teaching was believed to encourage close relationships and understanding between the students and their teacher, as well as lend to the homeroom group a strong sense of "unity" and security. Individual identity and membership in the homeroom were perceived not as coming into conflict but as mutually supportive. The structure of the homeroom forced every student, even the most shy or reticent, to be responsible to the group. This mandated involvement insured that students were, as one teacher put it, "productively occupied in the collective. At the core of whether this is successful is whether students have the spirit of collectivism. They must help and love one another. A group of students must be pervaded by this class spirit."

Establishing a unified sense of belonging was considered crucial to future academic success, and the efforts by teachers to assist young students create a home base within the school was reflected in the relative warmth of younger students' classrooms. The walls of junior one and junior two homerooms (seventh and eighth grades) were covered with bright paper left over from parties and large posters of heroes such as the selfless PLA soldier Lei Feng. Blackboards were more elaborately decorated than in senior classrooms. In one homeroom a "merit board" displayed the "good deeds" performed by students in the class. A horizontal graph also recorded individual student performance in a campaign to Study the Example Set by Lei Feng. Next to each student's name a red, arrow-tipped line pointed to the right side of the graph. The line grew in length as the student performed good deeds.

A colleague who taught younger pupils remarked, "In our school, we have students develop the three loves: of the party, of socialism, and most important of China. For younger students these things have to be concrete. We must enable them to see clearly what they are studying. They learn about models and national heroes so that their minds are filled with those people. Advanced homerooms are held up to the rest—we want to reap a bumper harvest. By doing this kind of thing every day students are brought together in the forming of good habits. From quantity to quality we say."

Teachers and administrators realized that in order to make the homeroom collective a meaningful social group for students, pupils must believe they were allowed to "organize themselves, run their own affairs." "The students must feel that the school is theirs," a teacher confirmed. School leaders were shrewd in giving students this sense of ownership, since many of the school's implicit lessons, how to act, how to behave, how to survive in a boarding school, were passed on from student to student.

Homeroom student officers were consequently elected by their classmates. The homeroom's chief student cadre was the monitor. In addition, there was a homeroom study officer, a physical education officer, a literary officer, a livelihood officer, a propaganda officer, and a labor officer. Each homeroom also elected four small section leaders, seven or eight representatives for each of the students' different classes, four or five dorm room leaders, a hygiene officer, and an officer responsible for "economizing," who made sure lights were turned off and water taps twisted tightly shut.

In addition, every student was a member of the student council and elected officers to council positions that corresponded to those in each homeroom. Since officers were used by adults primarily as an extension of official school culture, and since there were literally no students who did not hold some school office, the homeroom was indeed a very effective method for simultaneously providing students a sense of control and reinforcing sociability and solidarity. Group unity minimized the possibility that students might gather in groups of their own choosing, and consequently the possibility that the goals of the school might be bent by any unsupervised social purpose. Not long after I began teaching at the LXLS, a homeroom teacher explained to me that strong peer pressure to conform to the plans of the homeroom group made it nearly impossible for students to disengage from formal school values and activities:

"Some students just pay attention to studies, but not homeroom duties, and we have to talk with them. "If your brother or sister lagged behind wouldn't you be worried?" That's all it usually takes. They get the point. Their classmates are their brothers and sisters. I had a student who was very good, but she kept all her knowledge to herself, locked it away, like some precious wealth. I didn't criticize her in front of her classmates, but I did say to the whole group that knowledge belongs to society, not to ourselves. If you have knowledge, it is your duty to give it to others. Students must understand that they must help classmates less fortunate than themselves. They cannot view their talent as private property. You don't lose any of your knowledge if you share it with others. This spirit of sharing is what their friendship should be based on. Lei Feng had an expression we remind students of: "One open blossom isn't spring. Spring is here only when 10,000 flowers are open" (*yi hua kaifang bushi chun, wan hua kaifang cai shi chun*). It means if you alone are good that isn't the purpose. We need everyone, every student's talents and energies."

The Homeroom
Teacher

Although the responsibility for running the homeroom collective was placed as much as possible in the hands of students, the homeroom teacher was ultimately held accountable for its success. As a result, homeroom teachers were appointed on the basis of "proven records in teaching, firm, reliable ideological positions, even but inspiring temperaments, and organizational ability." At the LXLS the position was normally assigned to teachers of mathematics, foreign languages, and Chinese, so all students would have a special role model in at least one of these essential subjects. "The successful homeroom teacher is one who really takes to heart our policy 'respect teachers, love students' (*zun shi, ai sheng*). It is this which is at the heart of the student-teacher relationship. What makes a good student and a good teacher are very much intertwined in this respect. All teachers must think about this, but for the homeroom teacher, it is crucial. The homeroom teacher not only teaches, she also educates."

"Educating" referred to understanding and then regulating all aspects of a student's life, from home problems to matters of the heart. The latter was especially time consuming, since the LXLS condemned what was euphemistically called "special relationships" between girls and boys. Although teacher attitudes toward romantic attachments between girls and boys have changed in the past five years, students in the early 1980s were forced to keep these hidden from adult censure, and expressions of affection were delivered secretly in love notes or poems.

Because romantic relationships, forbidden by school regulation, were made visible only through discovery and criticism by a homeroom teacher, it was the homeroom teacher's job to deliver the constant message that "unhealthy attachments between students ran counter to the purposes of hard work, all-round development, and concentrated study." Consequently, students were treated as children, and junior secondary school students were unwilling to call upon classmates of the opposite sex in class, and when this inadvertently happened, they giggled and glanced nervously at one another. The teachers with whom I worked found this reaction natural and attributed what they believed to be rampant sexual promiscuity among North American children to a lack of consistency, even a fundamental hypocrisy, on the part of American adults, whose media encouraged students to act like adults while educational and religious institutions still treated them like children.

Older LXLS students commented upon the behavior of their younger classmates sympathetically. A 17-year-old pupil reflected, "They are still children ... well, maybe we all are a bit. We are not, well, open about our favorite boys, if we like one better than the others. That is supposed to be for college students, you see, and the junior students don't want their actions to be misinterpreted. But we are not like that now. We are such good friends, the members of our homeroom. We've been with one another for so long now. But most of us don't have boyfriends or girlfriends. We're just good, good friends."

The school's attempt to manage student sexuality grew more difficult when students entered their senior year. Their last semester of high school was directed by pressures to pass the college entrance examination, a single-minded goal that drew students together in anxious, late-night study. Older students were careful to arrange clandestine tête-à-têtes outside the school grounds on weekends. They were fiercely protective of each other's relationships and acted as classmates' alibis and go-betweens.

Because of the complexities that the homeroom teacher's job entailed, most of my colleagues were wary of taking on such a responsibility, even though being assigned as homeroom teacher was a tacit recognition from the school leadership that they were doing a good job. First, the position of homeroom teacher required many additional hours of keeping reports at the end of the term, meeting with parents, and grading weekly journals in which all pupils were required to deliberate upon their lives, their successes and failures, their personal problems. Second, the homeroom teacher's position occasioned envy. When one successful homeroom teacher in the English department was relieved of her duties to prepare for an assignment abroad, a colleague announced to everyone in the office, almost as a dare, "Who's going to take care of her darlings *now*?!" While all teachers were expected to act as moral exemplars, the job of the homeroom teacher could be an onerous task:

"You see, being classroom teachers we are responsible for whatever occurs in the class, everything, anything that happens in any student's life. The job goes way beyond academics. We have to create a healthy and productive collective, since it is from this group that the students receive their school identity, their images of themselves as students, as a member of our whole school. This is the group in which they learn and grow, come to relate with other human beings, change. They have to share in this process, to learn the group point of view and how that relates to their own ideas. This, you see, is what collectivism is all about. It doesn't mean that everyone is exactly the same, but that everyone is cared for equally. Collectivism demands a correct relationship between the state, the individual, and the unit. No matter how hard it is, the collective's interests must precede our personal desires. Well, I tell you, keeping track of this all for each child, to do the job seriously, not just play the game I mean, it's really exhausting. We make a distinction between teaching by example or just talking (*shen jiao yuyan jiao*). Do what I say, not what I do—that's totally meaningless. If students are going to be persuaded to do what is right, well then, they have to see that we all take what's right seriously. The purpose of the homeroom is to give the kids a sense of physical and ethical place, security in the broadest sense of the word. By the end of the day I feel as if I've crawled in and out of so many lives."

Homeroom Rivalry

One of the important outcomes of homeroom solidarity was the manner in which it contained and directed academic and social competition. In a school where individual students were continually subject to public evaluation and pressure toward ever more exacting performance in their academic, moral, and physical lives, one might logically predict, as I did at first, that extreme competition among individual pupils would erode homeroom allegiances. In fact, the opposite occurred. The structure of the homeroom, in conjunction with the way students were rewarded for achievement, minimized competition among students, who competed instead against other homeroom groups to prove their "spirit of unity."

Interhomeroom competition was most visible when a homeroom group was rewarded for exceptional unity, perhaps even receiving the municipal distinction of "model three-merit homeroom." Because the ensuing efforts by other homeroom groups to prove their own solidarity could not be directly waged inside the classroom, it shifted to the playing field and other extracurricular activities. After a surprising victory over a model class in a volleyball match, students in one of my English classes recounted breathlessly, "We couldn't believe we did it. Everyone assumes they'll do everything better than us." A colleague who taught these same students remarked:

"It's so typical of them. When they do well they are really in high spirits, but when they have a tiny setback they get depressed. No confidence. It's funny how the classes all have a different personality. The Japanese-language group, they don't like their work, they read Chinese history in Japanese and find it extremely boring. Yet, they are very capable. To me they even look at least a year older than the rest, very tall and mature. Then there's class two. Since elementary school they've always been the reserved ones, grown-up. They always do things right. Then there's class one. Like younger children, they have always been completely open with one another. They hang around with one another, look at them, hanging on each other laughing. They don't have a strong sense of themselves, but I like their openness. They don't lie, they're not coy."

Being number one placed unwelcome pressures on students to "do things right." To brush off this stigma, model groups sometimes appeared sarcastic or self-effacing about their record of "superior service and attitude." On a blustery afternoon I accompanied one such group of students on a walk to Hongkou Park to visit Lu Xun's tomb. When I asked them what they wanted to do, they shouted, "Nothing!" "Just hang around." "We never have a chance to do that." They recalled how during one Grave Sweeping Holiday they were asked to place a paper wreath at Lu Xun's grave. "We were told we had to hold our heads in silence for three minutes. Three minutes! Oh, we were *so* pious!" "Was that difficult for you?" I asked. "Not at all!" they laughed. "We're good at it."

When I told a colleague I questioned the consequences generated by homeroom rivalry, she surprised me by saying, on the contrary, there wasn't enough competition. "They're friends. They simply won't compete. Actually, if they competed more it would be better. They'd work harder." It was only then that I understood that the tendency for homeroom groups to become the unit of competition reinforced the school's ability to control students. It provided students competitive goals while keeping competition at the group rather than individual level. By restraining close friendships and small cliques of students within its legitimate confines, the homeroom directed peer pressure in what school leaders and teachers considered productive directions.

Political Activism
and Identity

"The first thing to ask about an ideology is not what is false about it, but what is true" (Apple, 1989, 36). Trained to ground their professional thinking in the Marxist presumption that social existence shapes consciousness, LXLS teachers asserted matter-of-factly that schools function to transmit to, legitimate for, and reproduce in young people a society's dominant cultural, social, and political values. Underlying their acknowledgment of the reproductive power of schooling was the assumption that knowledge is inseparable from human values and purposeful action. The colleagues with whom I worked never viewed schools as neutral purveyors of cognitive skills. Instead they accepted them as agencies with tremendous power to shape ideology, the "terrain where people acquire their views, allegiances and world outlook" (Kwong, 1979, 129). We have seen already that this did not mean that foreign-language instructors enacted this activist pedagogy in critical reflection of their own foreign-language lessons. They defined political action in terms of the CCP and trusted that these lessons for students would take place in the school's Young Pioneer and Communist Youth League organizations.

The Young Pioneers

The stated objective of the Young Pioneers, to which all Chinese students between the ages of 7 and 14 belong, is to provide "a school in which all children study Communist ideology."[3] What this meant in practice was that Young Pioneer activities were designed to help students make a certain kind of sense of their social world. The homeroom was the structural unit or "team" in which Young Pioneers learned to appropriate the vocabulary of Communist ideology to understand their own lives. Consequently, homeroom solidarity, with its obligations and privileges, became intimately connected to and often expressed with the vocabulary of communism, and students were directed toward orthodox political behavior by the subtle, continuous winning of their consent through the daily actions they performed in their homeroom classrooms.

Young Pioneer cadres, like homeroom officers, were elected by their classmates. These cadres were highly visible students, distinguished from their Young Pioneer classmates who all wore red scarves, which symbolized the corner of the Chinese national flag, by red and white badges they wore pinned to their sleeves. The chief officer, the school's brigade leader, wore a badge with three stripes, the commander and officers of each homeroom group were identified with two stripes, and squad leaders, roughly corresponding to class officers in charge of each subject area, wore badges with

---

3 A detailed description of the goals of the Young Pioneers in the early 1980s in Shanghai is available in "*Shanghaishi xiaoxiandui gongzuo dagang,*" 1983. Martin Whyte provides an overview of how youth organizations have been used to foster moral, behavioral, and political attitudes. See Whyte, 1974.

one stripe. Homeroom teachers acted as "team leaders" to "assist students assume the initiative in study, develop a respect for labor and the common laborer, appreciate the benefits of physical activity and a healthy body, love artistic, spiritual, and natural beauty, organized activities for them during the holidays" (*Beijing Review*, 7 December 1981).

Young Pioneer events at the LXLS were rich in symbolism and ritual designed to appeal to young students while they submerged them in a belief system and a hierarchy of political authority. Such activities were organized to complement the school's dedication to three-merit development, an interrelationship that homeroom team leaders characterized by using an automotive metaphor. The car's steering wheel was the ideological and moral clarity gained through membership in the Young Pioneers; the motor was a sharp intellect gained through persistent study; and the car's frame was physical ability gained through rigorous physical exercise.

Above all, the Young Pioneers, assisted by its location within the homeroom collective, was designed to help students find personal meaning in social responsibility. Political symbolism and ritual were constantly evoked to assist students in creating meaning out of their personal histories and identities, in essence to manage their images of childhood:

"Ten years ago, you were still in your mothers' arms. Now, you wear red scarves, you've become glorious young pioneers, good children of the Motherland and Chairman Mao. This certainly is a thing worthy of celebration. ... You are called the reserve forces of the building of socialism and communism ... because you are still young. However, just because you are young I hope you do not think of yourself as unimportant. You should think like this: 'Now, I am a child, but soon I will be a mature adult; today I am a reserve force for the building of socialism and communism, tomorrow I will be a member of the shock brigades in building socialism and communism, in the future I should become a pioneer in the building of socialism and communism.'

Children's Day
Ceremonies:
Entering the
"Spring of Youth"
Hu Yaobang spoke the preceding words in 1959 at a ceremony celebrating the tenth anniversary of the founding of the Beijing Young Pioneers. His address was reprinted on the first page of Shanghai's *Wenhui Daily* on 1

June 1982, in celebration of Children's Day. Hu's military allusions not-withstanding, the theme of the holiday in Shanghai was rebirth, the eternal spring of youth. Advertisements for children's products were displayed in bookstores and pharmacies. Upbeat messages featured characters well known to Chinese children, such as Shanghai artist Zhang Leping's *Sanmao,* whose Charlie Brown-like countenance had for four decades paid witness to the state of Chinese childhood.

In honor of the holiday the LXLS's Young Pioneers sponsored an assembly for all junior secondary school students. The number of students involved required that the program be held at Fudan University's Branch School auditorium, a five-minute walk from the LXLS. Red velvet drapes on the high stage in the auditorium were drawn back to reveal a large golden "6–1" attached to the backdrop. Twenty eighth-grade students marched up the aisles, holding brass horns draped with red and gold banners. Lining up at the bottom of the stage, they blew their horns, calling the crowd to order.

What flowed across the stage that afternoon was a procession of dramatic springtime metaphor. Winners of recitations, mathematics, and spelling contests were honored while choirs of children sang out the joys of a socialist childhood. A well-known Shanghai tenor entertained the audience between homeroom skits. Finally, 10 girls in swishing skirts, holding aloft green bamboo branches, swirled round and round a boy in a red track suit who symbolized the coming of age of a new generation.

A colleague seated next to me reflected that these students would soon be leaving the Young Pioneers. She mused, "This is their last year as children. They are glad to be leaving the Young Pioneers, but they are also apprehensive. This is a way to make those feelings concrete for them."

Despite great differences in how the life stages of individuals in China and North America are socially and politically construed, Chinese educators agree that adolescence, called in Chinese the spring of youth (*qingchunqi*), is a universal touchstone of the human experience (Song, 1985). The LXLS students dancing upon the stage were the pupils described in Chinese educational literature as "half-child, half-adult." They were youths at a critical juncture, experiencing the confusion of puberty, eager to experience life firsthand, but without the requisite moral sense to guide them. While teachers rejected that adolescence is a period of inevitable crisis, they also eschewed idealized versions of youth as a golden age. Instead, they viewed young teenagers as idealistic, easily moved by the sacrifices of heroes, but fickle, experiencing shifts of mood that could lead them dangerously far down the road of cynicism. Fourteen-year-old students were thought to be particularly susceptible to peer influence and the temptation to form cliques with which to shield one another from adult criticism. They needed, it was thought, a gradual orientation to the independence required by young adulthood.

Three weeks after the Children's Day celebration all Junior 2 pupils gathered in the LXLS's tiered auditorium for an elaborate birthday party. Plays were performed, songs sung, dances danced. After several inspirational speeches about their futures, the students untied their red scarves in unison. Each student was presented with a piece of frosted birthday cake and a bowl of "long life" noodles, a fitting cross-cultural expression of leaving childhood. Students in my senior classes who were left out of these celebrations looked upon them with wistful nostalgia. "I'd rather be young again, no worries," mused one. Praised as precocious children, they felt beleaguered, exhausted, and irritated as teens.

Joining the Chinese Communist Youth League

After leaving the Young Pioneers LXLS students encountered subtle—and successful—pressure to join the Chinese Communist Youth League. League members were responsible for establishing their own recruitment plan and sponsoring and then electing new members. The general pattern of recruiting league members was begun long before students left the Young Pioneers. In their first year at the LXLS students were introduced to what League membership entailed in small groups for the study of the Youth League Constitution. By the time the students had "taken off their scarves" each homeroom had established a Youth League core. Students who wished to join the League were required to gain the support of two sponsors, who were responsible for introducing the candidate to other League members. The applicant was required to write a statement of purpose, a short description of family background and interests, and his or her motives for applying for membership. These materials, in addition to any pertinent information included in the sponsors' written reports, were discussed at a meeting of League members convened to select new members. Applicants attended the meetings, and final votes were taken by a show of hands.

While this process sounds painstaking and cumbersome, nearly one-half of the school's tenth graders were members, as a round gold and red League insignia pinned to their outer jackets indicated. Unlike the Young Pioneers, the Youth League is not a "mass organization" for all youths. Rather, it is intended for young people between the ages of 14 and 25 who are "advanced" in attitude and understanding of labor and Communist politics, philosophy, and ideology.

The Youth League organizational structure did not correspond to home-room divisions and was identified much more closely with the school's CCP branch. In fact, the Youth League was explicitly designed to act as a training ground for the CCP, which was described as the Youth League's organizational and spiritual "lifeline." The faculty advisor of the LXLS Youth League was a CCP member and a graduate of the Beijing Foreign Language Institute. She had majored in Spanish and once acted as language instructor at the LXLS before that language specialty was discontinued. She worked closely with the League's student secretary and organization officers, and represented their position to the LXLS's party secretary.

League members at the LXLS formed, according to their advisor, "the advanced core of a new generation." Because League membership entailed increased effort in both political and academic study and school meetings, it required of students rather constant public displays of both their weaknesses and strengths. These were documented in each member's League file which, in addition, contained the student's application form, League appraisals, commendations, and disciplinary action.

Despite this emphasis upon advanced merit, 90 percent of LXLS students became Youth League members before they graduated. League membership was described by one student as "the thing to do, after all." Another remarked, "I wanted to join. It's important for college, and all of my friends belong. You're either a member or trying to become one." League membership also provided bright students inclined toward "finding out how things really work" a small voice in running the school. Being active League members gave students the right to make known their grievances. Youth League membership injected into the tightly organized lives of students a sense of empowerment, even if it was expressed within the limited confines of what school leaders called "democratic centralism."

A stated goal of both the Young Pioneers and the Youth League at the LXLS was to create opportunities for assisting students to become more independent, self-reliant individuals. "These organizations," teachers stated, "belong to the students and must run on their initiative." They repeated popular slogans: "Where there is a red scarf, there is a new morality. Take the initiative into your own hands." Such rhetoric, like the constant calls for creativity in academic pursuit, however, could not alter organizational constraints that demanded of largely passive students conformity to prescribed patterns of behavior. From my perspective, the important lesson LXLS students learned through their participation in Young Pioneer and Youth League organizations was how to conform (or at least appear to conform) to the rules of the group and the limits to individual expression, rather than its possibilities.

The Children of Mao or the Children of Deng?

In 1983 Stanley Rosen predicted that "the gap between the model citizen and the Chinese students will only be reduced by altering the characteristics of the former and accepting the desires of the latter." This process was already under way at the LXLS and would accelerate throughout the decade. Despite the intrusive mechanisms at their disposal for insuring student alignment with the reified knowledge of the school, controlling adolescence through explicit political socialization became problematic in the eyes of most teachers at the LXLS. Teachers had to compete with a growing influx of foreign cultural values and a diversifying economy to capture their students' attentions. At the same time, how to provide knowledgeable students with "real answers" to life problems filled the pages of Chinese education journals. As schooling and psychological development became a legitimate area for social science inquiry, numerous articles were written about the attitudes and aspirations of adolescents. By the end of the 1980s my colleagues turned away from politics and toward research in the fields of human development and psychology to accommodate the concerns and desires of their students.

How teachers have viewed the development of this literature in relationship to their own role as moral exemplar reflects just how much adolescence is a socially constructed concept. The LXLS's youngest teachers, who had experienced the Cultural Revolution as children or youths, were often sympathetic to the concerns of their students, who were, they claimed, the children of Deng as well as the children of Mao (Chan, 1985, 225). Sometimes younger members of the teaching staff even expressed envy of their students' precocious abilities "to see through the system." In contrast, their veteran colleagues, brought up or educated in the 1950s, were perplexed or even angered by their students' refusal to bow to collective will. These veteran teachers, themselves likened in educational publications to flowers at the tree line, hardy, capable of withstanding adversity, saw their naughty charges as greenhouse plants and "pearls in the palm," polished, pampered, demanding (Cang and Cheng, 1988).

The LXLS attempted to balance its students' sense of entitlement, and the persistent celebration of excellence that unintentionally reinforced it, with annual and state-mandated requirements that all students participate in manual labor. "In China," explained a colleague supportive of this technique,

"labor constitutes a very important part of education.... Labor has a special connotation, because China is backward, and the Chinese people have suffered terribly. We Chinese have a particular feeling for labor—you might say hard work is a special tradition here.... Students are encouraged to labor—the party and the government don't want them to go back on history. Too, education has to be a combination of theory and practice. All our students are basically good at books, so we have to work on the other. Some people think it's just show. But that's missing the point. The students don't do that much work, but it's a symbol for them. Of course, the students perform the routine chores of everyday living, but that's not the same. Their week of labor is to show them what many people in China must do all their lives. They have to respect manual work, regardless of the fact that they probably will never do it."

"Combining education with productive labor" had changed greatly over time at the LXLS. The oldest LXLS students had experienced going to the countryside when they were primary school pupils during the Cultural Revolution. They remembered their two-week trips to a nearby commune fondly and indulged in scatological jokes (in English, since they sounded less offensive that way), practicing vocabulary they had learned on the farm.

By the early 1980s productive labor had been streamlined. Students worked for one or two weeks each year in a makeshift printing room collating materials that would later be published by the college with which the LXLS was affiliated. "Freed from class a whole week," students viewed the task gratefully. They did not come to respect the job itself but reported gaining a heightened awareness of the tedious labor others must tolerate a lifetime. One student remarked that he had learned "how it feels to be on an assembly line." What teachers and administrators "really care about," he continued, "is everyday labor. You know, whether we help out at home, keep our rooms and the cafeteria clean, and wash our clothes."

Ironically, the students' most persuasive lessons regarding status and the social meaning of work were delivered implicitly from the very structure of the LXLS and reinforced, rather than diminished, their sense of privilege. Students were constantly reminded that individual achievement was meaningful only when grounded in allegiance and responsibility to the homeroom, the school, the nation, and the CCP. Students were urged to think "outward" for their answers, to find meaning and solace in the sociological, rather than the psychological. Yet teachers justified what appeared to the outsider as elitist educational procedures in precisely those terms. "That this student will go to a key university is not only good for her, but will eventually benefit *everybody*," the Chinese term for which, incidentally, is "big family."

Like all educational work units, the LXLS had a strict division of labor and status. Those engaged in manual labor, such as school custodians, ground workers, and cafeteria personnel were obviously at the bottom. These distinctions were pointed out to students by well-meaning teachers who saw them as providing powerful incentives for students to study hard. After all, they maintained, meritocracy was now pragmatically defined: "from each according to his ability, to each according to his work." Since class background had been declared inoperative, achievement was judged across all backgrounds "rationally" or "scientifically." My colleagues believed, in a way reminiscent of their Confucian ancestors, that their pupils were destined to lead and deserved their privileged environment. I believed that though students were cautioned their ambitions must not lie solely with the advantages collegiate education could confer, their presence in a school whose prestige was based on its tertiary connection encouraged them to do exactly that.

Students at the LXLS also received daily messages about the social position accorded to foreigners residing in China. I provided the discomfited object of one such lesson delivered to students on a schoolwide outing to Jiaxing, the site of the First National Congress of the CCP. The students were initially excited by this adventure, because few had opportunities to travel outside Shanghai. They had all heard of the wooden boat at South Lake where Communist representatives had fled after their original location in Shanghai's French Concession was discovered. In addition to having offered sanctuary to hunted revolutionaries, the lake had been celebrated for generations in idyllic poetry and paintings. Unfortunately, like many scenic spots in China whose beauty has had centuries in which to be overdrawn, South Lake disappointed the students. No trailing mists obscured the sprawling development surrounding the lake, the train trip was crowded and slow, and the quality of snacks found wanting. The students were especially annoyed that their foreign instructors were met by a special escort from a nearby commune. "We saw *you* being whisked around," they later snapped at me when I asked them whether they'd had a good time. "*We* had to walk everywhere! *We* never have any choices."

The "Two *Jiao*"
of Entitlement

Of course, LXLS adults would have disagreed with the students' assessment. In fact, most shared the perception that their pupils suffered from an arrogance of privilege and relatively unrestrained choices, and supported the school's campaign against "the two *jiao*" of pride and indulgence. Pupils at the LXLS heard so often that they were special that they were in danger of becoming, in the words of a concerned colleague, "too good for their own good. The students are proud and blindly optimistic. We must solve how to make proud students more humble." Teachers were advised not only to "beat the drum" (encourage and reward outstanding student performance) but also to "use the hammer" (remind students that they also had weaknesses).

The campaign against the two *jiao* did not engage students through field trips or spirited service. It was carried out with no fanfare by all teachers in all classes on a daily basis. The first *jiao* of pride was perceived at school as a problem manifested most strongly by female students. Teachers believed that because girls were "more mature than boys," and because "they were more willing to listen to the teacher and study," they became "overconfident," "haughty," and "too self-assured. We have found that especially among girls there is vanity. If being arrogant and conceited is the enemy of study, we've discovered that vanity is a hindrance to progress. They correct mistakes but do so in a hasty manner, writing over previous work, and in so doing fail to record their past mistakes. This is no way to learn from mistakes. They simply don't pay attention to small errors. They feel they're too good for that."

The second *jiao* referred to being spoiled. This characteristic was most often, although not exclusively, attributed to male students. While girls were expected to help with chores at home, and were willing to participate in group work at school, boys were generally freed from domestic duties at home and disdained routine homeroom responsibilities. Teachers sometimes tolerated or even condoned this behavior on the part of their male students, with familiar-sounding resignation: "Well, you know, boys will be boys!" Yet, at the same time they blamed their male students' penchant for childish behavior on parental attitudes, "one of the unfortunate consequences of China's single-child policy."

By 1982 the impact of China's one-child policy on schools was gaining national attention. Thirty-two books on the topic were published that year alone, and the topic was frequently addressed in the media. Administrators at the LXLS were beginning to monitor their students' attitudes and behaviors from that perspective. Children from one-child families had the reputation for being stronger and smarter, certainly characteristics rewarded at the LXLS, but they were also perceived as the pampered centers of family attention, the "suns about which other members of the family revolve as planets." They were considered egotistical, headstrong, and uncooperative. Teachers characterized these students by saying, "When they want to eat they just opened their mouths; when they want to get dressed they just raise their arms."

Senior students were accused more often for their pride than their spoiled behavior. They made light of students who went to less prestigious schools and were complacent about their foreign-language studies, which they perceived (rightly) as "far above the level of other secondary school students." Their contact with foreigners on a regular basis gave them an air of cosmopolitan smugness, and their frequent jaunts to the school's affiliated college made them feel assured of their opportunities for a good college education. This adolescent affected nonchalance exasperated teachers, of whom students expected a great deal and complained if those expectations were not met: "No, that's too much work! You're not serious!" Or "The other class learned that word for the test and we didn't! If we don't learn the word, of course we get the question wrong!" Or "This book is so boring! There had to be a better choice!"

Such pupils recognized that the education they were receiving was providing them with an influential mode of discourse that was associated with a life-style of privilege. This shared symbolic universe, coupled with the LXLS's collective ethos of high achievement and its teachers' pedagogical belief that success came from hard work, reinforced their belief that they, in fact, deserved privilege. "Why shouldn't we feel good about being here?" declared a student. "We've worked hard, accomplished a lot. One has to be realistic. It would be a lie not to recognize our strengths." Pragmatic to the end, they were indeed as much the children of Deng as the children of Mao.

Chapter 7
The Three-Merit Ideal

Shanghai schools are back in session. Nearly 1,300,000 students have happily packed their book bags and returned to school. For the coming semester, schools have adopted positive measures to foster ideological and political education. In placing emphasis on training in Communist morality and thinking, Western Secondary School is helping its students acquire the attitude of loving the Motherland, loving the unit, and loving labor. Shanghai Normal University's attached primary school, among other area schools, is organizing Socialist Ethics Month "love your Motherland, love your school" and "learn from Lei Feng" activities. Number Two Secondary School is promoting an effort called "further the five stresses and the four points of beauty and be worthy of the name teacher," and helping educators become models for their pupils. Many schools have encouraged teachers to cherish their students, especially those who lag

behind their peers (*WHRB*, 15
February 1982, 1).

Lunar new year celebrations were over. Students longed for mornings when they "got to stay in bed until 10:00 A.M., watch television, and eat, eat, eat." They whined that they were bored, that there was nothing to do. Eyeing me sullenly, they griped about being forced to do homework during the holidays, rather than being allowed to "goof around," "hang out."

Unlike many vocabulary items introduced in English class, these phrases, which I had once included in a preposition exercise, students used immediately, never forgot, and animated with what may be a universal adolescent body shrug. This particular morning I could not get the lights to come on in the classroom. A student nicknamed Egg was stretched across two benches. Leaning on one elbow he shook his head. "No electricity." A girl stared quizzically at Oil, a classmate who was doubled up beneath his desk. "What are you *doing*?" she cried and ducked her head under to see. The two began to laugh in muffled sounds, then crawled out red-faced and hiccoughing.

A tall girl was drawing a huge, pink Chinese character, *PIAO*, across one side of the blackboard. "I don't get it," I commented. She sputtered, "It's, it's Gourd!" Gourd protested from her desk. "Because," Oil explained, "Gourd used to sit with Lu who had to leave school because of poor grades. Gourd's last name is Hu, so together they make *hulu* [gourd]. Since a *piao* is a ladle cut from half a gourd—"

The tall girl interrupted, gasping between laughter, "And Gourd is only a *Hu* minus the *Lu*, she is half a gourd. Ta dah! A *piao*!"

Delighted laughter mingled with a metallic clanging that drifted in the classroom window. The gatekeeper, ever resourceful on days when industry's demands for electricity took priority over those of education, stood in the courtyard and beat a gong to mark the end of midmorning break. Two boys rushed into the classroom and glanced in my direction. "No eye exercises so we're *not* late!" The taped recording to which students performed ritualized eye exercises was simply set aside on days without electricity.

As the gatekeeper's operatic banging died away, the students were sitting at their desks, pencil boxes and books at hand, waiting. I had said as yet not one word. I made a mental note, not for the first time, how effortlessly these young people shifted into the role of compliant student. In less than 30 seconds, each student bent to the lesson plan's first activity, a 10-minute writing exercise. They were to select one vocabulary item they had learned during the past week, generate a list of 20 words that came to mind from that word, then write a brief narrative incorporating as many words from their list as possible. Gourd's paragraph has stayed with me ever since:

"I have never found out who put the little cross (X) on the wall. But for years, it had been there. Twenty. I'd made twenty mistakes on my math test paper. My mother's angry face. I could hear her frightening voice: 'If you keep on doing so badly, I'll drive you out of the house!' I was scared. Walking down the street alone in the dark, begging for food here and there, sleeping in a dirty corner, and...I suddenly woke up from the nightmare. Flops! Pops! The balloon in one of the boy's hands burst. He began crying loudly. Words of comfort never help. My grandmother stayed with me until midnight. 'Child, don't cry. You'll feel O.K. soon.' No, I doubt it. My friends don't get scolded if they get poor marks. Why must I? Life is so unfair. 'Eat the small apple. Leave the big one for your brother.' Just because he is a boy, everyone loves him. Boys and girls are equal, aren't they? Madame Curie is female. She reaches what many males can't reach. That shows it precisely. Oh, if only I were Madame Curie! Twenty crosses, nineteen, eighteen... three, two, one, zero! No, no mistakes at all. My mother's warmest smile I have ever seen. A tight hug. A kiss. The cross is still there. I wonder if it will ever be wiped off.

Tenth-Grade English, Section 1: "The Best and the Brightest"

Gourd was one of 10 girls and 8 boys in Section 1 of the LXLS's Senior 1 (tenth-grade) English homeroom. Although she was unquestionably the LXLS's most accomplished linguist, her talents remained controversial. Teachers placed bets on her potential as if they were entering an office football pool.

A commonly held conviction among Chinese foreign-language instructors is that one of the most reliable indicators of foreign-language ability is facility with one's native language. One of Gourd's faculty admirers believed, "Particularly to translate a foreign language into Chinese you need three parts foreign language, seven parts Chinese (*sanfen waiwen, qifen zhongwen*). And it's more than that. It's a feel for communicating. She will do well, because she's really very good at communicating her feelings and thoughts in Chinese."

"We'll see," interjected a skeptical colleague, who was a proponent of an equally widespread belief that all-round student achievement and potential was best predicted by proven analytical and mathematical ability. Gourd was a mediocre science and mathematics student. "I don't know whether she has the stuff to make it or not," the teacher concluded.

Gourd and her classmates were 16 years old in 1982. They had entered the LXLS as primary school students in 1975 and were openly referred to as "the last pupils to carry the mark of the Cultural Revolution." Infants at the beginning of those tumultuous 10 years, they had participated in primary school campaigns criticizing Lin Biao and Confucius. They would, on occasion, shout songs "from those days," a pastime they found hilarious in my presence. "It's so ironic after all that," they grinned at me, "having 'an imperialist' for a teacher."

Because their recruitment to the LXLS had been contingent upon faultless family background rather than rigorous examination, the students' academic abilities were suspect. Frequently, they were held up to younger schoolmates and found wanting. "They lack something," a colleague worried, "perhaps a firm academic foundation." The school's younger pupils, who had been admitted to the LXLS primarily because of their outstanding scholastic records, were considered quicker, more academically prepared.

Despite this perceived limitation, Section 1 students were considered "the best and the brightest" English students of the class of 1984. Each pupil's academic, personal, and physical characteristics had been examined with the detailed appraisal common to evaluation of "three-merit" students in China. Nearly every Section 1 pupil had gained (or been given) a reputation for excelling in some area—student cadre, outstanding artist, musician, journalist, runner, mathematician, prankster. Teachers had worked assiduously to judge and then rank these abilities. Once this task was accomplished, students could be "assisted in overcoming their weaknesses and further developing their strengths." Occasional doubts about the negative consequences of labeling students remained secondary to the educator's responsibility to mold and counsel students.

Long before I set foot in Section 1's classroom I was informed by my colleagues that two of the class of 1984's most popular boys were Section 1 students. Their popularity stemmed in part from their identification as "future scientists," in the early 1980s still a noble appellation among students in China's elite urban secondary schools. Both were active Youth League members. One of the students was an exceptionally tall, nearsighted boy who was a favorite of teachers and school leaders. In spite of the glasses he had acquired after entering the LXLS, he radiated three-merit confidence. He assumed a role of leadership but remained self-effacing. Teachers described him by commenting that despite his "ordinary worker background," he was one of the school's most promising students, not only in foreign languages, but also in physics, mathematics, and "unity" with his peers.

Section 1 also included two of the class of 1984's most well-liked girls. A tall, athletic pupil enjoyed the most relaxed relationship with her male classmates. She was a Youth League member with consistently meritorious academic performance in all classes. The second girl was described by her classmates as "easygoing, always willing to lend a hand, not a cadre, just an ordinary student." She, too, excelled in foreign languages, mathematics, and science.

Reflecting the politicized era in which they were born, several Section 1 students were named for their nation, *Hua,* China. Most of them, however, embodied their parents' gendered expectations and dreams. In daughters parents longed to see grace and beauty, and calling upon a female student in class evoked the lightness of a lute's song, the swift agility of a swallow, the supple green of springtime. In contrast, when addressing male students, teachers heralded the cries of earthquakes and the crash of tides, the military and glorious, the inventive and strong.

Just one student in Section 1 was an only child, four had two siblings, and the remainder one brother or sister. Five students had at least one grandparent living with their parents at home. Only four of the eighteen students were considered from working-class backgrounds. Six of the pupils' fathers were high-level cadres, in area shipyards, metallurgical and paper plants. Four were workers, numbering two drivers, a lineman in an electric fan plant, and a quality control officer in a brick factory. Three were educators, including an administrator of a district Children's Palace, a teacher of secondary school politics, a secondary school administrator. Two were engineers, in naval and mechanical design, and two were in foreign-language work, one a clerk for the International Travel Service, one a German-language specialist. One was a medical researcher. Two fathers were abroad for study and research in 1981, in West Germany and the United States.

All of the students' mothers worked outside of the home, at jobs they had been assigned by the state. A number were highly educated women, including a chemist already retired from a materials factory. Three were members of the medical profession, a factory medical doctor, a nurse, and a cadre in charge of a medical college's foreign student office. Two were teachers, of secondary school geography and of fire prevention at a research institute. One was a technician who designed electrical fixtures, another a telephone operator. Two were factory secretaries. Eight were line workers in plants producing radios, thermometers, clothing, and machine parts.

Section 1 pupils generally exuded the academic and social optimism that their teachers and parents incessantly worked to instill. They had learned so well and had been rewarded so often for evidencing the characteristics demanded of the good student that they had, in part, become that ideal. Did they like school? "Of course we like school. We can be together with our friends." "It's boring at home. The teaching is good." "We'll get into college from this school. We're lucky to be here."

Less often students were moody, sulking at their desks in silent acquiescence. The perennial "Who am I?" questions of growing up concerned them mightily, especially when they felt misunderstood or infantalized by parents and teachers. Some went through periods of what they described as "fatalism" or "depression," scribbling dark comments in the margins of their exercise books: "My young life is not, repeat *not,* worth living!" Did they like school? "Are you kidding?! I can't stand this prison." "The food is lousy. We can't watch TV." "All we do is study. Study our brains out."

These contradictory feelings of resentment at and belief in the public and ordered discipline of school routine were captured by a Section 1 pupil in an essay entitled "My Ideal School." In it she reflected back to her teachers the central dilemma of Chinese pedagogy: how to nurture student initiative and independence while guiding both toward the perfection of basic skills. The student began her essay with the sly assertion "As I haven't seen an ideal school, I am forced to imagine one." She continued:

"The student's life is rich and happy. They can do anything they like with their spare time. The food at school is fine. Students don't have to eat the same things, but can buy anything they like. Students can spend their money freely to buy nice things to eat or use at the school shop. The teachers never prevent them from doing any of these things. Every student can choose to learn one other skill besides the subjects they ought to learn. In study, teachers are very strict with students, and make them learn as hard and as well as they can. Teachers are excellent, skillful, and make students interested. Discipline isn't too strict in class, for if so students will be too quiet. An ideal school makes students feel much more interested and happy to stay at school than at home, but won't put on pressure to confine students to school."

The pressures of confinement kept students locked into much more than campus grounds. They resented having no control over their use of leisure time and no choice in academic endeavors. Yet they willingly granted teachers the right and duty to be strict disciplinarians, having been long convinced that expert knowledge was crucial to their future lives. Section 1 pupils devoted considerable energy working with their teachers to embody school values. While I remained skeptical, even irritated, at the stylized essays I received from pupils who recounted their efforts to attain three-merit status, I came to understand how well such portraits reflected the students' contradictory relationship with authority.

Three-Merit Students

"How to Be an Ideal Student

Every student should do his best to be an ideal student. And an ideal student first of all must study hard. He must listen carefully in class and use his brain all the time. He must do his homework well and hand it in on time. Then it'll stand to reason that he can get good marks.

An ideal student not only must study well, but keep good discipline as well. He must always be strict with himself. He must take active part in every activity including having meetings. He must always be ready to help others.

On the other hand, an ideal student should also keep fit. He should have good health. I think this is important for every student. One could do nothing without good health.

Let's work harder together. I'm sure we'll make good in the future after our hard work."

Asked to describe a good student, Section 1 pupils responded like their teachers with quick and predictable renditions of three-merit development. They associated good ideological and moral character (*sixiang pinde hao*) with loyalty to the group (usually "the socialist Motherland" or "the people"), respect for teachers, unity with classmates, and compliance with student regulations. They equated good health (*shenti hao*) with participation in vigorous exercise and recreational activities, proper hygiene, and good grades in physical education class. Being good at study (*xuexi hao*) signified having a clear understanding of the purpose of mental labor, a firm grasp of the basic skills and knowledge of each major subject area, and excellent grades. Significantly, student descriptions like the one provided above almost always diverged from Mao Zedong's original three-merit formula, which we follow below, by inverting its order of goodness. Students were quite correct in assuming that academic achievement, not moral development, was the LXLS's prime directive.

The First Merit of Moral Development

One of the most noteworthy characteristics of the LXLS's attempt to insure the moral and ideological health of its students was the breathtaking speed with which political campaigns launched from the nation's center were incorporated into local rhetoric and practice. As rapidly as huge banners were unfurled down the sides of the city's tallest department stores, meetings were convened to summarize the major goals of the country's newest campaign and bring them to bear on the lives of students and teachers. The coordinated efforts of thousands of organizations, federations, and unions that made such superbly orchestrated public outpourings possible revealed the comprehensive scope of China's formal political apparatus and infrastructure for dissemination of state policy.

The most visible campaign mounted at the LXLS during my stay began in March 1982 in conjunction with CCP efforts to strengthen China's "spiritual civilization." The campaign proved a remarkable example of how national policies became intertwined with ongoing school conventions, creating for students and educators alike exceptional opportunities for sharpening their dialectical wits. Section 1 pupils and their teachers became finely balanced weather vanes as they were mobilized by pageantry and dramatic slogans. Their political acumen taught me that conformity has an ironic twin in China, the flexibility and adaptability to be able to cover oneself smartly when ideological winds shift.

National Civic Virtues Month

The issue at stake was a familiar one that cut close to the bone at the LXLS. National Civic Virtues Month was to promote a code of socialist ethics that could "resist and overcome the corrosive influence of exploiting class ideologies and other ideologies running counter to the socialist system, such as capitalist ideology, surviving feudal ideology, anarchism, ultra-individualism and bureaucratism, and oppose and crack down on unlawful or criminal activities undermining our socialist economy and socialist cause" (*China Daily*, 16 December 1981, 5).

Students began participating in related activities during their three-week winter holiday. Shanghai municipality organized a community service drive called "new practice week" in which one million students engaged in sweeping city streets and sidewalks, and promoting public health. Students at the LXLS chose to become involved in traffic safety, an issue they felt strongly about since many traveled hours through hazardous traffic to return to school after weekends at home.

Pink and green "five stresses and four points of beauty" (*wujiang simei*) posters appeared on school walls at the beginning of the new semester to encourage students and teachers to uphold high levels of decorum, manners, hygiene, discipline, and morals, and to cultivate a noble heart and mind, polite language, proper manners, and a wholesome environment. As in all comprehensive movements, these words meant different things to different people. For some of my colleagues they symbolized CCP concerns that efforts to insure the Chinese population's moral rectitude must complement China's developing material economy. While the material base of China was the preeminent measure of success for a socialist civilization, ethics could exert a powerful influence on the overall health of the nation, as well as the rate at which material improvement would occur.

English teachers tended to articulate such concerns in pedagogical terms:

"The five stresses or graces are education's method, while the four beauties can be thought of as education's purpose. We teachers must worry about the five stresses, how we approach students. Are we good models for them? The four points of beauty in mind or soul, in language, in behavior, in the environment, are what we hope they as human beings will someday embody. That is, our job is to cultivate students who have high ideals, morality, intelligence, and strength. Civilized behavior can't be separated from intellectual training. It's really the same thing. We have to get students to think about what is really beautiful in life, what is not, what it means to treat others with respect, what their attitudes about the health of the country should be. This means not just how they look or talk, but what's in their hearts, their actions towards others, the purposes of their lives."

National Civic Virtues Month was formally launched on the last day of February. Chinese Communist party leaders took to the streets of Beijing to sweep away what became known as "the three *d*'s." Asked by their homeroom teacher to watch television that Sunday evening, students heard Premier

Zhao Ziyang dedicate March to the elimination of dirtiness in the environment, disorder in public places, and discourtesy among salespersons, attendants, bus and trolley conductors, doctors, and police officers. March already commemorated Mao Zedong's first "Learn from Lei Feng." campaign. Two decades of schoolchildren had been encouraged to follow the example of the selfless army hero who was crushed by a truck at the age of 22. Now, public service was being extended to include the creation of a clean and ordered social environment befitting a modernized China.

On Monday, 1 March, the door to the Section 1 English classroom was locked. I was surprised to note that a couplet brushed in black ink on deep red paper had been pasted on each side of the door. "Be civilized," it advised. "Strive to be in the vanguard, establish a new atmosphere, and achieve three merit development." A horizontal scroll over the top of the door exhorted, "Study Lei Feng." My first thought was that the demonstration class I had conducted the previous Friday was either being honored or rejected out of hand.

"Oh, Teacher!" A breathless student ran up to me in the hallway. "We've had to change classrooms for the month so class two can make this their exhibition room. *You* remember!" Despite the flags all around me I had no idea that this exchange was to take place. After lunch the pupil gave me a tour of "the Lei Feng room." Its walls were hung with certificates and prizes class two members had received in dictionary contests, foreign-language recitations, and mathematics competitions. An especially talented student had drawn a stirring portrait of Lei Feng on the board. An electricity experiment was set up in a corner of the room, and a guest book lay opened next to a bound school history, completed by a student who had submitted it as a "history investigation." My student guide viewed her schoolmates' accomplishments with studied detachment. "Class two, you know, is an advanced class for the whole municipality. They have answered the party's call to take part in this month's activities. They have formed some youth service groups, and they have made this exhibition room to show the good deeds they've done."

She paused for a moment, frowned, then broke away from her formal lecture. "Actually, I must tell you none of my homeroom likes to come here. We're always sort of held up and compared with class two." She added quickly, as if regretting her criticism, "Although we also respect class two's work, of course."

The following afternoon I walked around campus examining the art teacher's oil paintings that had been hung on corridor walls. During the students' lunch break they had set up tape recorders that blasted Chinese Muzak through the school's corridors. Red banners flanked a sign that read "Youth Service Team." Beneath the banners two girls ran a bank so popular it would later become a permanent student enterprise. Several boys had set up a barber shop and were shearing their homeroom teacher.

Section 1 students spent little time waxing philosophical about what they dubbed "just one more campaign." "Well, let's see," said a student considering the significance of her participation. "We must all do our bit for the country, to be clean and polite and help others." "And learn from Lei Feng," added another student. "Yes," giggled the first. "And learn from Lei Feng."

As March progressed National Civic Virtues Month took several turns in Shanghai. On the first Thursday morning of the campaign two and a half million Shanghai residents, including government officials and military personnel, joined student efforts to clean Shanghai's streets, parks, and bus stations. Flags along major thoroughfares marked makeshift sanitation stations. Media accounts proclaimed that National Civic Virtues Month was to be more than an abstraction. It was to be the concrete product of one billion peoples' daily acts. The following Sunday two million youths, from over ten thousand service teams, took to the streets as part of an "at your service to lend a warm hand" activity organized by the city's Youth Leagues. League members who worked in electronic factories repaired television sets and radios. Young artists handed out calligraphy. Apprentice tailors carted sewing machines to city curbs.

Most LXLS teachers and students believed Shanghai's spirit of public service was a short-lived phenomenon. "Come April," they remarked, "people will return to their old ways." Socialist ethics would be difficult to, in the words of the media, "regularize, systematize, and habitualize." Nevertheless, Section 1 pupils excised private doubts from their more formal commentaries. "On TV our Premier Zhao called upon us to learn from Comrade Lei Feng and try to be a polite person. This Monday morning as soon as we arrived at school we discussed how to do this all during the month. First, we thought maybe we can do some sewing for the youngest pupils. Then we thought we could go to the street and help people. Finally, our class teacher suggested we clean the school's toilets. Yesterday we divided into three groups, and armed with brooms and mops we began. We smiled sweetly from the bottom of our hearts as we did this good deed for others."

What reservations they did express were cautiously noted. "There is a saying: 'well begun is half done.' If we begin this month's work well, we're sure to have a beautiful school. My class teacher asked us to answer the party's call by cleaning the toilets each week during March. We were not very happy about it, but we have to do it. I think it's of little use, but I'll do my best."

Even the few students who openly complained that they were "sick of hearing about Lei Feng" were enthusiastic about activities that gave them legitimate reasons to "get out of the school for a while," to feel "as if they were participating in something real for a change." One student remarked, "Because we're here at the boarding school we really can't get out and see what's going on. Sometimes I get the feeling I'm missing out on something."

On Thursday, 1 April, the flags that flanked the LXLS's entrance disappeared. Lei Feng posters remained in classrooms, but the exhibition room was dismantled, and Section 1 pupils returned to their familiar room. When I walked into the classroom our first morning back, students joked that since it was April Fool's Day, they had decided to honor the occasion by forgetting about civic virtues. I shared this reaction with my colleagues, and they admitted feeling less than sanguine about the efficacy of the school's month-long activities:

"Young people in senior secondary schools are especially confused. There's been so many political movements, and who knows what the future will hold. Anything could happen. We don't know, you see. That's the root of the problem. I have a friend who is a politics teacher and over the last three years everything, literally everything, has changed! So the kids have to be parrots. Well, these students have got to have more to convince them than that. We can't just say, 'Believe this!' These kids are smart. It's what we want them to be, right? We must give them real answers, not just empty talk."

The Second Merit of
Physical Development

On a Sunday evening in October 1981, China's national soccer team defeated Kuwait in a 3–0 match. The victory was celebrated with uncontrolled exuberance in Shanghai. Fans wrote poems in honor of their team. College students burned their quilts in bonfires. When China's team defeated Saudi Arabia in a much-publicized match one month later, Shanghai's evening catharsis was even more electrifying. Thousands of supporters swarmed the sidewalks. Celebrants hung out of bus windows screaming, "Long Live China!" "We're number one!" College students took to the streets in discordant processions of drums and horns and cymbals. Section 1 students were jubilant. "Do you know what we did last night? We got to watch the game on the school's televisions. And we got to stay up late. We piled our desks on top of each other, three on top of each other. The boys climbed up there. We're never that crazy! And we got our bowls and spoons from the room and beat on them like mad, screaming and yelling. We were so happy!"

A month later the students entered their classroom in agitated conversation. I assumed they were discussing results on a difficult chemistry test I knew they had just received. Earlier in the week they had complained that the test was "excruciating." "It was just death. That's what it was!" I was wrong. In fact, they were delighted that the Chinese women's national volleyball team had the previous evening been victorious in a match with the United States. "You didn't know that?!" they cried in disbelief and disappointment when I was found to be sincerely ignorant of the competition. "You're just pretending!" The women's volleyball team went on to defeat Japan in the Third World Cup Women's Volleyball Tournament, making the captain of the Chinese team, Sun Jinfang, a national heroine. Her picture dominated the students' homeroom classroom.

Strong Children, Strong Nation

The students' avid devotion to national athletics invigorated the more mundane physical activities in which they were required to participate daily. Each morning LXLS pupils lined up, as did students throughout China, for broadcast exercises. When the "Number six broadcast exercise for adults" boomed over the outdoor loudspeakers, students, led by a physical education instructor, stretched and extended their ways through a five-part routine designed to exercise the body's major muscle groups.

Constant reminders about physical fitness appeared to students from every corner of the school. Even the back covers of their exercise books were printed with "the four diligences" of trimmed nails and clean hands, clothes, hair, and teeth, as well as "the four don'ts:" don't drink unboiled water, don't spit, don't eat tainted food, don't pollute. These themes were repeated by school nurses who taped to the clinic door a notice reminding students "To become a three-merit student you must protect your health and vigorously take part in physical training." At the beginning and end of each semester the school's medical staff of three doctors, two nurses, and one pharmacist examined every student, measuring height, weight, and checking the students' eyes and ears. Although the clinic staff did not administer inoculations, they did insure that all students were regularly examined for encephalitis, hepatitis, and tuberculosis.

Field Day

Classes were canceled one day each semester when the LXLS paid formal tribute to the importance of physical fitness. Section 1 students were selected as flag bearers for an opening ceremony in 1982 and donned the school's limited number of red tracksuits to lead the entire student body out onto the parade ground.

Teachers charged with evaluating each homeroom's martial performance lined up at the base of the school's sports platform. A huge banner raised over the platform swung in the wind, proclaiming the opening of field day. A scratchy march boomed over the school's loudspeakers. Four boys, all Youth League members, proceeded onto the field, holding the Chinese national flag by its corners. Two of the boys were Section 1 pupils, and neither wore the glasses that both owned and certainly needed. Later they admitted that they felt "silly" wearing glasses, that "it would be ridiculous, you know, there with our thick glasses and leading in the students for field day."

The boys were followed by the rest of their homeroom classmates, who carried aloft red flags. Students squared off in practiced military formation in the front right corner of the playing field. They were followed by Junior 1, Junior 2, Junior 3, and finally all senior classes. Each homeroom group was identified by a class placard that whipped wildly in the brisk wind.

The students stood at attention as the assistant headmaster read a brief address into a microphone set on the platform. He reminded them that "not only is moral and intellectual work important, but so is athletic activity." He encouraged them to "take physical activity as a significant—even essential" part of their training, stressing "the vital importance of meeting the party's call to become all-round students."

He also chided the students for reading without proper lighting. They were to protect their eyesight. They did not take care of themselves. In one class, he warned, only two out of twenty-six students had decent eyesight. They must realize that without their health their future contributions to China were in jeopardy.

The headmaster ended his opening remarks on an upbeat note, wishing the students "great success" and stepped away from the microphone, making way for a tall girl. A colleague turned and whispered, "See her? She's a very likely choice for this kind of thing. She's really very bright. Even the boys can't beat her in math and science." The girl stepped to the microphone and barked, "Let the field day activities begin!" She turned to her left, everyone taking her lead, and the four flag bearers raised the flag while China's national anthem played over the loudspeaker. When the flag raising ceremony was completed, each class of students ran off the field in unison.

The English staff was, as always, responsible for directing shot put competitions. Two section-one girls, both in tracksuits, wandered by to watch the proceedings. One smiled wryly, pulling the red, baggy shirt away from her slender frame. "This is the first time in my life I've worn such an outfit." Her friend smiled. "She thinks it looks awful on her." The two students, who were inseparable friends with birthdays only a few days apart, began discussing whether either would do well in competitions, basing their conclusion upon their biorhythms, which they had read about in a magazine. "We don't really know if it's significant or not, but we think it's interesting. During tests do you know all three of my lines combined at a low point? I did quite well in English, as you know, and in Chinese, but in math and science, my god, I averaged a 69!"

Pointing to her classmate she exclaimed, "But that one got a 95 in math! That was the highest in the class, better than all the boys."

Watching two English teachers supervise shot put activities, one of the girls turned to me and asked, "Do you know what we used to throw in this game when we were in primary school?" The girl paused for effect. "Hand grenades!" she cried. "And do you know what the targets were?" Another pause. "American imperialists!" Her friend continued, "This is what the English teachers always judge. It's a tradition. See the French teachers at high jump?" "Yes." "And see there, at long jump?" "The Japanese teachers." "Right! You see, the school's found out that language teachers just can't handle stopwatches. So they're given something easy to measure." It was only after I recounted this conversation to a colleague that I realized the student had been serious. The teacher laughed. "Foreign-language specialists have a reputation for being awful at space and numbers, you see. All we have to do here is use the tape measure."

Midmorning snacks were specially prepared and carried out onto the playing field in steaming aluminum trays. When students were not engaged in competitions, they milled about, considerably more relaxed with their various teachers than when in the classroom. "Do you know what?" a student asked. "See that science student?" I looked, remarking that I didn't know her. "Of course you don't!" the student replied impatiently. "You don't have her in class. But she has contact lenses. They cost 40 *yuan*."

The Virtue of
Clear Vision

The pursuit of accurate vision is one of the most unique and fascinatingly metaphorical aspects of physical training in Chinese schools. Keen eyesight is symbolic of the all-round development and well-being of children. Visual acuity serves as a measure for educational concern, indicating the availability or deficiency of resources to insure appropriate levels of lighting and nutrition. Municipal and provincial educational bodies distribute awards to communities for their "nearsighted free" homerooms and schools. While faulty vision portends education limited by poverty or narrowed to excessive and effete scholarship, good eyesight spanning childhood is indicative of education on track and explains why primary and secondary schools throughout China require their pupils to engage daily in a national routine of eye exercises.

As mentioned earlier, the virtue of clear vision was of such paramount concern at the LXLS that nearsightedness precluded admission. Although becoming nearsighted during one's LXLS career was allowed, it was not desirable. Pupils engaged in eye exercises thrice daily and were given eye examinations by the clinic staff as often as once each month. The back covers of their exercise books outlined "the two do's" of protecting keen eyesight. When reading, the books advised, sit up straight, hold your book about one foot from your eyes, and after reading continuously for one hour, rest or look into the distance. Likewise, students were warned to avoid "the two don'ts" of reading in poor light or while lying in bed, walking, or riding in a moving vehicle.

Not surprisingly, nearsightedness took on rather fantastic proportions for Section 1 students, signifying everything from "a bookworm mentality" to blatant disregard of physical fitness. They deplored their "failing eyesight" with a touching mixture of self-mockery and despair, and associated glasses with weakness, frailty, even decadence, characteristics from which specially selected children must remain disassociated.

The three-merit student foiled by nearsightedness was a common theme in the students' weekly compositions. One descriptive essay entitled "The Bicycle for Nearsighted Students" was accompanied with an elaborate illustration of a "bicycle built for two, modeled after Shanghai's Forever brand," complete with two sets of brakes, handlebars, hooks for book bags, bells, flags, and "two, flip-up bar attachments, adapted for quick and easy removal of your eyeglasses." Two classmates handed the assignment in as a joint project and demonstrated the bike in operation, hunching over a class bench and peering squinty-eyed through their real glasses, which both wore unfailingly.

Many of their classmates were self-conscious about wearing glasses, and not every student who needed them owned a pair. When a note on the board was important enough to write down, students passed their glasses around the room, from one to another. Eyesight also provided a source of competition, and homeroom classrooms posted each member's "eyesight history" and monthly rate of progress or decline.

The Third Merit of
Intellectual Development

"My winter vacation was simply busy and boring. I didn't have much fun for I was always worrying about my homework. My homework was accumulating all the time, and even the last day of vacation was spent on homework, even though I had been doing my sums all the time. I complained about the teachers, especially my science teachers. They had said so sincerely that they hoped we would have a good time. However, they asked us to do a lot of homework. We had to do seventy math problems, fifty physics problems, and forty chemistry problems. And what is more, the problems were very difficult. I have to call them 'cruel creatures' as they never take pity on their dear students."

The student who handed to me, quite unsolicited, this description of her so-called vacation expressed a common sentiment among her classmates that school represented an interminable cycle of homework and examinations. Chinese schools, in sharp contrast to their North American counterparts, are roundly disparaged for their excessive academic demands, to the point that bulging book bags, the symbol in China for overworked schoolchildren, are literally weighed by some communities to guard against unreasonable homework.

Homework and
Examinations
The Shanghai Bureau of Education stipulated that no more than three hours of homework could be assigned secondary students daily, and to insure compliance with this guideline homeroom teachers were asked to keep weekly records of how much time their students required to complete their assignments. Despite such precautions, my colleagues found it difficult not to equate quality education with large quantities of homework, and their assignments

for Section 1 students often exceeded municipal guidelines. Educational excellence was ultimately identified with outstanding examination results, and preparation to guarantee that outcome became a kind of "academic steroid."

Faced with hours of such intense study, students bickered constantly about its efficacy. "I just get fed up with it all. Why not just take the tests and be done with it? Just sitting and going over what we've already done. It's stupid! It's boring!" "It's useful and you know it. Or I suppose you think you'll get everything right!" "Don't be ridiculous. The point is, who cares?"
"You do!" "That's right! You do!"

Their final if reluctant recognition of the importance of academic achievement led students to view their teachers as allies more often than adversaries. We have already seen that teachers' reactions to the pressures of examinations mirrored their pupils' sentiments. One colleague particularly frustrated by the frantic cramming of her charges watched in dismay as they stalked through hallway and courtyard memorizing lessons. "Look at them. Just look at them!" she cried. "I can't stand that endless circling. We can't always hold their hands. They must strike out on their own. What are we doing?"

Teachers and students became exhausted as spring wore on. Harried teachers grumbled that the blossoms of the scholar tree were turning yellow, alluding to the classical period in spring when imperial examination candidates immersed themselves in mind-numbing study. May came and went, and drenching, wearisome rains encouraged thick undergrowth in the school courtyard, then roses, which grew prolific and heavy, lolling extravagantly in the heat. Their fragrance mixed with exhaust and hot roof tar and the whine of saws from the school workshop to make teachers groggy and vexatious. Students fearful of examinations rotated round the athletic track in wobbly, short circuits, dizzy with their lessons.

Finally, examination schedules were chalked in large block characters on a small blackboard that was propped up in the school's entrance:

Wednesday	Thursday	Friday	Saturday
chemistry	English orals	mathematics	English writtens
Chinese	physics	politics	geography

Students saw little connection among these subjects. Some even denied the possibility that a coherent pattern could emerge from their stress-filled lessons. Yet they tolerated sleepless nights of tedious review because they realized the system of assessment upon which their futures hung was designed to produce more failures than successes. In 1980, when fewer than 5 percent of Chinese youths attended post-secondary institutions, 95 (81 percent) of the LXLS's 107 graduates were accepted into colleges and universities. Six of these students ranked in the top 10 of students on Shanghai municipality's foreign-language examination takers, including first place. The following year 128 of 149 (84 percent) graduates enrolled in colleges and universities, again with 6 LXLS students ranking in the top 10 on foreign-language examinations. Of Shanghai's 58 students who scored over 400 points on the entire entrance examination, 33 were LXLS pupils. A student who received the highest score on the municipality's science examination was from the LXLS's experimental science homeroom. All but one of the 34 students in this homeroom were accepted by a tertiary school for college training.

The anxieties such expectations elicited in Section 1 students surfaced visibly during the oral component of their English examinations. After listening twice to an unfamiliar story that had been prerecorded on tape, students came individually to a staff office and were asked to answer five questions. They then reached into a bowl and fished out one of eight passages from their language text that after a few moments of thought they were asked to "retell." Performing valiantly as her fingers folded and unfolded the little slip of paper upon which her question was typed, one student asked in a trembling voice, "How much is this worth? How much is this worth?" The retelling exercise was worth 40 points. She blinked back tears of disappointment when she received a 33.

Just as there were no back row seats for students in their classrooms, there was no escape from the persistent demands of study. "Do you want to know what I figured out?" asked a second student after his examination. "I like this place. Yes, I do. But I'll tell you what our lives are all about! Eat, sleep, and study like hell! It's true, too. But it binds us together. Do you see? In fact, we will probably be friends for life, going through all this."

College-Bound Scientists and Humanists

Academic courses in China are broadly divided into the sciences and the humanities. Concentrated emphasis on improving the quality of secondary schooling during the early 1980s led to the streaming of senior secondary school pupils into science and humanities tracks. The LXLS began tracking its Senior 2 and Senior 3 students in 1980 for reasons that went beyond national concerns about educational quality. As foreign-language training in regular secondary schools gradually improved after the Cultural Revolution, LXLS leaders hoped to maintain the school's academic edge by offering first-rate training in all subject areas. According to the headmistress, "most students who enter pay more attention to humanities and foreign languages than math and physics and chemistry. To counteract this we repeatedly carry out propaganda work to encourage students to be the best in both foreign languages and other subjects."

Section 1 pupils were required to choose their specialization by the end of the second semester of their Senior 1 (tenth grade) year. Although the decision was ostensibly their own, parents and teachers figured heavily in their determinations. A girl who initially hoped to enter the science section was persuaded by her parents, and then on their behalf by an English teacher, not to. Her parents worried that her life would be "harder" in the sciences and that even if she did "stand the competition" she might, upon graduation from college, be assigned a job far away from their home in Shanghai.

The girl was disappointed and confided to me that she felt "sciences and engineering were more important than languages." Many of her classmates, even those who wanted to enter the humanities classroom, agreed. In fact, the teacher who counseled her against entering the science homeroom seemed to regret her decision. "If students further their studies in the language class it's safer and they can enter the institute. But some pupils still should enter the science course. They're promising students and they can contribute. They can't only think of their own security. Also they are strong in that area. In our daily life, we are assigned jobs. When we do labor, someone will always need to sweep the floor. In this tiny act, still some students complain. You can't just go through life saying this is what I'll do because I'm fond of it."

A number of teachers feared the implications of the tendency to celebrate science in the school curriculum, even though this inclination was frequently criticized by the media as "emphasizing science to the neglect of humanities":

"People have become especially interested in our school because of last year's science class [the Class of 1981]. Thirty-three of these students entered the university and one student entered a technical school. The top student placed number one in the municipality on the science test. People were shocked that this could happen at a language school, and now many parents think, well, this would not be a bad place to send their children. But you see, we are not here just to teach science. Yes, it is wonderful that students be all-round youth, outstanding in all subjects. But language is our specialty, we shouldn't get carried away and lose sight of that."

Actually, such a possibility was slight. Specializing in humanities at the LXLS virtually assured students entrance into a tertiary institution. As the headmistress indicated, the humanities homeroom offered most students the path of least resistance to college. Each year since tracking began three-quarters to two-thirds of LXLS students have chosen to specialize in the humanities. By the end of the 1981–82 school year 25 members (26 percent) of the class of 1984 had decided to enter the science homeroom class. Twenty were male students (43 percent of the male students in the class of 1984). Five were female students (just under 12 percent of the female students in the class of 1984). "Perhaps," mused a Section 1 girl, "science would be more useful, more practical, although I like English, you see. People say that armed with math, physics, and chemistry, you can go anywhere in the world and not be afraid (*xuehao shu li hua, zou bian tianxia dou bupa*). Well, that's too bad for me, then."

College-Bound Boys and Girls

Exploring the connections between Chinese schooling and gender, defined here as the ways in which a particular culture (and its parents, teachers, and students) gives meaning to biological difference, is complicated because, on the one hand, so much seems so familiar. Schooling in China is central, as it is worldwide, to the social construction of concepts such as intelligence and success. Women in China have struggled valiantly and often in vain to embrace these concepts as competing cultural and economic demands, specifically those involving interpersonal and family obligations, are separated from and discounted in dominant images of excellence.

However, North American conceptions of gender, which often make natural and essential sexual opposition and which are based upon notions regarding an autonomous human subject, differ from those in China. Consequently, Chinese educators rarely adopt what many of their North American counterparts identify as "feminist" perspectives on schooling, nor do they necessarily agree with or find especially relevant the assumption that gender is a political, socially constructed category of analysis. To most of my colleagues, gender (*xingbie*) connoted biological difference, and their examinations of its relationship to academic achievement, when they considered the connection at all, commonly began with the assumption that "the special needs of girls" distinguished female education from an established (male) norm. One female colleague gave me this essay:

"I Like My Pupils

Though I have only sixteen pupils (since I have only three years of teaching experience), I like them very much. I like the ten girls in my class because they are well behaved and hard-working; I like the six boys in my class because they are clever, though they are sometimes naughty.

Why should I write about the girls first, instead of the boys? That is because I like the girls in my class better than the boys. The girls are always well behaved. Never once have they made me angry or cross. In class they never talk with each other or fidget. They always greet me politely whenever they meet me. They are not only well-behaved but also hard-working. That is the main reason I like them. They always listen to me attentively and answer my questions actively in class, and do their homework carefully after class. Thus, even though they are not as clever as the boys in my class, they usually get better marks than the boys.

I like the boys in class, too, because they are clever. They learn things quickly. If I teach them some new materials, they will learn them quickly. But they are naughty. However, I don't mind this naughtiness, for they are boys after all. Perhaps I wouldn't like them if it weren't for their naughtiness."

The essay and Gourd's appeal earlier in this chapter speak powerfully, although in startling different voices, about one of the least explicitly discussed and most implicitly acknowledged determinants of the aspirations of Section 1 pupils. Gender (my word) influenced whether students would specialize in the humanities or the sciences, what colleges they would eventually attend, and, as the above essay indicates, how they were perceived and treated by their teachers.

During my stay at the LXLS I concluded, although my colleagues did not necessarily agree with me, that dominant definitions of educational excellence were often, if unintentionally, based upon assumptions about human development and learning that derogated the capabilities and hopes of female students. Beginning in 1982 the school implemented a new enrollment procedure stipulating that boys and girls were to be admitted at a ratio of approximately two to one. The school's policy was partially a response to a standard practice in key secondary schools of requiring female candidates to have higher examination scores than their male classmates. The policy was commonly justified in developmental terms. "In the past, when students entered at the elementary level, they were very young and immature. The boys were especially childlike, and they didn't study well. When it came time to take the matriculation exam for junior middle school, they didn't do well enough and had to be dismissed to other schools. Therefore, there is now an imbalance between girls and boys."

In fact, in all homerooms, with the exception of one Junior 2 section, which had 11 boys and 19 girls, the number of male and female students was nearly identical. In addition, at the end of 1982, the two junior secondary school graduates asked to leave the LXLS were not boys, but girls. One of these students had good marks in English and was one of the school's most talented female athletes. The handful of boys who did poorly in foreign languages all remained at the school.

A girl asked to leave the school explained in tears that she was forced to do so because her mathematics and science grades were poor. She had the reputation of being a sophisticated girl, and her father was a high-level army officer. The school had arranged for her to enter a specialized senior high school that trained nurses and midwifes. A colleague reacted to my skepticism that this particular student should be asked to leave the school by responding, "Oh, but look at the school she'll be going to. Nurses are in high demand. Her future will be secure."

After one semester the girl said she had become reconciled to her new school. She had shed her boarding school persona and permed her hair, an act that received public censure at the LXLS. As my colleague predicted, she also felt she had gained self-confidence and a position of leadership at her new school, something she never experienced at the LXLS. "Because my English is better," she told me, "well, you see, I have been given a firmer foundation in languages than the other girls, and I am now a leader in this school. I wasn't before, as you know."

The prevalent perception held by Chinese teachers that girls struggle to achieve excellence in higher levels of schooling was examined in a 1981 *Wenhui Daily* report that raised the question of whether high school girls were indeed intellectually weaker, with less academic potential, than their male classmates (*WHRB*, 26 November 1981). Was it true that "girls are at the top of the class in primary school, are at the middle of the class in middle school, and at the bottom of the class in college" (*xiaoxue jian, zhongxue ping, daxue cha*)?

Many of my colleagues expressed this view, implicitly through their actions, or explicitly when prompted to discuss their views on the relative academic abilities of girls and boys. "Usually the girls' elementary school scores are better, and if we treated them the same way the percentage of boys and girls would be thrown off. We all know girls develop more quickly than boys through junior middle school, but once in high school they drop off and the boys excel. Perhaps this is biological, but we have to consider it. We penalize the boys by not taking this into account."

Others agreed with the basic premise but explained it much more elaborately. They contended that sociable and nurturing "by nature," a girl excelled in the primary school grades when verbal skills honed through early social interaction were rewarded. A female student's descriptive capabilities enhanced her aptitude for memorizing basic information, in short, to be a good student. However, being a good student became equated with getting good grades (to please the teacher) rather than understanding (to please themselves). Thus, a girl's capacity to think logically and abstractly remained underdeveloped, and, finally, her propensity to care for others rather than herself came to an inescapable fruition with the onset of puberty. Bound by her physiology to a holistic, "unfocused" view of the world, a girl turned away from the intellectual and leadership arena of males ("*Yanjiu nu zhong jiaoyu de tedian*," 1983; Ge, 1982; Zeng, 1981).

A teacher who had attended an all-female secondary school in her youth once told me that

"in junior secondary school some girls are good. Boys, if they can't concentrate, can't control themselves, they just while away the time, and then they lag behind. But when they reach senior secondary school if they know that they want to study they can *easily* catch up with the rest, and sometimes will, upon graduation, become the top students. But if a girl student didn't study well during the junior years, she couldn't be good in the senior years, I don't know why. I think that if she is not so good at studying, I mean to *me* I found that if her logical thinking is not so good, then she just can't catch up. I haven't thought about this problem deeply. Well, when the boys are in junior secondary school, maybe they haven't developed, their minds aren't developed, and they didn't get good marks, so they didn't pass the examination. It's because they didn't study hard enough. A girl usually concentrates. She listens carefully, and she works very hard, but she still lags behind. For these students it's not a question of work. I don't know how to answer your question, but even though she works very, very hard, even then she can't achieve."

When I asked her whether she treated boys and girls differently in her teaching work, she responded, "yes, I am usually more strict with the boys in the junior years; as for the girls, I think they can control themselves. If they can't get good marks, or can't meet my requirements, sometimes I found perhaps this is something here [pointing to her head]. I will just excuse them. But for the boys I will usually be very strict. I will ask them to concentrate in class."

Even the college entrance examination was designed to take into account the common belief that boys would eventually out-perform girls. Despite the fact that teachers believed that this happened in senior secondary schools, girls managed to score well enough on the entrance examination to warrant policies stipulating that those wishing to attend the best key post-secondary institutions had to have higher scores than male applicants, "to avoid skewing the proportions of male and female college students." Not surprisingly, 39 percent of all general secondary school students and 24.5 percent of all college students were female in 1981.

Chinese educators attempted to refute the pervasive logic of this system not by denying its validity, which could have been done by a quick perusal of entrance examination results, but rather by encouraging female pupils, "What boys can do girls can do" (*nan tongxue keyi zuodao de, nu tongxue ye keyi zuodao*). Ironically, they reinforced the message that areas of achievement are biologically fixed with their pedagogical strategy of "nurturing female strengths and overcoming female weaknesses" (*yang qi suo chang, bu qi suo duan*).

Small wonder, I thought, that girls between the ages of 13 and 16 were considered especially susceptible to "regressive tendencies" (*huigui xinli*), described in Chinese handbooks as a peculiar affliction of girls who do not want to grow up. Slogans did little to remove the obstacles females faced in continued study or starting a career. Initial efforts (that would quickly escalate throughout the decade) at maximizing productive efficiency in the home, at school, and in the workplace, coupled with long-standing perceptions of female talent and a backlash against the Cultural Revolution model of the strong, "unfeminine" woman, reinforced discriminatory practices in educational entrance requirements and hiring (*Xinmin Wanbao*, 13 August 1989; Honig and Hershatter, 1988). Such discrimination was perpetuated by school administrators who tolerated disproportionate enrollment of males in senior secondary schools and colleges, because work units considered women (because of their family obligations) "inefficient" workers.

This is not to suggest that my colleagues did not recognize that female students were responding with concern as schooling became increasingly stratified by material resources and educational purpose. However, because they lacked a vocabulary for examining how newly initiated economic and educational reforms based on efficient management of resources might influence the aspirations of girls and boys differently, they rarely challenged views of adolescent development that demanded female students achieve higher scores before being accepted into secondary and tertiary institutions. Thus, the same female teachers who sparred with male colleagues, proclaiming, "We hold up a good deal more than half the sky around here!" simply advised their female students to "follow the example of Madame Curie."

Recall the Children's Day skit described in chapter 6 that featured a male student presented to the audience as the symbol of Chinese youth. Female students danced at the perimeter of the stage, forming a pastel frame for their classmate's glorious coming of age. As I was watching this performance, I turned to a colleague and whispered that this arrangement was hardly a coincidence. She was startled at my interpretation and wondered why I always looked for hidden meanings, chased after my own stories. Later, when I asked her to help me sort out her views on boys and girls, she told me:

"I don't know what it is. Women worry more. About other people. About the world. Maybe that's why the girls seem more narrow. They memorize well and they're responsible, there's no doubt about that. But the boys are always thinking, doing things with their hands. They don't care as much about marks, like they don't need those symbols so much. They focus on themselves, right what they're doing now. I wonder sometimes if boys and girls are really different. It seems to me boys are more creative, but I have no strong proof or evidence. I also think it has something to do with history. In traditional China, girls were deprived of the right to go to school. But now there are more and more career women. For instance, our Madame. She's very capable. Boys may have different aptitudes, but we can't say who is more clever. Some girls have an inferiority complex. They are content with low work, they don't consider themselves very promising. Whenever girls think they are handicapped intellectually, I give them the example of Madame Curie—you must not be downcast. I say jokingly, 'Look at our school—more female leaders, and our teaching group leader is female, too.'

The Foreign Idiom
and the Three
Merit Ideal

"Language is the place where actual and possible forms of social organization and their likely social and political consequences are defined and contested.

Yet it is also the place where our sense of ourselves, our subjectivity, is constructed" (Pierce, 1989, 401).

At the beginning of the 1990s Shanghai confronts head on what James Clifford has called a global "predicament of culture," where "identities no longer presuppose continuous cultures or traditions," where "individuals and groups improvise local performances from (re)collected pasts drawing on foreign media, symbols, and languages" (Clifford, 1988, 14). Although this process was just becoming apparent in Shanghai in the early 1980s, the recurrent *ti-yong* dilemma of Chinese modernity that foreign-language training represented, and which education at the LXLS necessarily attempted to resolve, made me wonder how much English might be operating in the lives of my students as a vehicle for presenting themselves, and, consequently, as a site for opposition to the explicit values and norms of the LXLS curriculum.

Clearly, the school's image of three-merit development was at once dependent upon, complicated by, and not wholly compatible with advanced foreign-language training. The foreign texts and foreign teachers that students encountered were neither mere objects for cultivating fluency nor representations of how people "over there" live and speak. Although teachers and leaders recognized the direct influence foreign teachers and the materials they brought with them had on their pupils, they also believed this influence could be anticipated and controlled. They were right to the extent that the LXLS's environment allowed constant monitoring of the consequences of teaching methods and student behavior.

Few limitations were placed upon the content of the Section 1 students' experimental American and English literature courses. These were introduced by foreign teachers and led to uncensured access to foreign texts and even lectures, upon student request, on European religious traditions and beliefs. One might conclude from the following program for a student-organized "English afternoon" that the LXLS had indeed achieved a workable balance between openness to foreign content and preservation of established values. Yet, this relatively open and certainly gracious stance toward innovation from without was predicated upon largely unanalyzed assumptions that students in such a privileged and protected learning environment would not stray.

Program

1. Girls' Choir	Class 1, Senior 1
2. *A Welcomed Lady Thief* (a short play)	Class 1, Junior 3
3. *The Last Leaf* (a short play)	Class 1, Senior 1

4. *Duet*	Liu Ming and Wu Wen
5. *Dustmen on Strike* (a short play)	Class 1, Junior 3
6. *Solo*	Fang Hong
7. *A Loveable Eccentric* (a short play)	Class 2, Senior 1
8. *Solo*	Wang Qian
9. *Aladdin and His Lamp* (a short play)	Class 2, Junior 3

All of the short plays on the students' program featured foreign settings. Four Section 1 pupils performed an adaptation of O. Henry's "The Last Leaf," their classmates predictably snickering at the final death scene. Another group of students dramatized an *English* passage, "A Loveable Eccentric," the principal character played by a convincingly bumbling student who had raided a relative's wardrobe for clothing from the 1940s. The music selections were also of foreign origin, including "Country Roads" sung by a John Denver fan. I had been asked to correct the script and find a costume for the larcenous character in the students' only original play, *A Welcomed Lady Thief*. The leading lady had decided to carry my shoulder bag, "So I can look the part," she informed me with a shrewd grin. I had no idea what she meant until I read the script:

A Welcomed Lady Thief

Characters

Narrator
The head of the shop assistants
Middle-aged lady
Guard

NARRATOR: This is one of the largest department stores in Japan.
(Middle-aged lady walks about store, examining clothes, etc., steals a scarf and a pair of sunglasses, puts them in a shoulder bag, leaves store. Guard and head of shop assistants watch, not trying to stop her.)
GUARD: Let me tell you the truth now. Our boss has recently found out that the woman has excellent taste in clothing. Last month she stole a coat and a pair of gloves from our shop. Strangely enough, these kinds of coats and gloves soon became the latest fashion.
ASSISTANT: No wonder the boss told you not to catch her when she comes in.

GUARD: I'm sure the boss will sign a contract with the manufacturer for more of those scarves and glasses. In this way the boss will get more profits.
ASSISTANT: Of course!
GUARD: It's really very interesting.
NARRATOR: Now, Comrades, please think about why this woman is so lucky! What have you learned about the capitalist countries from watching this play?

Thus was foreignness safely contained and student encounters with foreign languages and knowledge resolved without chaos or uncertainty. Or were they? One striking by-product of the school's decision to adopt foreign-language textbooks published abroad was that the students' language lessons rarely conveyed overt political messages. Whatever political and moral significance teachers wanted to attach to language study had to be supplemented. On occasion, the *English* series was used for this purpose. Yet students, ever alert to their teachers' attitudes, were aware that lessons from this textbook "were not really important" and prepared them with anything from bored, dutiful precision to a quick, indifferent skimming of the text passage.

A colleague seemed genuinely surprised and amused when I asked her whether any political significance should be attached to the LXLS's use of foreign-published texts. I had related to her an incident in which Section 1 students had balked at studying one of their *English* passages. The story described the life of Old Li, a commonplace but heroic socialist who "was unselfish, modest, always putting the interests of the people before his own" (see Appendix D). Old Li was apparently impossible to take seriously in English.

I wondered whether part of their difficulty in relating to the passage's moralistic tone was that they felt odd doing so with an American teacher. Foreign instructors at school had but to mention a politically loaded name—Lei Feng, for instance—to bring the house down. Yet, it seemed more likely that pupils did not wish to drag into their English classrooms political ideology they were constantly reminded about elsewhere. Had the students decided that subtly different rules operated in the foreigner's classroom?

"You're worried about our students' morality!" my colleague shrilled, clapping her hands as if she had been waiting all along for me to walk into some trap, and in finally having done so I would now understand her problems. "We teach this series because it fits the needs of our students quite well. You know that.... If you look carefully at the contents of the senior one text, I should say you will find a wide variety of passages. Some encourage students to model their lives after good people, heroes. Most are simple, interesting narratives, that's all. The Cultural Revolution is over."

The Cultural Revolution may have been over, but foreign-language proficiency did urge students to assert control in unusual ways. They used English for the creative violation of school norms, for devising simple pranks calculated to rupture school routines just enough to cause minor adult displeasure. Older students who were most fluent phrased misbehavior so cleverly or with such precocious cross-cultural intent (jokes on teachers and classmates on 1 April, for example) that their infringements of school regulations were overlooked. By offering an alternative vocabulary for mild acts of student rebellion, whose meaning could be conveniently lost in translation, English acted as a safety valve when the boarding school environment grew too oppressive.

On a Saturday morning a colleague walked into his classroom to find the letters *T.G.I.S.* scrawled a meter high across the board. He related the incident with humor and curiosity. "I saw those letters and had absolutely no idea what was going on. I asked the students, and they finally told me. You taught them that, didn't you?"

When I sheepishly admitted having done so, my colleague assured me that he was not chastising me. "It's appropriate. The students told me the background of being glad the weekend has arrived. It's not exactly how we're supposed to view things around here. Oh, let me tell you, I quite understand how they feel. It's just, well, not something I expected."

I understood, of course, that I had once again proved myself foreign, presuming that "excitement is a goal, not a worrisome by-product" of teaching (Rohlen, 1983, 167). I could not help myself. Especially during the final weeks of the semester as examinations loomed, students vented their short tempers in their second language. "I can't wait to get out of here!" they cried in English. "These reviews. Boooooring! They're driving me mad!" Their cultural code-switching turned classroom blackboards into surreal collages of adolescent taunts and fantasies, presumably less threatening inscribed in a foreign idiom. "You chicken!" "John: gifted disco dancer." "Let's party!" "T.G.I.S." was accepted by students naturally in such an atmosphere, and just as naturally their heteroglossia brought them into collision with accepted LXLS norms.

Admittedly, potential conflicts were usually precipitated by special events such as the celebration of exotic foreign holidays. A chaotic storeroom on the school's first floor provided unlikely props for numerous good-natured and confused meetings of divergent cultures. Mobilizing their vast familiarity with performance, Section 1 students transformed themselves into bizarre Halloween crowds of mad scientists, huge-headed clowns, revolutionaries, Jane Eyre. "Do you know who I am?" shouted a student, peering gleefully through glasses that perched precariously upside down on his nose. He thwacked across the gray cement floor of the classroom like a tall Chaplin. I was astonished that perhaps this was who he was trying to impersonate, until I noticed that his shoes were on the wrong feet. We all stepped back as the boy twirled, revealing that his clothing was on backward and as much as possible upside down. "I'm Mr. Backward," he screamed. His classmates took this as an indication the party had commenced and began a fervent bobbing for apples. I reacted with apprehension when in the middle of their merrymaking the foreign affairs officer stepped into the classroom with a camera. During the following week I was relieved to hear that the party had bothered no one in the least. "Why should it?" asked one of my administrative officers. "It's important that our students learn about other societies. There's nothing wrong with having a good time."

The exuberant cultural stereotyping that accompanied major European and North American holidays lent a curiously traditional note to "foreignness" at the LXLS, as that of something wondrous and not quite real. Pictures of foreign instructors with students at parties were displayed in the school's most public symbol of foreign interest, "The Friendship Room." Here items presented to the school by visiting tourists and dignitaries were carefully preserved. The unwrapped Frisbees and postcards captured a sense of disparate traditions brushing up against one other but never quite interpenetrating.

With this much contact—exposure to a cosmopolitan world of symbols—school leaders expressed favor. Yet, two students who became close friends with a 16-year-old daughter of a foreign teacher (after being explicitly asked by the school to do so) were eventually criticized for the relationship. The American girl had given the students her teen magazines, which promptly circulated through the girls' dormitory. Counseled to restrict further interaction to formalities, the two students were reluctant to maintain any friendship at all.

Foreign-language instruction at the LXLS recreated and legitimized a very important part of the knowledge and culture of China's well-educated elite, but it also subverted its apparent ideological closure. On the one hand, education was guided by the demand that students draw their own identities from socialism's most laudable models. On the other, relatively unrestricted foreign-language study presented students with "a moral system outside the political one established by the state" (Barlow and Lowe, 1987, 45). The school's success at realizing its ideal image of education depended upon providing students an identity that was inherently compelling rather than forced. And students found their sense of identity in both their public image and the ways in which they asserted themselves against it.

"Seventeen in Shanghai"

As the school year drew to a close, the LXLS came under the scrutiny of China's massive 1982 census. There had not been so many posters in the lobby since National Civic Virtues Month. As Shanghai's primary and secondary schools broke for summer vacation on 10 July 1982, district census workers counted 435 pupils living in the LXLS's dormitories. At the same time, the papers revealed that 10.5 percent of China's workforce had a high school education, and less than one percent had received a college education.

During the first Saturday of their seven-week vacation Section 1 students gathered in my room at the Jing Jiang Hotel for a party. The boys wore shorts and the girls wound their bright skirts around their bare legs as they argued about attending the school's summer camp in Nanjing. Some were delighted at the prospect of traveling up the Yangtze River. "I've rarely been outside Shanghai," said a boy. A classmate retorted, "Who cares? You know what they say about Nanjing, that it's a furnace in the summer. Well, it's too hot. I'm staying in Shanghai, because what if I got sick?" "Well, I'm going," his classmate replied. "I'm bored by vacation already." "Hah!" laughed another. "What we'll do is complain all summer about how bored we are, and then after the first day at school we'll wish we had another vacation."

"My friend here is going to stay with me for a few days instead," remarked Gourd, who pulled "Japan" onto her lap. "Great!" muttered a male classmate. "So the two of you just stay in Shanghai and do your homework!" "Oh, God!" screamed one of the girls. "Do you know we already have a ton of homework to do this summer? Especially in Chinese and math."

"Don't you gripe," complained one of the boys who had decided to enter the science homeroom. "We also have tons of physics problems to do." "Well, that's your own fault, isn't it, Mr. Scientist?!" the girls retorted. "Oh, come on!" another student intervened. "It doesn't matter. We all just let the whole lot slide until the end of the summer, anyway."

The students mused about what it would be like when they could attend college and "do whatever they wanted to do," a thought that rapidly precipitated another round of loud bantering. "All I know is that I don't want to leave Shanghai." "Oh, neither do any of us." "Speak for yourself!" "I'd like to go to Beijing University." "Oh well, good luck!" "Yes, getting in and eating *mantou* [steamed bread]!"

The students burst into laughter. They detested the bread, more commonly eaten in northern China than in Shanghai, and were rebuked when they left bits of it in angry twists on the cafeteria floor after breakfast. "Fudan's better than Beijing." "No it's not." "Better than the Institute." "Anything's better than the Institute!" "You don't know what you're talking about." "Well, I don't want to go there and become some interpreter. All this work just to become an interpreter for a bunch of stupid tourists? That's not enough."

What is so striking about this conversation is not so much what it said, but what it took for granted. Students did not discuss whether but where they would go to college. At least in this outcome, the LXLS was not so different from America's most prestigious preparatory schools. It is no coincidence that in 1984 when the LXLS established an exchange relationship with a North American school it was with Phillips Exeter Academy.

By recruiting the crème de la crème and infusing it with high expectations, the LXLS became a center for cultivating an elite group of students that looked to the future with an expansive and sometimes unrealistic sense of possibilities. Their graduation commencement, held at the end of August only after students had received the results of their college entrance examinations, celebrated not what students had accomplished in the past, but what doors those accomplishments had opened for them. For the one English-language major in the class of 1984 who was not accepted by a college, it was a poignant celebration indeed.

In her second year of college Gourd wrote an essay entitled "Seventeen in Shanghai." In her preface she observed that "the voices of China's insignificant 650 million little ones are seldom heard. Shanghai is a place where, like anywhere else in the world, good and bad, courage and cowardice mix. Only here, one seems to be more willingly coerced into abandoning one's dreams. So while they still exist in the hearts of the young, a record of them appears to be all the more precious." Gourd warned of the consequences of dreams early and effectively silenced, and recalled a lesson she learned at the LXLS "five years ago. . . . I've already forgotten the name of its author. But I do remember his words: if you tell me what the

new generation thinks, I will tell you what the future of the nation brings."
Gourd illustrated this point with the words of a fifteen-year-old student. The
girl employed "cunning innocence" "to play the fool" with her parents and
teachers. Docile on the outside, the girl kept the furious secret that "deep
inside me, I know everything." Gourd felt a keen sense of connection to the
girl's silent anger and wisely associated it with a nationwide cultural and
political legitimation crisis, one that had already begun to erode the LXLS's
collective.

Chapter 8
Conclusion

Many of the characteristics of schooling explored in the previous chapters have been identified by North American educators as the hallmark of excellent education. The LXLS's dynamic leadership, vital sense of mission, stable and committed faculty, high expectations for scholastic achievement, and sustained parental support created a school climate that nurtured outstanding academic accomplishment.

In fact, the LXLS exuded such pedagogical consistency that one is almost compelled to take its earnest public account at face value. The optimally sized boarding school embraced and enhanced with rituals of entitlement China's long school calendar. The specialized foreign-language curriculum, unabashedly elitist by design, privileged students who in return for highly valuable training complied with its uncompromising regimen. Collective planning and evaluation procedures placed strict demands upon teachers to structure and then assist students to meet common learning objectives. Pupils were publicly held accountable for their academic efforts, and they studied with persistence and concentration. Administrators were adept at mobilizing the energies and ambitions of hand-picked teachers and students and making them a unified group possession. This pervasive school ethos provided members of the LXLS community with a clear sense of identity and self-representation.

Yet, the LXLS's relentless effort to secure educational goodness bred tensions that compromised that outcome. Its prestige derived from an extraordinary material buffer and political mandate but left the school ideologically vulnerable. Teachers took pride in the LXLS's key school status but struggled for greater professional autonomy. The steady pressures applied to students to conform to adult images of the three-merit pupil made not just disruptive behavior but also individual innovation close to intolerable. Driven by an externally imposed entrance examination, students defined school—not happily—as hard work. At the same time that they resented the scholastic marathon into which they were drawn, they accommodated its demands with a single-minded fatalism that made teaching as disturbingly predictable as it was comfortingly explicit.

Throughout the 1980s these tensions heightened as definitions of excellence forged immediately after the Cultural Revolution were called into question by policies associated with China's open door. In particular, economic and educational reforms embodied a contest between popularization and diversification that mirrored efforts to balance demands for socialist equality and ideological rectitude with the needs of rapid economic development (Ross, 1991).

This contest was reinforced by two major reforms in secondary education initiated in 1985 (*Reform of China's Educational Structure*, 1985). The first reform redefined basic schooling in China by advocating the extension of compulsory education from six to nine years. While the task of making possible and desirable for all Chinese children the now constitutionally guaranteed right to a junior secondary school education remains daunting,[1] external studies of Chinese schooling express cautious optimism about the likelihood of achieving a nine-year compulsory system without massive increases in material commitment (Noah and Middleton, 1988).

The 1985 decision's second assignment for secondary schooling was its continued diversification. Insufficient vocational schooling, identified in the report as the "weakest link in China's education," was blamed for the misalignment of formal schooling with the employment options of Chinese youths. By the end of the 1980s China had come close to meeting its goal of vocationalizing one-half of its senior secondary schools (*RMRB*, 22 February 1990). The expanding employment opportunities in major metropolitan centers like Shanghai had made vocationalization efforts so successful that as many as 60 percent of senior secondary school students were enrolled in technical-vocational programs (Lamontagne, 1988).

The simultaneous effort to increase access to and stratify educational opportunity benefited the LXLS and its key school counterparts, even though debate about the social and political consequences of concentrating scarce resources in such highly selective institutions remained contentious. Key schools thrived as formulaic, centralized control of curriculum and financing was replaced by local and regional planning. Keys schools also dominated the creation and distribution of knowledge about secondary school education. Their veteran teachers were called upon to write and grade national examination test papers. As publishing researchers, these teachers set the terms of

---

1 The national average rate of entrance into China's junior secondary schools hovers just below 70 percent, placing it eightieth among 139 countries and regions of the world. Nearly 7 percent of the 38,380,000 students who do attend drop out before before completion of grade nine. In 1988 33.2 percent of China's counties lacked the resources to universalize junior secondary schooling. See *JYB*, 31 December 1988 and 16 March 1989, and State Statistical Bureau, "Education and Reform" in *Beijing Review* 31, no. 45 (7–13 November 1988): 31–32.

secondary school debate in district and municipal education bureau publications. Some schools even reestablished connections with overseas alumni associations from which they derived prestige and hard currency, and came to embody China's modernization goal of defining success in relationship to international standards.

The LXLS enjoyed the particular advantage of Shanghai's diversified economy, that afforded access to the alternative forms of financing increasingly required to fund exceptional programs. In addition, the city was experiencing something of a cultural renaissance evidenced by a "Shanghai boom" in television dramas, documentaries, and scholarly revisions of the municipality's unique role in the development of modern China. This self-conscious pride of place generated optimism even in the face of environmental degradation and a transportation and energy infrastructure stretched beyond the breaking point, and encouraged unusual, if unrealistic, plans for social rehabilitation and innovation. By the year 2000, the city's schools were to be made the best in the nation, its key schools and technical institutions reaching international standards and the entire metropolis transformed into a center for worldwide exchange.

Unfortunately, invigorated teaching and leadership in institutions such as the LXLS were accompanied by shortfalls in educational provision in less prosperous, primarily rural regions of China, where 3.8 percent of the population had attained a senior secondary school educational level, a proportion identical to the number of urban Chinese who had attained a college education. Illiteracy rates for rural youths between the ages of 12 and 19 were three times the level of their urban peers. As many as one-third of all rural pupils were undernourished, and many attended schools that failed to meet national standards for such basic facilities as chairs and safe drinking water. The collapse of dilapidated classrooms became a national symbol for schooling that lacked substance and relevancy for the majority of China's children (*JYB*, 15 September 1988, 31 December 1988, 19 January 1989, 18 March 1989).

State Education Commission officers countered widespread disillusionment with schooling by declaring that "education needs modernization and modernization needs education." Efforts to implement this slogan equated educational modernization with a school responsibility system in which increased autonomy and experimentation were overwhelmed by the quest for economic efficiency. *Modernization,* the most salient word in educational reform programs during the early 1980s, was replaced by *efficiency,* seemingly its most important measure.

The efficient school had become crucial as state educational funding failed to keep up with teacher salaries and material costs. Financing formulas designed by bureaus of education to encourage schools to initiate profit-making schemes became remarkably widespread. By the end of the decade school-run enterprises engaged three-quarters of China's primary and secondary school students.

While some educators justified this entrepreneurial wave as "a way out of Chinese education's quandary" (Li Daoping, 1990, 52), most complained that schools were corrupted by commodity consciousness (*shangping yizhi*). Dropout rates for students rose dramatically in prosperous coastal regions that offered employment opportunities to students with little formal education. "Dropout teachers" left their positions in search of more lucrative careers. Efforts to introduce "competitive mechanisms" into the classroom aggravated public perceptions of cynical teachers and students who abhorred their respective roles. The LXLS's expectation that the "principal must enter the classroom" was replaced by the image of the profit-driven administrator "grasping grades in one hand, and money in the other," selling diplomas, renting out vacant classrooms, or even, as in the case of the LXLS, leasing the rooftops of schools for billboards and microwave transmitters.

Five years after Deng Xiaoping challenged schools in China to move in the "three directions" of modernization, world, and future, secondary education had emerged as the most problematic and crisis-prone level of Chinese schooling. The significance of this crisis may not be readily apparent to North American educators who assume that defining educational excellence is a controversial task. The expectation that the quest for good schooling will inspire intense debate and even confrontation is reflected in the tendency to contextualize goodness, to applaud schools that are "different by design" (Metz, 1986). It does not surprise us to hear a colleague ask, "If public schools were authentically about a public sphere... Would not the curriculum incite?" (Fine, 1991, 199)

In 1988 Deng Xiaoping made official the perception that China's schools were in a state of crisis by admitting that neglect of education was the gravest policy error of the post-Mao era. To redress this oversight, 1989 was proclaimed the Year of Education in the People's Republic of China, and so the decade ended with a brutal reminder of the centrality of education to social change and conflict. The lesson learned was far more complex than the one that my colleagues already knew: inciting controversy within the public sphere of Chinese schooling is a dangerous proposition. In fact, the notion that a good school might just be one that "anticipates change and imperfection," and that "the former usually ushers in the disorientation and im-balance of the latter" (Lightfoot, 1983, 24–25), no longer seems to LXLS teachers a necessarily irresponsible compromise with goodness and harmony.

The Erosion of the
Unit Family and the
Moral Crisis of
Chinese Secondary
Schooling

In 1984 the LXLS's headmistress retired after two decades of service. Though the chief administrator was highly respected as an effective leader, her power was also resented, and some teachers welcomed her retirement, expressing the "need for new blood, someone less conservative." Their relief turned to dismay, however, when they discovered that the headmistress was to be replaced by the controversial "special teacher" discussed in chapter 4.

"She's a creative teacher for young students, true," a colleague admitted grudgingly. "She gets them singing and talking. She works actively. But she is not a leader, not a model for older students. Not enough presence, you see. That's it. There are others more qualified."

A second group of teachers considered the replacement justified and timely. They were viewed by disapproving colleagues as "conservatives" content with their stable teaching positions, "secure in their little worlds." The latter description was put forward by a veteran foreign-language teacher who contended her misgivings stemmed from being "interested in really good education." This reaction was criticized by an equally experienced "conser-vative" colleague, who dismissed such comments as coming from frustrated teachers "ambitious, after prestige themselves," "disgruntled by someone they think is less qualified becoming their superior."

Contention over the headmistress's successor was hardly overlooked by LXLS students and parents. Their concerns were sharpened by persistent uni-versity-level appraisals that LXLS graduates simply were not living up to their reputations. In addition, growing opportunities for highly trained foreign-language experts had drawn some of the school's most experienced teachers into prestigious positions in other units. Quite suddenly, the LXLS was per-ceived as lacking both the firm leadership and the accomplished staff it had once enjoyed. This loss of mission was especially troublesome for a school where privilege, in order to be justified, must appear to be earned.

Concern about the school's future was crystallized when a first-year LXLS pupil drowned in the college's swimming pool. At the best of times such events are institutional tragedies. Blame is directed in petty or even cruel ways, but survivors are drawn together in the process of providing meaning to a senseless accident. Far from bringing the school closer together, however, the student's death lay bare the fundamental nature and contradictions of the LXLS, confirming suspicions about the school's institutional malaise. "Why wasn't someone responsible there?" The drowning recalled to minds another student death at the LXLS, the unresolved murder described in chapter 3.

The connection of these "two black marks" against the LXLS now provide teachers with a reference point for the moment when the LXLS's strong collective ethos began to erode. The crisis faced by the LXLS is not primarily material, they say, but "something deeper, much more fundamental, linked to inexorable changes in our society." My colleagues' concern is visible in the marked contrast between their present apprehensions about education and the confidence they expressed a decade earlier. As if unable to believe that she had ever told me she was certain about her professional responsibilities, a veteran teacher mused in 1989, "Well, these things are no longer clear to me *now*." She located the source of her disquiet in the distance between the stated purposes of schooling and the daily lives of her pupils, as well as in her inability to understand, let alone direct, the current path of growing up Chinese.

Attempts to understand why schools are in trouble have led adults throughout China to criticize their children as arrogant youngsters whose lack of maturity, ethical standards, and discipline are made up for only by a self-centered world outlook that derogates diligent study and political rectitude. Some teachers still identify these characteristics as products of Cultural Revolution reforms that "egalitarianized" schools at the price of weakening their power as socializing agents and failing to educate properly an entire generation of Chinese students who have now become parents. Others attribute selfish and unruly behavior to the one-child family policy, or to the frailties of parents who are preoccupied by their own financial difficulties and divorces.

This evaluation of inescapable social disruption has been reworked by Chinese leaders who, well before 1989, identified the problems of schooling and youth with a lack of ideological guidance. For them, the course of Chinese adolescence *is* the healthy development of Chinese socialism. And the composite image of adolescence in China is not a happy one if adolescence is taken as a metaphor for the good society. A typical analysis of the younger generation, entitled "From 'I Do Not Believe' to 'I Have Nothing,' " contrasts a well-known poem written in 1976 by dissident Bei Dao to the title of a pop song fashionable a decade later. "This generation has absolutely nothing to worry about regarding food and clothing; they have the possibility of getting decent jobs and making money; and they have an enormous abundance and freedom of choice with regard to spiritual, mental, and material products—something that this nation has never had. And yet, to the amazement of their parents, they yell: 'We have nothing!' " (Liu Qing, 1990, 87–88).

In such portraits secondary school pupils are portrayed as a passive audience to the epic of the Cultural Revolution, around whom "the collapse of historical traditions, the absence of any basic awareness of a dominant guiding trend or direction" has generated "a sense of bewilderment and frustration with regard to the unknowable and uncertain future." What separates them from older generations is a different vision of self and collectivity. Their elders are wary of their "vagabond spirit," and unprepared for their judgment that morality is just a matter of taste: "I do whatever I feel is right" (Liu, 1990, 88).

Providing moral direction for this generation has involved continuous efforts by the state to insert into the secondary school curriculum ideological training that can both speak to students' desires for relevance yet mitigate the threat of "bourgeois liberalism." The most comprehensive recent program began in 1988 with the promulgation of new rules of conduct for secondary school students. Programs designed to help teachers make these rules "live in the lives of students" have included informing students with "four haves." The "four haves" movement defines socialist ethics in terms of ideals (*lixiang*), morality (*daode*), culture (*wenhua*), and discipline (*jilu*), and was launched with a reproach to teachers who had failed to cultivate these qualities in their pupils.

Since June 1989, this criticism has sharpened as leaders attempt to solve China's youth problem not by accommodation (an economic solution) but rather with ideological control (a political one) (Burns and Rosen, 1986, 53). Secondary school teachers, ironically reprimanded for treating schools as the "Land of Peach Blossoms," that is, a haven from the turmoil of a complex society, react with dismay or bitterness at being blamed for failed political socialization. Their analysis indicates that it is the CCP's failure to reform, as well as its naive or disingenuous dismissal of the power of popular culture, that estranges a supposedly "conscienceless generation" from social responsibility. Not surprisingly, programs for moral education designed by teachers proceed not from socialist politics but from theories of human development.

Significantly, this direction has been reinforced by greater provision of media, social, and judicial services designed specifically to protect and advise teen-agers caught in the upheavals of societal change.

In addition, educators have added to Mao Zedong's tripartite definition of the all-round student a fourth merit of goodness, a developed aesthetic sense, an appreciation of beauty (*mei*). A veteran teacher defined such ap-preciation as "simply the ability to choose proper entertainment when you see it." That beauty is equated with entertainment whose appropriateness lies in the eye of the beholder suggests just how much Chinese schools are accommodating to students who do whatever they feel is right.

Foreign Languages as Tools for Limited Cultural Access

Developments in foreign-language education have mirrored the quest for a coherent set of moral-political values appropriate to China's current level of economic and social development. Condemnation of foreign knowledge as a vehicle for cultural contamination temporarily subsided after 1984. The implementation of market socialism and a widened open door initiated com-plex changes in the structure and organization of knowledge in China (Hay-hoe, 1989a). Reforms in college-level foreign-language education challenged "the compartmentalization of language as an isolated discipline of study, urging it become a more vital aspect of human learning with greater social status, purpose and impact" (Cumming, 1987, 213). Research in applied linguistics and interdisciplinary specializations that combined the study of one or more foreign languages with economics, sociology, history, journal-ism, and computer science were initiated in 1985 at the college to which the LXLS is attached.

A growing perception that foreign-language proficiency increased eco-nomic and social mobility also enhanced the popularity of English-language study. Nursery school children in Beijing and Shanghai learned English in a "relaxed, communicative manner" as their parents studied "Everyday En-glish" by following the frustrations and discoveries of three Chinese teachers studying in Canada. The prime-time "living English" television show, "Fol-low Me," was China's longest-running program of the 1980s, with an au-dience of twenty million and a successful spin-off, "Follow Me to Science."

This popularity insulated LXLS teachers from many of the contradictory tensions in their eclectic approach to teaching examined in chapter 5. Articles in professional journals designed for secondary school foreign-language teachers, and contributed to by them, expressed cautious optimism about pedagogical reform. Increasing numbers of secondary school foreign-language teachers participated in in-service training programs at local colleges or in special centers established by municipal bureaus of education. Teaching methods for the encouragement of communicative language skills proliferated, some gaining national recognition. Foreign studies emerged as such a "hot" college specialization that students vied to gain entrance to departments "prefixed with the word *foreign*."

Secondary school foreign-language teachers have responded to the challenge of promoting a more "communicative" approach by reconceptualizing the three-centered approach to teaching that reigned so tenaciously at the LXLS during the early 1980s. As in their efforts to meet the social needs of adolescents, teachers have begun to "psychologize" foreign-language teaching. Although journals continue to feature articles designed to help teachers infuse their foreign-language lessons with explicit ideological content, for example, on "How Marx Learned Foreign Languages" and "Good and Bad Manners" (Chen and Gong, 1990), more commonly educators emphasize that foreign-language learning will be anchored by the establishment of emotional, rather than moral or ideological, bonds (Hu, 1989; Gu, 1989).

The gradual shift away from text and teacher-based authority in the foreign-language classroom has been incorporated into the most recent national secondary school English-language teaching outline (*Quanrizhi zhongxue yinyu jiaoxue dagang*, 1987). The outline emphasizes diversity in teaching practice to meet the varying developmental needs of students. Comprehensive ability in pronunciation, vocabulary, and grammar is called the means to— rather than the end of—language learning, whose ultimate goal is communicative ability.

The conflicting pressures on teachers to transmit (testable) linguistic knowledge and facilitate communicative ability are being addressed in Shanghai through extensive reform of the examination system. No longer justified as an admittedly narrow but essentially meritocratic sorting procedure, the college entrance examination is criticized as an overly centralized, pressure-laden, and exclusionary device that effectively "colonizes" secondary education. The State Education Commission has honored Shanghai's senior secondary school competency examinations as a "pioneering" effort to break the stultifying effects of the college entrance examination system (*JYB*, 25 October 1988; Shanghai Educational Testing Center, 1989).

Fully implemented since 1988, competency examinations in Shanghai are credited with improving educational quality and balancing attention to the teaching of both humanities and sciences. The tracking of students into science and humanities classrooms discussed in chapter 7 is now blamed for a premature narrowing of intellectual pursuits and is being discontinued in many schools. Competency examinations in nine subject areas are advocated as a more well-rounded assessment of every student's achievements.

Though competency examinations have not alleviated student perceptions of being overburdened by constant testing, most foreign-language educators agree that examination reform has provided an incentive for replacing a heavily grammar-oriented foreign-language curriculum with a "problem-oriented" approach to teaching and learning languages (Shanghai Educational Examination Center, 1988). Yet, detractors argue that the test's multiple choice format has encouraged teachers to teach for the test, rewarding an even more narrow competency than that embodied in teaching that emphasized translation. Critics also suggest that the current "fad" of emphasizing active speaking ability discriminates against older students and can be culturally biased. They contend that well-meaning foreign teachers give Chinese students the faulty impression that "it was satisfactory if students could only understand 70 percent of what they read and guessed the rest" (Qian, 1990, 39–40). The proposed solution will sound familiar to educators in North America: "We have to go back to the basics, intensive reading based on a good textbook combined with many oral and written exercises. Students must be able to understand texts completely and read them fluently" (Qian, 40).

Although LXLS teachers debate the merits of recent reforms in teaching and evaluation, they are unanimous in their indictment of the commodity consciousness which has altered the shape of foreign-language education. They blame the profit-driven English-language craze for generating "unhealthy" competition among students, parents, even foreign-language teachers. Opportunities for advanced study and job mobility, rare in 1981 to 1983, are now cause for a different sort of grievance. As secondary school educators with foreign-language expertise secure lucrative careers or opportunities to study abroad, departments are left severely under staffed. The LXLS has suffered from a nearly total depletion of its senior secondary school English-language teaching section. Teachers are in such short supply that veteran teachers are retained well past the age of retirement, and all those who remain are swamped by increased classroom demands that leave little time for the extracurricular activities and in-service training crucial for the continuation of teaching reform.

Nor has foreign-language education escaped the critique of benefiting students in key schools while derogating students in regular and rural schools (Shanghai Jingan District Wanan Secondary School, 1988). At the same time foreign-language education has been relied upon to reduce inequalities between China and other nations, it has clearly exacerbated educational stratification within China. Foreign-language proficiency varies widely from the best municipal key schools to regular academic and vocational secondary schools in rural areas, which may offer foreign-language instruction only in senior secondary school.[2] Foreign-language teaching is called a "breach in the defenses" of quality education in schools that can neither recruit primary school students with three years of foreign-language training nor meet national guidelines requiring that every student attend a language lab at least once each week. In urban Shanghai, where private short-term English language training programs proliferate—some to assist even junior secondary school pupils in their efforts to travel abroad—a large number of senior secondary school graduates fail their English-language minimum competency tests (Ying, 1988).

Finally, despite efforts to nurture creativity and independence in foreign-language classrooms (Qian, 1988), 4 June 1989 indicated to teachers how ambivalent their leaders remain about the consequences of independent thinking. Consequently, they are uneasy about uncontrolled pedagogical settings, because these seem to imply ethical or academic ambivalence. In fact, their dominant interpretation of independent thinking is still "being in control," "having a firm sense of what's right," and "performing correctly." From the outsider's perspective, students are thereby pressed toward conformity by the very manner in which they are expected to be creative. The LXLS's boarding school structure reinforces this dichotomy, for its protective environment can both censor popular culture and ingeniously, if temporarily, reconcile rival ideological claims. Predefined roles, a hegemonic political ideology, the external imposition of an entrance examination, all make individual preference potentially threatening to institutional need.

Still, Chinese educators and students view the study of English as more

2 The policy of beginning foreign-language instruction in senior secondary schools is designed for institutions located in rural or remote regions with a shortage of teachers and facilities. Students study a total of 552 sessions of English. Shanghai 1987 examination scores ranged from an average of 80.83 for pupils in municipal key schools (out of a possible score of 100) to 70.98 for pupils attending district key schools to 50.57 for pupils in regular senior secondary programs. Ninety-six percent of municipal key students, 82 percent of district key pupils, and 32 percent of non-key students received passing marks on the examination.

than simply information to be memorized, or a tool for translation, or even modernization in commodity form. Teachers at the LXLS grapple with the reality that while the world forces Chinese students to be bilingual, the converse is certainly not true. "Making foreign things serve China" in an atmosphere where exchange is such a one-way proposition entails for them a difficult balancing act. Likewise, LXLS pupils learn that their foreign-language ability is their passport to the world. They have become so notorious for streaming abroad to attend Exeter, Andover, St. Paul's, and thus preparing themselves for a spot in a prestigious North American college, that the school is colloquially referred to in Shanghai as "the prep school for studying abroad."

Leaders and Teachers of the Class of 1984

The open door and the perception of crisis that jeopardizes it has had practical ramifications in the lives of LXLS teachers. Improved living conditions facilitated by promotions and the completion of a faculty apartment complex have addressed some of the teachers' personal complaints. Forty-two teachers received the title of lecturer, and as members of the teaching staff have left the LXLS to teach in tertiary institutions, new teachers have taken their places. After the English department's "special teacher" disrupted her controversial tenure as headmistress for a permanent life in the United States, changes in administrative staff have placed the school in the hands of leaders who are apparently more open to granting limited professional autonomy to teachers and staff.

In fact, the school's current headmistress is the only secondary school principal in Shanghai to have been elected to her position by coworkers. She calls herself a communicator, a role crucial to the maintenance of the complex personal and institutional relationships upon which the LXLS's financial and political stability depends, and identifies her chief responsibility as "public relations." When a reporter for a well-known Shanghai magazine once exclaimed, "But you can't spend all your time on PR!" the headmistress retorted that she had become an official by moving up the ranks the hard way. "Everyone carries on about the need for emotional investment, but this is only one aspect of the principal's job. After all, the cleverest housewife can't cook a meal without rice."

Clearly, being an effective leader at the LXLS no longer means being a parent. At any rate, the family has dispersed. As of this writing, all of the individuals who served as the LXLS's chief administrators during the early 1980s are abroad, and the school's English teachers have taken up other positions at such alarming rates that the senior staff is virtually without experienced instructors. Teachers are no longer required to stay at their posts eight hours every day—they come to school only for class sessions and meetings. Especially in the English department, the opportunity, even necessity, for mentoring relationships between younger and older teachers as they worked hour upon hour in teaching and research groups is gone. The French and German departments face a different problem. "Veteran teachers remain," explained a colleague, "but they have no successors."

The difficulty in recruiting qualified foreign-language students into the teaching profession, as well as the inability of exceptional schools to keep their English-language teachers, is described by remaining LXLS instructors as "the crisis in foreign-language education." Although efforts to increase the status of teaching throughout China have prompted increases in salary, teachers have had to settle for primarily symbolic compensation. A token few are wined and dined on National Teacher's Day, 10 September, and assured that their "voices" will be heard. A ubiquitous modernization slogan that proclaims "in projects of vital and lasting importance education is central" (*bainian daji, jiaoyu weiben*) has even been amended to affirm the pivotal role of teachers in that process (*jiaoyu daji, jiaoshi wei ben*). Yet, to educators weary of balancing ideological rectitude with the pressures to develop a pedagogy appropriate to an era of the open door, such proclamations sound hollow.

The irony is that at the very moment teachers question the school's authority to define and influence success, they have been placed squarely in the position of mediating China's most troubling social contradictions. Teachers who decry the impact on learning of commodity consciousness are castigated for not establishing a behavioral ethics that can counteract the dark side of a commodity economy and an open door. They and their schools have become both scapegoat and solution for China's cultural crisis.

Students of the Class of 1984

When Section 1 students graduated in 1984, less than one-quarter of all secondary school graduates who sat for the national college entrance examination that summer were accepted into some form of post-secondary schooling—including secondary technical schools. All but one of the 52 LXLS

English-language graduates were accepted by colleges, institutes, and comprehensive universities.

Ten of 45 of these students, six boys and four girls, studied advanced foreign languages, journalism, and social sciences in China's two most prestigious language institutes. Nine graduates (five girls and four boys) enrolled in four-year teacher training institutions, all specializing in English, with the exception of one student who entered a library science program. Seven students (three girls and four boys) majored in English departments in Beijing, Fudan, and Nanjing universities. Six students (three girls and three boys) concentrated in diplomacy, law, and international relations at two prestigious institutions in Beijing. Four students (three girls and one boy) attended Shanghai University in English and international business relations. Three girls studied accounting at the Shanghai Finance and Economics Institute. A boy at Fudan University majored in world economics, a girl at Shanghai Machinery College specialized in English for Science and Technology, and a boy at Tongji University majored in German.

Only two section one pupils, both boys, specialized in the sciences. One described his first semester with pride, as he numbered among "100 first-rate students from different provinces of China." The "drastic rivalry" among these classmates was muted by the "friendship and modesty in the atmosphere" of the college. "Almost every day," he wrote, "we receive new ideas which may be incompatible with our daily experiences." The single section one girl who chose to enter the LXLS's science homeroom enrolled in a program in English for Science and Technology. Even though most of her mathematics, physics, and computer science courses were taught in English, she complained, "my English studies in middle school helped me so much that the studies here do not seem challenging at all. The deans have granted me permission to skip some of the reading classes, so I don't waste time."

Other section one pupils fretted about the demands of college life, "staying with my schedule so everything won't dissolve into a state of chaos." "There are so many things to learn, and I am so ignorant." Some were torn between studying and socializing with classmates, which they "never really had a chance to do before." Two section one girls who wanted to study in Beijing attended Shanghai institutions instead. Of the two section one boys who were adamantly opposed to leaving Shanghai because "while the schools in Beijing might be good, the weather is terrible and the food worse," one did study English at Beijing University, an offer, apparently, he could not refuse. The other entered Shanghai's Fudan University and, in addition to section one's most talented language student, was selected to study abroad during his junior year.

By their second and third years of college, most section one students became increasingly disillusioned, some by difficult living arrangements. A male student who commuted daily to school complained that "to some extent home is merely a hotel for me. The family is such a catastrophe, with mother's endless chattering after you and father paying no attention whatsoever. Maybe this is the so-called generation gap," he mused. Others who had aspired to better schools or greater challenges looked back on their years at the LXLS with regret and wonder. "I so wanted to be a scientist then. I thought such a life was glorious. I really believed this. Now, I don't think China needs scientists. Each unit has so many. Now, I think China needs spiritual improvement. There's no motivation, no spirit of hard work . . . . In my high school I would never have imagined my life now. Useless. The best are wasting their time and lives playing poker. They have nothing to do. Research is impossible or meaningless."

Those who studied in prestigious, comprehensive universities were generally more optimistic about their futures, their course work, and their opportunities for finding challenging careers or traveling abroad. Students studying in highly regarded institutes of diplomacy or international relations also expressed little dissatisfaction with college life. Even students who entered language institutes reluctantly were fortunate in their timing. The newly achieved university status and expanded curricula of language institutes, coupled with China's English-language "craze," had made interdisciplinary foreign-language departments one of the most popular destinations for high school graduates.

Students in teacher training institutions expressed the most disenchantment with their studies and career opportunities. They believed the skills they had worked so hard to acquire were not being put to good use and were envious of classmates who were more successful on the college entrance exam. "I have been frustrated from the first day of entering the university." "Life here is not nearly as interesting as I had imagined it would be." "I hear about everybody else going abroad and I feel left out." That some of these students were able to complete their university studies in three rather than four years was little consolation.

"I had imagined that I would learn much more English in the university. But to my disappointment, it is actually quite the opposite. The problem is that I learned more English in middle school than my classmates. In order to fit teaching to the average level of the class, we all have had to start from the very beginning. My only option is to study by myself. And what's more, my spoken English is worse now than when I was in secondary school. I just don't know what to do. I'm quite desperate."

This student's desperation was echoed by a number of her female classmates who expressed dissatisfaction with restricted college training and occupational mobility. One described her college life as filled with meaningless hours of playing Monopoly with friends, "disconnected from everything." Although she consoled herself, hoping that "there is always the blind belief that some day all will be fine again," she eventually left China.

One can only speculate, from these various experiences, about the relationship in China among family background, gender, and access to elite secondary and post-secondary training—although this question certainly deserves attention by educators who are evaluating the success of China's trickle down approach to universalizing quality education. Section one pupils from working-class backgrounds have studied at the world's most prestigious universities; children whose highly educated parents were influential cadres have not. It must be remembered that even though the class of 1984 was the last group of students to enter the LXLS without taking a written examination, they were still very carefully selected pupils. All were chosen for their prospective success as "advanced foreign-language specialists," and it is not surprising that nearly all have succeeded.

Only four 1984 female graduates (compared to ten boys) studied in schools outside Shanghai, an expected pattern, since urban Chinese girls are typically encouraged to stay close to their parents. In addition, the only pupil who did not enter college is female. Nevertheless, these young women have experienced nearly as much diversity and opportunity in training as their male counterparts. Twelve (compared to fifteen of their male classmates) studied in prestigious national key institutions. Three of six students who studied diplomacy and foreign relations are female. Five female and four male students trained to be teachers, increasingly considered a feminine occupation.

Since graduation, both male and female members of the class of 1984 have worked in secondary schools and colleges, banks and travel agencies, research institutes and foreign affairs offices, television stations, luxury hotels, and joint venture companies. Yet, young women have experienced more job disappointments, or at least express such concerns more openly than their male classmates. "We just earn money by selling time," complained a young woman, sometimes enraged at the dreariness of her position at a large bank, sometimes resigned at the predictability of the routine she had established. "The problem is that you cannot spend your working time reading your own books. So most of us usually sit there without doing anything." One of her classmates wrote asking me, "Have you read Sylvia Plath's *The Bell Jar?* I think she sums up my present life well." And another reported grave disappointment with her teaching assignment in a non-key secondary school.

Now everything is over, and I've been assigned to teach at a middle school near my home. My friends are shocked, for they thought I was sure to gain a very satisfactory job. Every one feels it, that I should be assigned to a middle school while those whose English level is much lower than mine have got better jobs. To the students of our university, middle school is considered the worst place to go—and I'm so lucky that I've been sent there, only because I was not good at licking the leaders boots, even though I worked hard and did well in my study.... I'm really wasting my time and energy working in such a place.

Most section one pupils, male and female, have left their first jobs or graduate school positions and gone abroad to North America, Australia, or Europe. Their exodus calls into question the consequences of the LXLS's extensive socialization process. The school's definition of loyalty to the state during the early 1980s and the definition now maintained by members of the class of 1984 are dangerously at odds. In her study of political socialization of the Cultural Revolution generation, Anita Chan rightly reminds us that the success of political socialization must be measured over the long haul (Chan, 1985). It is likely that the LXLS, at least for these particular students, reinforced a pattern of questioning that has brought them not into alignment but confrontation with the state.

The contradictory role of foreign knowledge in these students' lives has been brought into sharp relief by the violence of 1989. While foreign knowledge embodies the "scientific, progressive, and creative" thinking China's leaders advocate for modernization, it also provides students with cultural and political alternatives to Chinese socialism. Because foreign-language students are so closely associated with, and even help popularize, such alternatives, one might predict that they would be at the center of efforts to redirect reform. Yet this does not appear to be entirely the case.

As we have seen, the Chinese government has periodically expressed concerns about the privileged educational and occupational access enjoyed by that segment of China's educated elite proficient in foreign languages (*Chronology*, 1983, 357–58). Even during the Cultural Revolution, steps were taken to protect foreign-language students, their language proficiency considered too strategic and dearly cultivated a resource to squander (Fu, 1986).

In the aftermath of June 1989, Hu Menghao, president of the Shanghai International Studies University, was named general secretary of the Shanghai Communist Party. His promotion rewarded his success in containing student demonstrations during the second half of the 1980s. In fact, the university's students were singled out by the media for their understanding of government policies.

That students at China's most prestigious foreign studies institutions have gained the reputation for sacrificing political ideals to pragmatic self-interest says as much about the consequences of the open door as the personal commitments of China's "thinking generation." In return for public loyalty, students are allowed privately to pursue their own careers and study abroad.

How do we see the class of 1984 in this light? Born at a time when "there was anger in everybody's guts" (Li Shaojun, 1990, 94), section one students embody characteristics drawn from both the "I Do Not Believe" and "I Have Nothing" generations. "After toiling away on the mainland for over 20 years, I have come to realize what a misery it is to be a Chinese; but after all, I've made the best of it to be a Shanghaiese. If some day we succeed in making not necessarily the wealthiest but one of the most dynamic nations out of the one billion weary population, I believe it can be a big contribution to human history. Of course, I can do very little for that course, but I hope it will eventually come true."

This passage was written by a section one student before 4 June 1989 and intimates the frustrations felt by many young people who took to the streets that spring. Generally, members of the class of 1984 were astonished, and temporarily heartened, by the democracy movement. However, others expressed fretful or angry misgivings about remaining on the sidelines. Gourd left China for Europe just after the events of the summer of 1989. Watching the swift changes in Eastern Europe with "fear, and perhaps envy," she expressed her sadness "after the angst, in Berlin," wondering "if there still is the possibility of forgetting," feeling the "shame of being just a donor, outside the action."

Rage soon turned for most of Gourd's classmates to a fatalistic, exhausted momentum that has taken the majority out of the country. "First we were very angry and indignant. Then we were disappointed. Now—now we are indifferent. There is no future for us here. There is nothing for us. If you want to improve your lot you must go abroad. There's no chance here. You just end up sitting and waiting, sitting and waiting. For what? What do they expect? We don't understand what they are doing. What do they care of the people? Power? Is that all? Just Power? So we go abroad. We can't say anything. We just go abroad."

In doing so, the students of section one have fulfilled, in a tragically ironic manner, their school's expectations that they become "bridges to knowledge" (Barber, Altbach, and Myers, 1984). They personify knowledge, in this case of the English language, as an international commodity and instrument of power. Skilled in its manipulation, they have become members of an "invisible college" with access to a global network of personal contacts and prestigious conferences and journals (Altbach, 1987, 169). However, that very knowledge has also prevented them from returning home. If nothing else, the presence of these troubled, creative individuals in our "own" system of schooling should serve notice to those who would ignore the interconnectedness of world crises.

The *Ti-Yong* Debate Revisited: International Literacy and the Challenge of Democracy

Today the LXLS's low profile is broken on its southern edge by a multi-story office and classroom building. The school's entrance crouches low before this soaring spire of post-Cultural Revolution prosperity. The idealized portrait of China's children in the front lobby has been replaced by a painting of boldly abstract red and blue figures. The canvas's careening forms invites multiple interpretations, providing a tantalizing portrait of China's "postmodern" generation and a sharp reminder that schools are not only the instruments of national policy but also the sites for constructing social alternatives, for rebuilding cultural authority on new foundations.

Chinese educational reformers recognize this when they lament that "within the sphere of education, the problems of how to teach and how to study have often hidden the problems of what ought to be taught and what ought to be learned" (Yang, 1990, 8). Significantly, in deciding what ought to be taught and what ought to be learned Chinese educators equate "modernized" pedagogy with the spirit of democratic administration (*minzhu guanli*).

What Chinese teachers envisage when they redefine modernization as a quest for democracy can be puzzling to North Americans. First of all, "the reproductive charter" of Chinese schooling has overwhelmed the qualities

A new painting for the front lobby: China's "postmodern" generation.

that North Americans often characterize as democratic education—"active involvement and authority that is distributed, constrained, and legitimized by its contribution to learning" (Samoff, 1991, 17). In addition, many Chinese teachers agree that "the reduction of democracy to freedom is a rich country's ideology" (Touraine, 1991, 28), and like their counterparts in other nations that have struggled with education based on the tenets of communism, hope for a place on the spectrum of educational reform that can avoid both the nihilism they see associated with excessive freedom in the United States and the mindless conformity they reject from their own experience (Shturman, 1988). In fact, democracy implies for many a quest for unity, where people share "identical ideals" (Esherick and Wasserstrom, 1990). Such a vision hardly embraces North American versions of participatory democracy or pluralism in the quest for a better society.

If in the global struggle for democracy China "marches to a different drummer" (Dewoskin, 1991, 50), how should we interpret the declaration by Chinese reformers that "democracy is international, and the efforts of pursuing democracy by one country should be supported by the people of every democratic nation"? (*Chronicle of Higher Education*, 1 May 1991, 37) Perhaps we can begin with a mutual understanding, as much a cornerstone of North American progressive educational thought as it is the socialist program, that the development of the capacity for informed questioning in students demands an appropriate balance of care for the individual and care for society. Here we worry together that a "modern" society promotes technical rather than ethical concerns and rewards efficiency and individual competition over commitment to others. Chinese and Americans both hope that education will help their children understand the practical consequences of their knowledge, and share the dilemma of shaping societies where moral discourse is possible. Though the quest for democracy in this context rarely implies for Chinese educators the critical empowerment of teachers and students advocated by North American critical theorists, it does demonstrate that the distribution of intellectual power and authority is a crucial, if not the central, challenge facing secondary schooling during the last decade of the twentieth century.

Nowhere is the extent to which we share these concerns clearer than in foreign-language teaching and learning. In both China and the United States linguistic ignorance is identified with scandalous indifference to high standards and a source of national insecurity. "Strength through wisdom" might well hark back to the slogans of nineteenth-century Chinese reformers who sought to use foreign languages as a tool to save China, although it is, in fact, a North American "critique of U.S. capability" (President's Commission on Foreign-language and International Studies, 1979). Perceptions of declining economic and international stature have motivated late-twentieth-century American self-strengtheners to lament their fellow citizens' limited international proficiency. "How," they demand, "are we to open overseas markets when other cultures are only dimly understood?" (National Governors' Association, 1989) Chinese leaders share this utilitarian desire for international literacy and, like their North American counterparts, blame schools for failing to lay the "cornerstones of competition."

At the heart of Chinese and North American anxieties about international literacy is that we both confront a global cultural "crisis" which stems from the recognition that in the interdependent world of the late twentieth century divergent cultural values and life-styles coexist as often within national boundaries as between them. While we hope to broaden our perspectives on the world, we also hope to secure that set of commonly held beliefs that can insure the survival and continuity of our respective nations.

The difficulty in doing both has prompted social critics in both China and the United States to retreat from the challenge of diversity. North American educators do so with the warning that when public values go unclarified the public school is in danger of losing its primary mission and justification. Critics more committed to pluralism seek schools "where freedom of expression is uncompromisingly protected and where civility is powerfully affirmed," where "the sacredness of the person is honored and where diversity is aggressively pursued," "where individuals accept their obligations to the group," "where the well-being of each member is sensitively supported," and "where rituals affirming both tradition and change are widely shared" (Campus Life: A Special Report by the Carnegie Foundation for the Advancement of Teaching, 1990, 7–8).

We have seen that Chinese educators grapple with the competing demands of diversity and community in a different but no less profound way. Although transcending culture has been the goal of Chinese educators since the May Fourth era, different ways of living and communicating have been presented to Chinese students predominantly as alternatives to rather than models for appropriate development. As we have seen throughout this study, rather than being appreciated for their capacity to alter an individual's sense of being, foreign knowledge and languages have been mistrusted precisely because they can change someone's mind. Thus, Chinese foreign-language students are advised, "Know thyself first." "Count the good things of your family." "Only when we know ourselves can we know others." The assumption underlying these admonitions—that "we" will be little changed by the experience of coming into contact with "others"—is rarely challenged.

So, what do teachers at the LXLS mean when they counsel students to "have the whole country in mind, and the whole world in view" (xionghuai zuguo, fangyan shijie)? Do they intend something different from North Americans and Europeans who equate international literacy with cultivating world citizens with a world conscience (Husen, 1986)? The answer to this question is yes and will remain so as long as the independent action and creativity for which young people are supposed to be trained are impossible for Chinese leaders to grant. Although Chinese leaders understand full well that knowledge has increasingly become "the political medium for collective organization" (Wexler, 1987, 15), they hardly agree that foreign-language study is a struggle for meaning whose ultimate goal is to empower individuals to question why a foreign language is being learned and for whose benefit (Peirce, 1989).

The power of foreign languages to transform so fundamentally, and even make individual and cultural identity deliberately problematic, is, of course, what Chinese leaders have struggled for over a century to minimize. Far from being celebrated for their capacity to alter an individual's sense of orientation, foreign knowledge and languages in China have been suspect precisely because they challenge national identity.

In a recent book entitled *Going My Way*, Li Hanhou captures this dilemma by reclaiming the *ti-yong* distinction for the 1990s (Li, 1986). Inverting the nineteenth-century self-strengtheners' prescription for national salvation, Li proposes that Chinese modernization rest upon "the West for fundamental principles, China for practical application" (*xi ti zhong yong*). Nevertheless, he simultaneously evokes Chinese tradition in the search for national identity: "In order to better understand Western culture, to assimilate Western culture, we must better understand ourselves." Li's insistence on eschewing wholesale Westernization in this process, coupled with his reevaluation of China's cultural heritage for the modern age, makes him a worthy ancestor of the self-strengtheners he evokes. It also makes him a sympathetic counterpart to American educators who contend that "if we truly want to educate our students for a global society, if we are serious about internationalizing, we have to realize that people need to understand their own culture before they can understand another" (Mossberg, 1990, A44).

As Chinese educators sort out what global citizenship (*qiuji*) entails, debate surrounding the necessity of foreign-language schools continues. Perhaps the study of foreign languages has become so common in China that foreign-language schools are superfluous. The possibility exists that they have outgrown their usefulness, as did their nineteenth-century counterparts. Or it may be that in attempting to produce young linguists who can communicate spontaneously, they have not been attentive enough to outside pressures and their own contradictory intentions.

Teachers at the LXLS believe that to survive their school must continue to reevaluate its contributions to schooling in Shanghai. It may respond by becoming less willing to take risks, to become more like other key schools. By doing so, however, the LXLS would lose its specialized identity and claim to superior resources. If the LXLS is to both enhance its one area of expertise and integrate that into a broader curriculum, more creativity and involvement in foreign studies, not less, will be needed. The question remains when LXLS teachers and their national leaders will be willing and able to respond to this challenge. Until influences across national boundaries are globally perceived and structurally permitted to encourage mutual enrichment rather than the means to absorption or conversion, the LXLS's uneasy compromise will continue.

Appendix A
"Suggestions by the Ministry of Education for Running Foreign-Language Schools Well," 1963*

The continuous expansion of our country's international relations and rapid advancement of all areas of socialist development have created an urgent need for the cultivation of high level foreign-language manpower. In addition to diligently managing tertiary foreign-language departments and institutes, greatly strengthening foreign-language instruction in regular middle schools, and under conditions where teaching staff and facilities allow establishing in a well-planned and step-by-step manner foreign-language classes in higher levels of full-time primary schools, one avenue for training high-level foreign-language manpower must be centered around the well-planned management of a number of foreign-language schools which begin instruction in the third grade of primary school. In accordance with instructions from the Central Committee Propaganda Department, and after preliminary study by concerned provinces and municipalities at the conference for making preparations for foreign-language schools, several problems concerning establishing foreign-language schools were identified and listed as follows:

1. The general instructional objective of foreign-language schools is in line with that of regular primary and secondary schools, the only difference being in somewhat divergent requirements in the area of cultural and scientific knowledge. In foreign-language schools teaching requirements for Chinese, foreign languages, history, and geography are increased while requirements for mathematics, physics and chemistry are suitably decreased. Consequently, both foreign-language schools and regular primary and secondary schools must thoroughly implement the party's policy that education must serve proletarian politics, must be united with productive labor, and help students develop morally, intellectually, and physically to become cultured workers with socialist consciousness.

* *Almanac*, 1984, 737.

Foreign language schools must especially emphasize strengthening ideological-political training and moral instruction to cultivate students with proletarian revolutionary ideals and Communist morality. Careful attention should be paid both to insuring that bourgeois thinking and other reactionary ideologies do not influence and corrupt students, and to preventing the development of an atmosphere of special privilege. Organizing students to participate in productive labor carries out an important aspect of party educational policy, strengthening political education, and it must not be even slightly neglected. Middle school students should be organized each year during definite time periods for one or two trips to peoples communes to participate in agricultural labor. Strict and conscientious effort should also be made to organize students to take part in labor at school.

2. System of study and curriculum. The course of study for foreign-language schools and regular primary and secondary schools are the same, that is a six year primary school program, and three year junior and senior middle school programs.

The curricula for foreign-language schools and regular primary and secondary schools are basically the same. At the primary school level great attention should be paid to instruction in Chinese language and arithmetic in order to establish a good foundation in these two areas. Foreign language classes should commence in the third grade of primary school. Classes in general production knowledge should not be held. At the secondary school level the number of class hours devoted to politics class should be the same as in regular middle schools. Time spent in classes in foreign language, Chinese language, history, and geography should be greater than, and time spent in classes in mathematics, physics, and chemistry less than, the time spent in these same classes in regular middle schools. Classes in general production knowledge should not be held. Middle school Chinese-language classes should include relatively systematic knowledge of logic and rhetoric; history and geography classes should include relatively systematic knowledge about the history and geography of the regions in which the target language is used. In mathematics analytic geometry should not be studied, and requirements for physics and chemistry should be basically the same as those in secondary normal schools.

In accordance with the teaching requirements outlined above, and with reference to the new "Full-time Secondary and Primary School Teaching Plan (Draft)," we have drafted a "Foreign Language School Teaching Plan (Draft)." This teaching plan has been discussed and studied at the Foreign

Language School Conference, and is being sent out along with this notice for trying out in foreign-language schools.

3. Teaching requirements for foreign-language classes. In foreign-language schools time spent in studying the foreign language in primary and middle school levels must not be less than 2,500 class periods. Upon graduation students should be relatively fluent in one foreign language, with correct pronunciation, a 5,000-word vocabulary, a good understanding of grammar, an ability to read most foreign-language books, newspapers, and magazines, and an ability to engage in general everyday conversation.

At the primary school level emphasis should be placed on training in pronunciation and spoken language, requiring correct pronunciation and stress to insure that a firm foundation in pronunciation and spoken language has been laid. In junior middle school continued emphasis should be placed on training in spoken language, a definite amount of vocabulary should be mastered, study of basic grammatical structures should be completed, beginning reading skills should be learned, and in addition attention should be paid to training student ability to use the foreign language in writing. In senior middle school continued emphasis should be placed on both training in oral language, reading, and writing, and providing appropriate training in translation skills.

In foreign-language classes, progressive steps should be taken until the target language is used to conduct class. For each year of study, text selections should include progressively more original materials. In various senior middle school classes (such as mathematics, physics, and chemistry) foreign-language texts and the target language should be used whenever possible, as long as the student's ability to understand correctly and grasp the basic knowledge and skills of these disciplines are not adversely affected.

In order to insure the quality of foreign-language instruction, foreign-language classes at both primary and secondary levels should be divided into small sections for instruction. The school should provide numerous facilities and conditions to assist study of the foreign language, such as providing tape recorders, record players, foreign language typewriters, and other modern equipment, ordering foreign books, newspapers, magazines, and extracurricular reading materials, actively promoting a diversity of foreign-language activities, and creating an environment beneficial to the study of foreign languages.

4. Establishment of schools. In the fall of 1963, in addition to the Beijing Foreign Language Institute Attached Foreign Language School and the Beijing

Foreign Language School, it is decided that in each of the six cities of Shanghai, Nanjing, Changqun, Guangzhou, Chongqing, and Xian one foreign-language school will be established, for a total of eight schools. In the fall of 1964 or 1965 Shanghai will establish a second school. It is recommended that Hubei Education Bureau should establish a school in the fall of 1964 in Wuhan. Within two or three years there will be a total of ten schools.

5. Selection and establishment of types of foreign-language curricula. In accordance with the availability of teachers in various regions, in conjunction with consideration by the foreign affairs office and other administrative departments of the kinds of high-level foreign-language manpower needed, it has been decided that the ten foreign-language schools mentioned above should teach classes in seven languages: English, Russian, French, Spanish, German, Japanese, and Arabic.

Appendix B
"Suggestions by the Ministry of Education for Running Foreign-Language Schools Well," 1979*

In 1963, the Ministry of Education, acting upon instructions from the Central Committee, sent out a "Circular Concerning Running Foreign-Language Schools Well," which stipulated that this type of school should admit students, who had completed the second year of primary school, into a 10-year course of study. (At that time secondary and primary school comprised a 12-year system.) Upon graduation these students would enter classes in foreign-language institutes and departments that were designed especially for continuation of their training and the cultivation of high-level foreign-language manpower.

Currently, the focal point of our country's work has been transformed into the building of socialist modernization, and all fronts are in urgent need of foreign-language manpower, especially highly proficient translators, research personnel, foreign-language teachers, engineers, and technicians. Therefore, training high level foreign-language manpower in order to meet the needs of realizing the Four Modernizations and developing international relations is a strategic responsibility of the utmost urgency. Toward this purpose, it is crucial that existing foreign-language schools are reorganized, recovered, and run well, and that a number of new schools are gradually established. Concrete suggestions are as follows:

1. The nature and responsibility of foreign-language schools. Foreign-language schools are schools that provide specialized training, and whose primary responsibility is to cultivate students of high foreign-language and cultural proficiency for tertiary institutions. These schools can link up with college-level foreign-language institutes and departments, and become part of a straight route of training from primary school to college [*yi tiao long*]. At the senior middle school level classes can be divided into humanities and

* *Almanac*, 1984, 742–43.

science sections. After graduating and meeting entrance examination requirements, students will primarily study in foreign-language institutes or departments, but they can also apply to technical-scientific universities or liberal arts colleges, or according to individual ability and available possibilities, be assigned to appropriate employment related to their specialties and training.

2. System of study, curriculum, and teaching requirements. For foreign-language schools enrolling primary school graduates, the provisional course of study is set at five years. Schools with the proper facilities can also admit primary school pupils who have completed two years of elementary school. For students beginning their studies in third grade, the course of study is provisionally set at eight years.

The curricula used in foreign-language schools and regular secondary and primary schools are basically the same. Time spent in foreign-language study at the primary school level should not be less than 600 class periods, and at the middle school level not less than 1,400 class periods. Upon graduation, students should be relatively fluent in one foreign language, with correct pronunciation, a 4,000- to 5,000-word vocabulary, a good knowledge of grammatical structure, the ability to comprehend simple original material, and the ability to engage in general, everyday conversation. The use of the target language in conducting foreign-language classes should be gradually increased until it is the sole language of instruction. With the prerequisite that unified teaching requirements set by the Ministry of Education are fully met, foreign-language texts and the target language should be used as much as possible in middle school mathematics, physics, and chemistry classes and senior middle school classes teaching the geography and history of the countries in which the target language is used. In order to insure teaching quality, instruction in foreign-language classes at all levels should be carried out in small sections. Schools should create diverse means to develop conditions and facilities beneficial to the students' foreign-language study, such as providing necessary tape recorders, record players, foreign-language typewriters, and other modern teaching media, subscribing to foreign-language books, newspapers, magazines, and extracurricular reading materials, actively promoting various kinds of extracurricular foreign-language activities, and creating an environment conducive to foreign-language learning.

Chinese-language classes should include some knowledge of logic and rhetoric. History and geography classes should include appropriately increased historical and geographical knowledge about the countries in which the target language is used.

Foreign-language schools can refer to the full-day secondary and primary school provisional work regulations (trial draft) in planning for part-time programs.

3. Foreign-language curriculum and school size. Speaking in reference to the entire country, six languages can be taught: English, Russian, Japanese, French, German, and Spanish. Each school should not teach an excessive number of languages. Schools in Manchuria and in the Northwest should plan to teach more Russian and Japanese.

Considering the necessities of administering boarding schools, the size of foreign-language schools should not be excessive; generally the student body should not exceed 1,000 pupils.

4. Student recruitment, promotion, matriculation, and job allocation. Recruiting students should involve examination and strict selection. Students of sound morals, excellent academic achievement, healthy body, clear enunciation, strong ability to model, and quick reaction should be selected from throughout a municipal area. After students have been enrolled, the school should reexamine them; if a minority is found unqualified, they should be promptly transferred to another school. Students should undergo especially rigorous selection procedures during promotion from primary and junior middle school. Those students who are not suitable for continued training in foreign languages should be transferred to ordinary primary and middle schools. The foreign-language school, appropriate education administrative organ, and the school into which the student is being transferred should all carry out good ideological work and make proper arrangements for the student. From primary school to senior middle school, matriculation rates should be limited to within 20 percent. The focal point of this work should be in primary and junior middle school levels. In as much as possible, students who have already been promoted to senior middle school should neither leave school nor be transferred. Foreign-language schools with the proper facilities can also admit new senior one students from regular middle schools.

After graduates from foreign-language schools test into post-secondary institutions, those schools should arrange separate sections, syllabi, and teaching materials commensurate with the foreign-language school graduate's actual level of ability, in order to avoid repetition or discontinuity in teaching content, and preserve the continuity of instruction.

Provincial or municipal education bureaus may work with local labor departments in accordance with government regulations and the students' individual abilities to help make suitable occupational arrangements for graduates who do not test into post-secondary institutions.

5. Teaching materials. Foreign-language teaching materials in foreign-

language schools should include a definite amount of original foreign-language material. The proportion of original material should increase each year until by the senior level it predominates.

The compilation of foreign-language teaching materials (including textbooks, teaching reference books, maps, and charts) should be organized in conjunction with the Ministry of Education; the writing of various language teaching materials can be entrusted to different post-secondary institutions and foreign-language schools, and selections can also be taken from teaching materials published abroad.

6. Teachers. Standards for foreign-language school teachers and staff should be higher than key secondary and primary schools and should be worked out according to actual needs (including small foreign-language instruction groups and the boarding school system).

Allocation of foreign-language teachers should involve consideration of such needs as small instruction groups, extracurricular foreign-language activities, the establishment of an environment conducive to foreign-language learning. Classes in higher grades should still be divided for foreign-language teaching, and it is provisionally decided that two teachers should be assigned to each class of primary school students and three for each middle school class. Every area should transfer a definite number of highly proficient and experienced teachers to foreign-language schools to direct teaching, as well as assigning a number of outstanding graduates from post-secondary foreign-language institutes and departments to foreign-language schools. The teachers sent to teach at foreign-language schools must be of high quality, especially in the areas of pronunciation ability, speaking ability, and ability to work with primary and secondary students. Teachers in other disciplines should be selected by local educational administrative departments in accordance with requirements for key secondary and primary schools.

Areas with sufficient facilities may contract overseas Chinese and foreign teachers to assume teaching responsibilities.

Continually improving the proficiency of the teaching staff is an important factor in running foreign-language schools well. The work of in-service training should be conscientiously carried out. Indeed, to assist continued training for teachers, facilities should be improved and opportunities should be provided, such as subscribing to foreign reading materials, receiving foreign broadcasts, watching foreign films. Foreign-language schools should have a separate quota for sending teachers abroad or to domestic short-term in-service training programs for study. In the area of teaching and in-service training, foreign-language teachers at foreign-language schools should get the same treatment as university foreign-language teachers.

Teachers who have been sent from post-secondary institutions to teach at foreign-language schools should receive the same kind of salaries and benefits they did at the post-secondary level. The salaries and benefits of other foreign-language school teachers should be studied separately in the context of reform of the salary system.

7. Funding. Funding for foreign-language schools should be higher than that of local key secondary and primary schools. Funding for foreign-language schools should generally be directly allocated by the education departments of provincial, municipal, or autonomous region governments. Those foreign-language schools attached to institutions of higher learning that are operated by ministries and committees of the Central Government should receive their funding from the relevant ministries or committees through their supervising institutions.

8. Leaders. Foreign-language schools are generally under the guidance of the provincial, municipal, or autonomous district education bureau and directly linked to local foreign-language institutes or tertiary foreign-language departments. In terms of foreign-language teaching and in-service training, they receive direction and assistance from the post-secondary school with which they are linked.

A foreign-language school can also be an attached affiliate to a tertiary foreign-language institution under a system of dual administration by both the provincial, municipal, or autonomous region education bureau and the tertiary institution to which it is attached, the latter taking primary responsibility. The provincial, municipal, or autonomous region education administrative department is responsible for general classroom teaching, as well as student ideological and political training, recruitment, and job allocation.

Responsibility for foreign-language school policy, teaching plan, and teaching materials is directed by and set in conjunction with the Ministry of Education.

Foreign-language schools are equivalent to provincial or municipal key point schools. The arrangements made by each provincial or municipal education administrative department for key schools (including allocation of personnel, funds, and equipment) should also be made for foreign-language schools, with due consideration given to their special character.

Foreign-language schools should be provided with a strong leadership group, with senior comrades being familiar with foreign-language teaching.

Presently, the first step is to reorganize and recover the eleven existing foreign-language schools and transform those that have been changed into foreign-language teacher colleges back into foreign-language schools. Beginning in 1979, no more teachers will be trained in these schools; the responsibility for training foreign-language teachers will be given to local normal colleges (junior middle school foreign-language teachers trained in two-year teacher colleges and primary foreign-language teachers trained in classes in secondary normal schools). Existing foreign-language classes for teachers should still be run conscientiously. In addition, following present and future developments in education, additional foreign-language schools can be established in accordance with actual conditions, but plans for development must be submitted to provincial, municipal, or autonomous region educational authorities and approved by the Ministry of Education.

Appendix C
"Full-Time Six-Year Key Secondary School English Teaching Outline," 1982*

I. Teaching Objectives and Requirements

Foreign languages are an important tool for the study of cultural and scientific knowledge and the promotion of international relations. In order to build our country into a modernized, highly democratic, highly cultured strong socialist nation, we must raise the scientific and cultural level of all Chinese peoples. We must train a great quantity of red and expert, highly qualified foreign-language manpower for all areas. Therefore, foreign languages are an important part of the middle school curriculum, receiving the same consideration as basic subjects such as Chinese and mathematics.

Use of the English language is very extensive, and English is one of the most important foreign languages taught in Chinese middle schools. The purpose of teaching English in six-year key middle schools is to provide students with basic training in listening, speaking, reading, and writing, to cultivate in students a basic ability to use elementary English, both orally and in written form, with particular emphasis placed on cultivating reading skills. A firm foundation must be conscientiously laid to enable students to progress in their studies and utilize English.

The six-year key middle school program begins in the first year of junior middle school. After completion of this study program, students should have acquired a knowledge of basic pronunciation and grammar, learned 2,700 to 3,000 vocabulary items and a definite number of commonly used idiomatic expressions, be able to read materials of the same relative difficulty as their textbooks with the aid of a dictionary, and moreover attained a definite speaking ability.

* *Zhong xiaoxue yingyu jiaoxue yu yanjiu,* 1982, 1–8.

II. Teaching Principles

1. Adhere to language-teaching principles to achieve thought education through teaching and learning. The responsibility of English teaching is to enable students to use English through training in basic skills. Teaching materials should be prepared according to the demands of the principles of English-language teaching. Language usage should be authentic; contents and organization should fit the needs of various training and should lead to efficient teaching. English class, like any other class, has the responsibility of promoting thought education. In all training, particularly in reading materials, attention must be paid to both the requirements of teaching and healthy content. Students must be helped to establish correct thinking and good moral character. In the relationship between thought and language education, students should study English well and at the same time receive proper ideological influences.

2. Explain clearly basic linguistic knowledge and emphasize training in the ability to use the language. English class should emphasis training in skills. The purpose of teaching students essential basic knowledge of pronunciation, vocabulary, and grammar is not to enable them gradually to understand and memorize this knowledge. Its importance lies in guiding them in practical language use, cultivating their ability actually to use the language.

    English classes should be characterized by a small amount of explanation and a lot of practice. Normally, teaching a new language point should begin with oral practice. Only after much practice has led to a definite automatic proficiency should a concise summary explanation be given. This is more efficient. If practice is thorough and explanations concise, practice can be more efficiently guided and students skill in using the language improved.

3. Consolidate training, emphasize stages. In studying a foreign language, practice in listening, speaking, reading, and writing cannot be separated. They are complementary and help promote each other. Coordinated practice in listening, speaking, reading, and writing leads to better and faster language acquisition.

    At various stages of learning, practice in listening, speaking, reading, and writing can receive different emphasis. In the beginning stages, listening and speaking training should be paramount, accompanied by appropriate reading and writing practice. After students have acquired a definite ability in and are accustomed to listening and speaking, and have acquired a certain amount of vocabulary and the majority of basic grammatical structures, reading comprehension can be of primary emphasis, complemented by aural-oral practice.

4. Use English as much as possible, use the native language appropriately. English should be used as much as possible in organizing classroom teaching, particularly in explanations. In introductory stages, use of audiovisual aids and demonstration while using the native language as little as possible or in fact eliminating it entirely is completely feasible. As students knowledge of and skills in English improve, the possibilities for using English in organizing classroom teaching and explanations become greater and greater.

However, for students of junior middle school age and older, the native language is relatively fixed, and in the study of English-language interference is inevitable. The problem lies in how to take advantage of the native language. If managed properly, through timely, appropriate comparisons, use of the native language can be effective in studying English. If managed poorly, if the native language is used too often, or if inappropriate comparisons are made, the native language will become a big impediment to learning English. Consequently, how to treat the native language in English teaching is worthy of study and continual consolidation of experience.

5. Bring into full play the guiding role of teachers, motivate the students' enthusiasm. In English teaching the leading role of teachers should be especially emphasized. Teachers should demand of themselves exact pronunciation, standard penmanship, and fluency to set an example. They should continuously improve their spoken ability and as much as possible use English to organize classroom teaching. In accordance with the special characteristics of youth, they should intensively study teaching methods and continually raise teaching quality. Teachers should maintain strict requirements of students, help them develop good study habits and acquire correct study methods. They should encourage student enthusiasm and help them fully recognize that studying a foreign language well requires hard work. They should encourage the students' progress and patiently help students with difficulties. They should devise extracurricular English activities so students study in an active and lively way.

III. Teaching Methods

1. Pronunciation. Learning pronunciation is the foundation of good English study. Pronunciation training is to a large extent a process of cultivating habits. From the very beginning strict requirements must be made, and training strictly upheld to help students form good habits.

   Studying pronunciation relies primarily on modeling. The teacher must supply many opportunities for listening; after the student has understood correctly, modeling can begin. In order to help students imitate more efficiently, explanations about the methods and skill of pronunciation can be given.

   Because of the relatively complex relationship between English spelling and pronunciation, it is difficult for junior students to master. The International Phonetic Alphabet (IPA) is a useful tool for both teaching and the students' independent study, and is required in the teaching of pronunciation.

   In the introductory stage, attention should be paid to syllabic and sentence stress, phrasing, smoothness, and basic intonation. If the simple sentences of this stage are to be read or spoken well, these skills are necessary. Training in reading aloud is one important path to improving students pronunciation. In addition, it is beneficial in raising listening ability and reading comprehension, and should be continually practiced.

2. Vocabulary. Teaching vocabulary requires not only that students learn a certain number of words, but that they also acquire the methods for studying vocabulary. Increased vocabulary and improvement in ability to acquire vocabulary are mutually related. Only after students have learned a certain number of words can they gradually improve their ability to study and remember vocabulary; grasping the methods of studying vocabulary can, on the other hand, raise the efficiency of study and increase vocabulary.

   Teachers should guide students in paying attention to the relationship between spelling and pronunciation, teach students basic spelling rules, help students develop the ability to determine pronunciation from spelling, and spelling from pronunciation.

   Students should grasp basic word formation, be able to determine part of speech and meaning from a new word's components, and determine part of speech from the position and use of a word in a phrase or sentence.

Another important aspect of vocabulary teaching is word meaning and definition. Before a student understands the exact meaning and usage of a word, the teacher must often explain the word, give examples, and the student must use it over and over again. It is impossible simply to take an English word and match it with a Chinese equivalent. Many words, especially verbs and adjectives, present problems of fixed and customary usage, and even syntax. It is more efficient to use sentence patterns to teach these words to students. It is also necessary to pay attention to phenomena such as words with changing or multiple meanings. In addition, during lessons teachers should consciously reintroduce previously studied vocabulary over and over again, for consolidation and review.

The vocabulary requirements in the teaching outline include correct spelling, reading, meaning, and understanding of words. The most commonly used items (approximately 60 percent) should be part of the student's active vocabulary.

Students should be trained to use the dictionary. When students begin extensive reading, students should use English-Chinese dictionaries.

3. Grammar. The purpose of middle school grammar teaching is to help students grasp basic grammar in order to understand, speak, read, write, and use English. Sentence pattern practice provides typical structures and is an effective method for introducing grammatical points.

When teaching a grammatical point, the teacher may first describe the structure so students have some understanding about it prior to practicing. After students have a beginning grasp of the grammar point, a concise summary can again be given. Simple rules can also be introduced, prior to the students' practice.

The purpose of giving concise explanations is to reduce the possibility of students blindly repeating exercises and to increase linguistic accuracy. Therefore, explanations must be well timed, direct, and to the point.

Grammatical points that have a number of varying uses or are relatively complex should be introduced beginning with most simple explanation and gradually working toward the difficult, using two or three sessions, gradually broadening and deepening the explanation.

Essential grammatical points that are rarely used in spoken English but improve reading ability should be simply explained and practiced a few times in written form.

4. Text Materials. The text consists of the comprehensive material used to teach linguistic knowledge and practice listening, speaking, reading, and writing abilities.

In teaching the text, more important than explaining is conducting practice in reading aloud, oral and written questions and answers, oral and written retelling, and translation. The textbook is the primary material for practicing reading aloud. Requiring students to memorize parts of the text is beneficial in helping them improve both their feel for the language and their ability to use it. When conducting question-answer practice, students should be required to ask questions as well as answer them. Retelling should be demonstrated to beginners by the teacher. Students should then be required to take dictation from this demonstration, and gradually with guidance from the teacher independently engage in retelling.

When explaining the text, the distinctive linguistic characteristics of English and common manners of expressions that differ from Chinese should be pointed out, explained, and practiced in appropriate exercises. A translation method may be used to assess the students' understanding of the text.

Sentence analysis is beneficial in improving the students' understanding. Teachers may analyze long or complex sentences, according to the needs of teaching.

5. Reading. Improving the students' reading ability will be difficult if the textbook is relied upon solely; teachers must also guide students in reading a definite amount of extracurricular materials.

Reading can help enlarge vocabulary, enrich linguistic knowledge, and raise ability to use the language. However, the primary purpose for teaching reading is to help students accurately understand reading materials. Requiring students to write summaries in English or Chinese or answer comprehension questions are effective methods for guiding reading and assessing whether or not students have correctly understood what they have read.

Students should read as much as possible easy, original works or original works that have been simplified. The difficulty of this kind of reading material is not just in vocabulary and grammar but also in manner of expression, common usage, and the ways of thinking and background knowledge it reflects. Therefore, these kinds of problems should be emphasized in teaching, directing students to use dictionaries and grammar texts to acquire the ability to solve problems independently.

6. Direct teaching, educational technology, and the foreign-language environment. Using a direct teaching style in introductory stages is very efficient, since students form direct and vivid links between objects, actions,

situations, and language. In addition to utilizing materials, models, and pictures, direct teaching also includes the teacher's expressions and gestures.

In situations where facilities permit, record players, radio broadcasts, tape recorders, slides, and filmstrips can be used to increase teaching effectiveness.

A foreign-language environment must be created for students. In addition to speaking English during classroom activities, it is necessary to develop all kinds of extracurricular activities that are appropriate to the students' level of proficiency and age group, such as recitations, story-telling, singing songs, performance of dialogues, exhibitions of hand-writing or pictures, wall newspapers, and so on. This provides students with more practical opportunities and improves their study, enthusiasm, and accustoms them to using English.

IV. Requirements and Content for Each Grade

Total hours: humanities, 960; science, 932; elective, 932

The purpose of six-year key middle school English teaching is to provide students basic training in listening, speaking, reading and writing, cultivate beginning ability to use English, both orally and in written form, with an emphasis on reading ability. In introductory levels, pronunciation training is primary. In junior middle school basic grammar instruction is completed through training in listening, speaking, reading, and writing. In senior middle school, emphasis is placed on reading comprehension, training should be given in more difficult grammar, and at the same time appropriate training in listening, speaking, reading and writing.

To insure the preceding goals, students must be trained in the following abilities:

1. Ability in vocabulary study skills, use of basic rules for spelling and word formation, use of the International Phonetic Alphabet to pronounce new words, use of English-Chinese dictionary, clear concept about parts of speech, identification of common expressions.

   By the end of the study program, the ability to read and spell 2,700 to 3,000 single words and a definite number of idiomatic expressions, knowledge of their basic definition, an active vocabulary of the most commonly used group (approximately 60 percent).

2. A grasp of basic grammar and ability to analyze sentences;
3. Ability to read text material aloud fluently, with correct pronunciation, intonation, stress, and pause;
4. Ability to retell and ask and answer questions, in written and spoken form, about text passages, and engage in simple conversation about everyday life;
5. Ability to read and correctly comprehend materials of the same degree of difficulty as the text with the aid of a dictionary;
6. Ability to write short, coherent 150 to 200-word essays and letters about familiar themes, with correct spelling, grammar, word usage, punctuation, and form.

Total class hours and class time for each academic year are actual contact hours. Hours for review and examinations are not included.

Junior Secondary School Grade 1
5 class hours × 34 (weeks) = 170 class hours

I. Teaching
Requirements

1. Alphabet: recognize, read, memorize, and write letters.
2. Pronunciation: use phonetic transcription and notation; use correct pronunciation and intonation when speaking and reading aloud or reciting lesson.
3. Penmanship: copy correctly from italicized models in text; write lower and higher case letters with correct form, punctuation, neatness; produce neat papers, and generally develop good writing habits.
4. Vocabulary: spell, write, define, and label part(s) of speech of all required vocabulary items; read according to previously studied phonetic and spelling rules.
5. Grammar: use correctly in spoken and written form simple sentence structures (including affirmative, negative, and interrogative), inflection, and tense.
6. Text material: read aloud fluently, memorize, and ask and answer questions about the text.
7. Understand simple classroom expressions; take dictation of one or several sentences.

1. Vocabulary: approximately 450 single items and a small number of common idiomatic expressions.
2. Pronunciation:
   a. Phonetic transcriptions for all vowels and consonants and several common consonant clusters.
   b. Basic rules of spelling.
   c. Syllabic and sentence stress.
   d. Fluent reading without stuttering.
   e. Falling and rising intonation.
3. Grammar:
   a. Parts of speech.
   b. Noun plurals, count or noncount nouns, nominative case.
   c. Personal pronouns, demonstrative pronouns, indefinite pronouns (*some, any, no*), interrogative pronouns (*what, who, whose, which*).
   d. Common prepositions indicating position and time.
   e. Cardinal and ordinal numbers.
   f. Affirmative, negative, and interrogative forms of the verbs *be, have,* and *there be.*
   g. Present and present progressive tenses.
   h. Adjectives, comparative adverbial.
   i. Sentence types (declarative, interrogative, imperative, exclamatory).

Junior Secondary School Grade 2
5 class hours × 34 (weeks) = 170 class hours

I. Teaching

Requirements

1. Pronunciation: pronounce correctly all vowels and consonants; read fluently with correct syllable stress of each vocabulary item; read without stuttering; use proper rising and falling intonation in short sentences; read text material fluently with correct pronunciation and stress.
2. Penmanship: copy the italicized text exercises correctly, with proper small and capitalized letters, punctuation.
3. Vocabulary: know correct spelling, parts of speech, and definition of each

word; determine correct pronunciation from spelling; using word-formation rules determine part of speech and definition.

4. Grammar: be clear about the structure of simple sentences; make no mistakes in written and oral work; be clear about the structure and usage of compound sentences; be familiar with inflectional changes already studied (noun plurals, past tense, past and present participles, adjectives, adverbial comparatives); be clear about the use of all tenses studied.

5. Text material: read aloud fluently and memorize parts of the text material; be able to ask and answer questions about the material, and use a dictionary to read materials with the same level of difficulty as the text.

6. Understand everyday classroom expressions and be able to answer simple questions; be able to take dictation from materials simpler than the text and understand the teacher's retelling of the text passage.

II. Teaching Content

1. Vocabulary: approximately 400 words and a certain number of common, idiomatic expressions.
2. Pronunciation:
   a. Phrasing and pausing.
   b. Stress.
3. Grammar:
   a. Be going to (future).
   b. Adjectives and comparative adverbial (continued).
   c. Reflexive personal pronoun.
   d. Modal verbs (*can, may, must*).
   e. Verb forms.
   f. Past, present, past progressive, and present perfect tenses.
   g. Sentence elements, five basic sentence patterns.
   h. Sentence types (simple, compound, complex).
   i. Adverbial modifier subordinate clause.
   j. Infinitives.
   k. Articles.

Junior Secondary School Grade 3
5 class hours × 32 (weeks) = 160 class hours

Appendix C

1. Pronunciation: read the text fluently with correct pronunciation, sentence stress, and pauses.
2. Penmanship: copy smoothly on regular or exercise paper capital and small letters, in script form with correct punctuation.
3. Vocabulary: use correct spelling, part of speech, and definition of vocabulary item; read vocabulary using spelling and reading rules; use word formation rules such as prefix, suffix, and roots to determine the meaning and part of speech of words; attend to phenomena such as various meanings and usages for one word, verb phrases, and common expressions.
4. Grammar: analyze compound sentences that are not excessively complicated, by ascertaining sentence units and function; attain preliminary understanding of the primary function of the five commonly used tenses (present, past, future, present progressive, present perfect); distinguish between past progressive, past perfect, and expressing future in the past, and state their significance.
5. Text materials: according to meaning and pronunciation, read aloud fluently; memorize sections of the text and with the guidance of the teacher retell the story simply; ask and answer questions according to the text; with the aid of the dictionary read materials of the same level of difficulty as the text.
6. Understand the teacher's explanations and stories that use language points already studied; be able to take dictation from material simpler than the text; use English to converse with teacher during class activities.
7. Use familiar sentence patterns, vocabulary, and common expressions to create sentences.

II. Teaching Content

1. Vocabulary: approximately 400 items and a definite number of common expressions.
2. Grammar:
   a. Object subordinate clause.
   b. Expressing future in the past and past perfect tense.
   c. Infinitives (continued).
   d. Passive voice.

    e. Indirect speech.

    f. Attributive clauses.

    g. The use of the pronoun *it.*

    h. Sentence formation.

Volumes 1 to 3 of the junior secondary school texts are primarily materials written by the editors, while one-third to one-half of the material in the fourth, fifth, and sixth volumes is compiled from simple original English material or edited original material. In the first texts in the series, dialogue and short passages primarily reflect the students' daily lives. Subsequent texts use stories, fairy tales, fables, short plays, diaries, letters, and short general-knowledge essays about science, technology and history.

Senior Secondary School Grade 1

5 class hours × 32 (weeks) = 160 class hours

I. Teaching

Requirements

1. Pronunciation: relatively greater fluency in reading aloud with correct pronunciation, intonation, stress, and pauses.
2. Vocabulary: spell, define, and label part of speech of studied vocabulary items; the most common vocabulary items (approximately 60 percent) available for active use in oral and written forms; use English-Chinese dictionary to solve problems such as definition of new words or familiar words with new meanings, collocation; in text material or material of the same level of difficulty point out common verb phrases and common idiomatic expressions.
3. Grammar: analyze more complicated sentences and understand the sentence's meaning; increase understanding of grammar and study several new grammatical points.
4. Text material: ask and answer questions about the text content; retell the story in oral or written form; with the aid of a dictionary independently read materials of the same level of difficulty as text, with basically no mistakes in understanding.
5. Take dictation from material simpler than the text; use English to converse with teacher during class activities.
6. Create sentences and narrate simple events and tell stories, within the boundaries of what has been studied.

II. Teaching Content

1. Vocabulary: approximately 550 words and a definite number of common idiomatic expressions.
2. Grammar:
   a. Object subordinate clause (continued).
   b. Infinitives (continued).
   c. Participles.
   d. Gerunds.
   e. Articles (continued).
   f. Modal verbs (continued).
   g. Subject clauses, predicative clauses, appositive clauses.

Senior Secondary School Grade 2
5 class hours × 32 (weeks) = 160 class hours

I. Teaching

Requirements

1. Pronunciation: same as Senior 1.
2. Grammar: same as Senior 1.
3. Vocabulary: spell, define, and label part of speech of studied vocabulary items; the most common vocabulary items (approximately 60 percent) available for active use in oral and written forms; study and memorize vocabulary items, increase ability in using idiomatic expressions.
4. Read aloud text material according to meaning and pronunciation; use text content to ask coherently and answer questions in written and oral forms; retell text and translate part of text into Chinese in oral and written forms.
5. Use dictionary to read materials of the same level of difficulty as text and translate a paragraph of the material into Chinese with no mistakes; gradually enlarge boundaries of reading material and increase reading speed.
6. Engage in simple conversation and tell stories within the bounds of familiar linguistic knowledge; write short essays and letters about topics that are familiar, with coherent meaning, correct spelling, grammar, word usage, punctuation, and style.

II. Teaching Content

1. Vocabulary: approximately 550 words and a definite number of common idiomatic expressions.
2. Grammar:
   a. Subjunctive mood.
   b. Absolute construction.
   d. The use of anticipatory *it*.
   e. Inverted word order.
   f. Elliptical sentences.

Senior Secondary School Grade 3
Humanities: 5 class hours × 28 (weeks) = 140 class hours
Science: 4 class hours × 28 (weeks) = 112 class hours
Elective: 4 class hours × 28 (weeks) = 112 class hours

I. Teaching

Requirements

In this year all requirements of the teaching outline should be achieved.

II. Teaching Content

1. Vocabulary: approximately 500 words and a definite number of common idiomatic expressions.
2. Grammar: new grammatical phenomena in text supplementary material.

In the senior texts selections from simple original English materials or other languages translated into English make up over 80 percent of all material. Selections include political, economic, social, cultural, historical, geographical, and popular science essays. Forms include narrative tales, short stories or excerpts from short stories, short plays, poems, biographies, short technical items, and descriptive and critical articles.

Appendix D
English-Language
Lessons Published
in China

"An English Class"[1]

LI: Stand up, please.
TEACHER: Good morning, boys and girls.
STUDENTS: Good morning, teacher!
TEACHER: Sit down, please. Are all the students here today, Li Ping?
LI: Yes.
TEACHER: Oh, Wei Fang. How are you today?
WEI: I'm all right, thank you.
TEACHER: That's good. Wang Lin, what day is today?
WANG: Today is Monday.
TEACHER: How many days are there in this month?
WANG: There are 31.
TEACHER: That's right. Come to the blackboard, Liu Ying. Write *Monday* and *month* on it, please.
TEACHER: Good. Now, go back to your seat. Boys and girls, open your books and turn to page 89. Let's read Lesson 18.

"An Old Scientist Speaks"[2]

I was born in 1912. A poor boy like me couldn't go to school. When I was your age I already had to work. The work was hard and the food was bad. After work I taught myself to read and write. But things are different now. Most children can go to school. You have fine schools and very good teachers.

Boys and girls, when you grow up, you're going to help build up our country. What must you do now if you want to do that job well?

You must work hard at your lessons. You must learn to write good Chinese.

1 [Junior Secondary School] *English,* vol. 1, lesson 19.
2 [Junior Secondary School] *English,* vol. 3, lesson 4.

Maths and physics are very important. If you do well in them, you can learn other sciences well.

You must be good at a foreign language. A good scientist must learn from the scientists of other countries.

You're all growing fast. Have plenty of exercise every day, children, and make yourselves strong. I needn't tell you that good health is a must for builders of socialism.

Above everything else, study Marxism. It's an important guide to the study of science.

"A Black Girl Speaks Her Mind"[3]

I've always been proud of being black. I think black is beautiful. Some girls ask me, "Don't you wish you were white?" I ask them, "What's wrong with being black?" One girl said, "A black girl can't be equal to a white girl, since white is clean and black is dirty." I asked her, "How can you wear your beautiful clothes? They must be very dirty, since black hands down in the south grew the cotton, and black hands in Harlem made the clothes."

Nobody in my family has been able to get a job since Dad lost his years ago. If Mum picks up an odd job, they stop our welfare money. Must we refuse to work so that we could live on welfare? Something must be wrong with this country.

They tell us blacks and whites are equal now. Last time my brother asked for a job. They said, "Sorry, why weren't you here earlier?" But a white boy came after him and got the job. This kind of thing makes you angry.

Mum and Dad can hardly write their names. They can't fight for their rights. They get bullied and cheated everywhere. That's why I'm working hard at my lessons. Nobody will dare to cheat me. I'll fight.

"Driver Lao Li"
[Senior Secondary School] *English*, vol. 1, lesson 19.

Lao Li, our senior hospital driver died yesterday. Today at the back of the hospital, in the open air, we held a memorial meeting, at which the hospital director, a young driver and Lao Li's second son made speeches. They told of his past, of his devotion to duty, of his revolutionary optimism in the face of fatal illness. They spoke of his fine qualities as a worker of New China.

3 [Junior Secondary School] *English*, vol. 4, lesson 23.

Appendix D

Lao Li came from a poor peasant family. He had hardly any schooling. Before liberation he was a cart-driver who could barely keep body and soul together, let alone support his family. So he came to Beijing to try to find work. He became an apprentice truck driver, living a life of grinding poverty. It was liberation that brought about a complete change in his life, and his gratitude and devotion to the party was boundless.

Lao Li had been a good friend of mine. He had driven me to and from work for many years and we always had much to say to each other. His attitude to me was that of a comrade. He had five children and never tired of telling me about them. All were at school and he was proud of them and loved them dearly. I once asked him if he had any difficulty in keeping five children in school. He said he had no difficulty at all, and he had never been so well off in his life.

A few years ago, while Lao Li was out with the hospital truck collecting supplies from a town several hundred miles away, North China was hit by an unexpected heavy rain that caused severe flooding. We were not surprised that he returned three days later than expected. He just said that the roads were flooded and some bridges had been washed away. We would have thought nothing more about it if we had not received a letter from a people's commune asking for the name of our driver.

As Lao Li was driving through the rain, the roof of a roadside granary fell in. The harvest had just been gathered and the food for hundreds of families was in danger. Without hesitation Lao Li stopped his truck and helped to carry the sacks of grain to safety. When all the grain had been removed, he set about helping homeless women and children to places of safety. For twenty-four hours he worked without food or rest and then without saying a word to anyone, went on with his journey back to Beijing. A villager had noted the number of the truck. The commune found out that it belonged to our hospital and now wished to write a letter of thanks to the driver.

That's the sort of man Lao Li was, unselfish, modest, always putting the interests of the people before his own.

Lao Li died of cancer. For months, it had been difficult for him to move about, but he insisted that he felt well enough for light work. He said he was fed up with resting at home and wanted to do something useful. So he was given a job in the inquiry office, where he set a good example to all by his deep concern for patients. Today we all felt that we had lost a comrade, a man we loved and respected, a man to learn from, a man whose death was weightier than Mount Tai.

Appendix E English-Language Lessons Published Abroad: New Concept English

"A Wet Night"[1]

Late in the afternoon, the boys put up their tent in the middle of a field. As soon as this was done, they cooked a meal over an open fire. They were all hungry and the food smelt good. After a wonderful meal, they told stories and sang songs by the camp fire. But some time later it began to rain. The boys felt tired so they put out the fire and crept into their tent. Their sleeping-bags were warm and comfortable, so they all slept soundly. In the middle of the night, two boys woke up and began shouting. The tent was full of water! They all leapt out of their sleeping-bags and hurried outside. It was raining heavily and they found that a stream had formed in the field. The stream wound its way across the field and then flowed right under their tent!

"By Air"[2]

I used to travel by air a great deal when I was a boy. My parents used to live in South America and I used to fly there from Europe in the holidays. An air-hostess would take charge of me and I never had an unpleasant experience. I am used to travelling by air and only on one occasion have I ever felt frightened. After taking off, we were flying low over the city and slowly gaining height, when the plane suddenly turned round and flew back to the airport. While we were waiting to land, an air-hostess told us to keep calm and to get off the plane quietly as soon as it had touched down. Everybody on board was worried and we were curious to find out what had happened. Later we learnt that there was a very important person on board. The police had been told that a bomb had been planted on the plane. After we had landed, the plane was searched thoroughly. Fortunately, nothing was found and five hours later we were able to take off again.

1 [Junior Secondary School] *Practice and Progress,* lesson 27.
2 [Junior Secondary School] *Practice and Progress,* lesson 79.

"Illusions of Pastoral Peace"[3]

The quiet life of the country has never appealed to me. City born and city bred, I have always regarded the country as something you look at through a train window, or something you occasionally visit during the week-end. Most of my friends live in the city, yet they always go into raptures at the mere mention of the country. Though they extol the virtues of the peaceful life, only one of them has ever gone to live in the country and he was back in town within six months. Even he still lives under the illusion that country life is somehow superior to town life. He is forever talking about the friendly people, the clean atmosphere, the closeness to nature and the gentle pace of living. Nothing can be compared, he maintains, with the first cock crow, the twittering of birds at dawn, the sight of the rising sun glinting on the trees and pastures. This idyllic pastoral scene is only part of the picture. My friend fails to mention the long and friendless winter evenings that are interrupted only by an occasional visit to the local cinema—virtually the only form of entertainment. He says nothing about the poor selection of goods in the shops, or about those unfortunate people who have to travel from the country to the city every day to get to work. Why people are prepared to tolerate a four hour journey each day for the dubious privilege of living in the country is beyond my ken. They could be saved so much misery and expense if they chose to live in the city where they rightly belong.

If you can do without the few pastoral pleasures of the country, you will find the city can provide you with the best that life can offer. You never have to travel miles to see your friends. They invariably live nearby and are always available for an informal chat or an evening's entertainment. Some of my acquaintances in the country come up to town once or twice a year to visit the theater as a special treat. For them this is a major operation that involves considerable planning. As the play draws to a close, they wonder whether they will ever catch that last train home. The city dweller never experiences anxieties of this sort. The latest exhibitions, films, or plays are only a short bus ride away. Shopping, too, is always a pleasure. There is so much variety that you never have to make do with second best. Country people run wild when they go shopping in the city and stagger home loaded with as many of the necessities of life as they can carry. Nor is the city without its moments of beauty. There is something comforting about the warm glow shed by

3 [Junior Secondary School] *Developing Skills*, lesson 41.

advertisements on cold wet winter deserted city streets at week-ends when the thousands that travel to work every day are tucked away in their homes in the country. It has always been a mystery to me why city dwellers, who appreciate all these things, obstinately pretend that they would prefer to live in the country.

Appendix F
1982 National College
Entrance
Examination:
English-Language
Questions

Name:

I. Vocabulary: Supply the English equivalent for each of the following groups of words. (total score 12 points, each item 3 points)

1. *January, February, March, April, May, June*
2. *Monday, Tuesday, Wednesday, Thursday, Friday, Saturday*
3. *military officer, police officer, professor, businessman, lawyer, nurse*
4. *village, hotel, garden, prison, classroom, supermarket*

II. Pronunciation: In each of the following groups of words, one word's vowel sound is pronounced differently. Underline the word with the different sound. (total score 8 points, each item 1 point)

example: be me wet need see

1. beat meat break heat freeze
2. have gave wave save slave
3. raise sail said lay tail
4. turn burnt hurt bury first
5. tooth food stool moon cook
6. box boss cost most lost
7. round bought house south mouth
8. hear dear bear near fear

III. Sentence Pattern Transformation: (total score 12 points, each item 2 points)

Change the following into the negative:

1. Peter does morning exercises every day.
2. Write it down in your notebook.

Change the following into indirect speech:

3. "Is it still raining?" the blind man asked.

4. "You will be hanged as a spy tomorrow at sunrise," the British general said to Nathan Hale.

Change the following into the passive voice:

5. They made the Negro slaves work long hours in the cotton fields.

6. If they grow rice instead of wheat on their farm, they will increase production.

IV. Multiple Choice: Choose the correct answer A, B, C, or D. No correction of the original sentence is necessary.

Example: (B) She _____ from the south.

    (A) are (B) is (C) am (D) be

1. My uncle lives _____ 105 Beijing Street.

    (A) on (B) at (C) to (D) of

2. "Whose room is that?" "It's _____."

    (A) my (B) ours (C) my brothers (D) of my brother

3. _____ he said he wasn't hungry, he ate the big breakfast.

    (A) Even (B) Unless (C) In spite (D) Although

4. He slept well _____ all the windows open.

    (A) when (B) while (C) with (D) because

5. If these trousers are too big, buy a smaller _____.

    (A) set (B) one (C) copy (D) pair

6. Some new oil fields _____ since 1976.

    (A) were opened up (B) has opened up (C) have been opened up (D) had been opened up

7. I didn't feel _____ going out for a walk.

    (A) so (B) as (C) rather (D) like

8. "Have you heard the news about Tom?" "No. What _____?"

    (A) is it (B) it is (C) are they (D) they are

9. We are going to learn _____ next week.

    (A) Lesson Twelve (B) Lesson Twelfth (C) Twelfth Lesson (D) the Lesson Twelfth

10. "Do you have a big library?" "No, we don't—at least, not _____ yours."

    (A) bigger as (B) as big as (C) as big than (D) as bigger than

11. _____ of them understood the old foreigner.

    (A) Someone (B) Anyone (C) None (D) Nobody

12. When my sister phoned me, I could not hear clearly what she was ___.

    (A) speaking (B) talking (C) saying (D) telling

13. That boy works hard. I _____ him to succeed in the exam.

    (A) like (B) expect (C) think (D) need

14. I _____ play football than baseball.
   (A) would rather (B) had better (C) like better (D) prefer
15. Helen doesn't like milk and _____.
   (A) so I don't (B) so don't I (C) either I do (D) neither do I
16. Would you mind _____ your radio a little, please?
   (A) turn off (B) turning off (C) to turn down (D) turning down
17. I don't think you can finish the work _____ my help.
   (A) since (B) because (C) without (D) unless
18. When you come to Wuhan, I can put you _____ for the night.
   (A) up (B) down (C) in (D) out
19. It will _____ you good to have some outdoor exercise.
   (A) make (B) do (C) be (D) feel
20. Would you be _____ to step this way, please?
   (A) too kind (B) so kind (C) so kind as (D) as kind as

V. Verb Tense: According to the meaning and structure of the following passage, select verbs from the list provided and fill in the blanks. Each verb can be used only once, and must be used with appropriate tense and voice. (total score 12 points, each blank 1 point)

ask, be, beat, carry, come, do, find, go, let, need, put, speak, take, tell

   After I finished school, I began to look for work. Now several months later, I _____ (not) the kind of work I was interested in yet.

   One morning I received a phone call. "_____ that Jenny Smith?" a man asked. I _____ you're looking for a job." I agreed. Then he _____ on. "I hear that you _____ well in your studies and that you were active in sports. Well, I might have a job for you. If you're interested, _____ over to my office. I'm Tim Brown of the All-Star Clothing Factory."

   I went to see Mr. Brown that afternoon. While _____ me questions, he looked at me, up and down, carefully. At last he said, "OK, I'll _____ you have the job." My heart started _____ faster. Would he _____ me on as a laboratory assistant? I wanted to become a scientist or an engineer some day. When he _____ again, I couldn't believe my ears. What he _____ was not a future scientist, but a model!

VI. Sentence Completion: Use English to complete the following sentences according to the Chinese meaning. No correction of the original sentence is necessary. (total score 18 each item 3)

1. Do you know the names of the two _____ (American astronauts [*meiguo*

yuhang yuan]) who _____ (most recently landed on the moon [zui xian dengshang yueqiu])?

2. I _____ (happened not to be at home [pengqiao mei zai jia]) when the _____ (fire started [shihuo de shihou]).

3. The old peasant suggested that a _____ (reservoir be built at the foot of this ([zai jei zuo shan jiao xia xiu zuo shuiku]).

4. There is _____ (a broken refrigerator [dianbingxiang huaile]). I must have _____ (it fixed [ba ta xiu hao]).

5. It _____ (was reported in yesterday's paper that [zuotian de baozhi baodao]) a Chinese woman doctor had come home from the United States soon after _____ (she had made a new discovery in a theoretical aspect of medicine [ta zai yixue lilun fangmian youle xin faxian]).

6. We _____ (were happy to hear that [gaoxing de ting dao]) all the school teachers in our country would _____ (soon get a raise [jiang yao tigao gongzi]).

VII. *Reading Comprehension: Read the following passage and answer the questions. (total score 18 points, each item 2 points)*
"How Can a Small Stamp Be Worth $16,800?"

Any mistake made in the printing of a stamp raises its value (*jiezh*) to stamp collectors. A mistake on a two-penny (*bianshi, yingguo fubi*) stamp has made it worth a million and a half times its face value.

Do you think it impossible? Well, it is true. And this is how it happened.

The mistake was made more than a hundred years ago in the former British colony (*zhimindi*) of Mauritius, a small island in the Indian Ocean. In 1847 an order (*dinghuodan*) for stamps was sent to London. Mauritius was about to become the fourth country in the world to put out stamps.

Before the order was filled and the stamps arrived from England, a big dance was planned by the Commander-in-chief of all the armed forces on the island. The dance would be held in his house and letters of invitation would be sent to all the important people in Mauritius. Stamps were badly needed to post the letters. Therefore, an islander, who was a good printer, was told to copy the pattern of the stamps. He carelessly put the words "Post Office" instead of "Post Paid", two words seen on stamps at the time, on the several hundred that he printed.

Today, there are only twenty-six of these misprinted stamps left—fourteen One-penny Reds and twelve Two-penny Blues. Because there are so few Two-penny Blues and because of their age, collectors have paid as much as $16,800 for one of them.

Choose the correct answer A, B, C, or D. No correction of the original sentence is necessary.

1. When a mistake is made in the printing of a stamp, the stamp
    (A) will be thrown away.
    (B) increases in value.
    (C) is not worth buying.
    (D) is worth no more that its face value.
2. The mistake on a two-penny stamp has made
    (A) a lot of trouble for the post office.
    (B) Mauritius the fourth country to put out stamps.
    (C) it worth half a million times its face value.
    (D) it worth as much as sixteen thousand and eight hundred dollars.
3. Mauritius is the name of
    (A) an Indian island.
    (B) a province of India.
    (C) a stamp.
    (D) a former colony of Great Britain.
4. When was the mistake in printing made? It was made
    (A) not long ago.
    (B) in the eighteenth century.
    (C) in the nineteenth century.
    (D) after some stamps arrived from London.
5. In 1847 most countries of the world were
    (A) not yet using stamps.
    (B) printing stamps in Mauritius.
    (C) printing their own stamps.
    (D) collecting valuable stamps.
6. Why did Mauritius print some stamps too?
    (A) London stamps were not well printed.
    (B) London would not print them.
    (C) Invitations to a big dance had to be posted quickly.
    (D) Mauritius had a very good printer.
7. The mistake on the island-printed stamps was in the
    (A) price.
    (B) color.
    (C) spelling of words.
    (D) wrong use of words.
8. "Post Paid" means
    (A) the same as "Post Office."

Barber, Elinor G., Philip G., Altbach, and Robert G. Myers, eds. 1984. *Bridges to Knowledge: Foreign Students in Comparative Perspective.* Chicago: University of Chicago Press.

Barendsen, R., ed. 1979. *The 1978 National College Entrance Examination in the PRC.* Washington, D.C.: U.S. Department of Health, Education, and Welfare.

Barlow, Tani, and Donald M. Lowe. 1987. *Teaching China's Lost Generation.* San Francisco: China Books and Periodicals.

Barnett, A. Doak. 1981. *China's Economy in Global Perspective.* Washington, D.C.: Brookings Institution.

Barnett, Suzanne, and John K. Fairbank, eds. 1985. *Christianity in China: Early Protestant Missionary Writings.* Cambridge, Mass.: Harvard University Press.

Basford, J. W. 1904. "The Rivalry of Government Schools." *Recorder,* p. 484.

Bastid, Marianne. 1987. "Servitude or Liberation? The Introduction of Foreign Educational Practices and Systems to China from 1840 to the Present." In Ruth Hayhoe and Marianne Bastid, eds., *China's Education and the Industrialized World: Studies in Cultural Transfer,* 3–20. Armonk, N.Y.: Sharpe.

Becker, C. W., et al. 1932. *The Reorganization of Education in China.* Paris: League of Nations.

Beijing shifan daxue xuebao (Beijing Normal University Journal).

Bellah, Robert, et al. 1985. *Habits of the Heart: Individualism and Commitment in American Life.* New York: Harper and Row.

———. 1991. *The Good Society.* New York: Knopf.

Benhabib, Seyla. 1987. "The Generalized and the Concrete Other." In Seyla Benhabib and Drucilla Cornell, eds., *Feminism as Critique,* 77–95. Minneapolis: University of Minnesota Press.

Bennett, Adrian. 1983. *Missionary Journalist in China: Young J. Allen and His Magazines, 1860–1883.* Athens, Ga.: University of Georgia Press.

Bennett, Adrian, and John Fryer. 1967. *The Introduction of Western Science and Technology in Nineteenth Century China.* Cambridge, Mass.: East Asian Research Center, Harvard University.

Bennett, Adrian, and Ching-Liu Kwang. 1974. "Christianity in the Chinese Idiom: Young J. Allen and the Early Chiao hui hsin pao." In J. K. Fairbank, ed., *The Missionary Enterprise in China and America.* Cambridge, Mass.: Harvard University Press.

Biggerstaff, Knight. 1965. *The Earliest Modern Government Schools in China.* Ithaca: Cornell University Press.

———. 1975. *Some Early Chinese Steps Toward Modernization.* San Francisco: Chinese Materials Center.

Bloom, Alfred. 1981. *The Linguistic Shaping of Thought: A Study in the Impact of Language on Thinking in China and the West.* Hillsdale, N.J.: Lawrence Erlbaum Associates.

Borthwick, Sally. 1983. *Education and Social Change in China*. Stanford: Hoover Institution Press.

Boyer, Ernest. 1983. *High School*. New York: Harper and Row.

Brown, Herbert O. 1982. "Politics: The Peking Spring of Educational Studies in China." *Comparative Education Review* 26:329–47.

———. 1986. "Primary Schooling and the Rural Responsibility System." *Comparative Education Review* 30:373–87.

Burns, John, and Stanley Rosen. 1986. *Policy Conflicts in Post-Mao China: A Documentary Survey with Analysis*. Armonk, N.Y.: Sharpe.

Campus Life: A Special Report by the Carnegie Foundation for the Advancement of Teaching. 1990. Princeton, N.J.: Carnegie Foundation.

Cang Gong and Cheng Yunti, eds. 1988. *Qingshaonian ziwo baohu* (The Self-Protection of Youth). Shanghai Translation Press.

"Caring for Middle Aged Intellectuals." 1982. *Beijing Review* 25, no. 33 (16 August): 5.

Carnoy, Martin. 1989. "Education, State, and Culture in American Society." In H. Giroux and P. McLaren, eds., *Critical Pedagogy, the State, and Cultural Struggle*. Albany: State University of New York Press.

Chan, Anita. 1985. *Children of Mao*. Seattle: University of Washington Press.

Chang Jian. 1983. "Putong zhongdeng xuexiao de gaige" (Reform of Regular Middle Schools). *JYYJ*, no. 6:11.

Chen Dongyuan. 1936. *Zhongguo jiaoyu shi* (China's Educational History). Shanghai: Shanghai Commercial Press.

Chen Guanbai. 1986. "Heisi de qiyue" (Black July). In *Baogao wenxue xuan* (A Selection of Reportage Literature), 418–47. Beijing: Peoples Literature Press.

Chen Hao. 1982. "Dui gaijin gaokao gongzu de yixie kanfa" (Some Thoughts on Improving the Entrance Examination). *RMJY*, no. 9:44–45.

Chen Hao and Zhou Xinying. 1982. "1982 nian gaokao mingti ceji" (Sidelights on the Setting of 1982 Entrance Examination Questions). *RMJY*, no. 8:36–46.

Chen Pu. 1982. "Tansuo buting" (Never Stop Experimenting). *SHJY*, no. 7–8:79–80.

Chen Qing. 1961. *Jindai zhongguo jiaoyushi ziliao* (A Collection of Materials on Contemporary Chinese Educational History). Beijing: Peoples Education Press.

Chen Shaomin, and Gong Zhiji. 1990. "Zhongxue yingyu jiaoxue ruhe shentou deyu" (Infusing Ideological Training in Secondary School English Teaching). *SHJY*, no. 7–8:25–26.

Chen, Theodore Hsi-en. 1981. *Chinese Education Since 1949: Academic and Revolutionary Models*. New York: Pergamon Press.

Chen Xilin. 1982. "Zhengdun jichu, zhuyi tingshuo, jiaqiang yuedu" (Consolidate the Basics, Emphasize Listening and Speaking and Strengthen Reading). *SHJY*, 7–8:66.

Chen Yi. 1962. "An Earnest, Well-Meaning Talk on the Study of Foreign Languages." *SCMP*, no. 2713:1–6.

Cheng Youxin, and Li Kejia. 1984. "Intellectuals: Their Class, Status, and Social Role." *Social Sciences in China*, no. 5:27–54.

The Chinese Recorder and Missionary Journal [Recorder].

The Chinese Repository [Repository].

Chow, Tse-tsung. 1960. *The May Fourth Movement.* Stanford: Stanford University Press.

Christian Education in China. 1922. New York: Commission of Reference and Counsel of the Foreign Missions Confederation of North America.

Chuang Chai-Hsuan. 1922. *Tendencies Toward a Democratic System of Education in China.* Shanghai: Commercial Press.

"Circular on Several Problems Involving Elementary and Secondary Education at Present." 1984. *Chinese Education* 17, no. 2:100–102.

"Clearing Cultural Contamination." 1983. *Beijing Review* 26, no. 45 (7 November): 13–14.

Clifford, James. 1988. *The Predicament of Culture: Twentieth Century Ethnography, Literature, and Art.* Cambridge, Mass.: Harvard University Press.

Clifford, James, and George Marcus. 1986. *Writing Culture: The Poetics and Politics of Ethnography.* Berkeley and Los Angeles: University of California Press.

Cohen, Paul. 1963. *China and Christianity: The Missionary Movement and the Growth of Chinese Anti-Foreignism, 1860–1870.* Cambridge, Mass.: Harvard University Press.

———. 1974. "Littoral and Hinterland in Nineteenth Century China: The Christian Reformers." In J. K. Fairbank, ed., *The Missionary Enterprise in China and the United States*, 197–211. Cambridge, Mass.: Harvard University Press.

Coleman, James S., Thomas Hoffer, and Sally Kilgore. 1982. *High School Achievement.* New York: Basic Books.

Collins, Randall. 1975. *Conflict Sociology: Toward an Explanatory Science.* New York: Academic Press.

"Cong Yucai de jiaoxue kan ketang jiaoxue jiegou gaige" (Yucai Middle School's Reform of the Structure of Classroom Teaching). 1993. *JYYJ*, no. 5:70–71.

Cookson, Peter W., and Caroline Hodges Persell. 1985. *Preparing for Power: America's Elite Boarding Schools.* New York: Basic Books.

Coordinated Fact-finding Group in Beijing Area. 1982. "Zhongxuesheng lixiang, dongji he xingchu de diaocha" (An Investigation of the Ideals, Motivations, and Interests of Middle School Students). *Beijing shifan daxue xuebao*, no. 1:7–13.

Covell, Ralph. 1978. *W. A. P. Martin, Pioneer of Progress in China.* Washington, D.C.: Christian University Press.

Cowan, J. Ronayne, R. Light, B. E. Matthews, and G. R. Tucker. 1979. "English Teaching in China: A Recent Survey." *TESOL Quarterly* 13:465–82.

Cuban, Larry. 1984. *How Teachers Taught: Constancy and Change in American Classrooms, 1890–1980.* New York: Longman.

Cumming, Alister. 1987. "Evaluations and Development of Foreign Language Teaching in China." *Canadian and International Education* 16:211–20.

Daily Report, China. Washington, D.C.: U.S. Foreign Broadcast Information Service.

Deng Xiaoping. 1983. "Respect Knowledge, Respect Talent." *Daily Report, China,* 8 July:K12–K13.

Dewoskin, Kenneth J. 1990–91. "Rhetorical Authority and Coercion in Chinese Statecraft." In *Rackham Reports.* Ann Arbor: University of Michigan.

Duggan, Stephen. 1933. *A Critique of the Report of the League of Nation's Mission of Educational Experts in China.* New York: Institute of International Education.

"Dui Waiguoyu xuexiao de you guanxi guiding" (Regulations Concerning Foreign Language Schools). 1984. In *Almanac,* 171–72. Shanghai: China Encyclopedia Publishing House.

"Dusheng zinu de zaoqi jiaoyu wenti" (Problems in the Early Education of Single Children). 1981. *JYYJ,* no. 6:37.

Duus, Peter. 1956. "Science and Salvation in China: W. A. P. Martin." Cambridge, Mass.: East Asian Research Center, Harvard University.

East China Normal University Secondary Education Structural Reform Research Group. 1981. "Shanghaishi de zhongdeng jiaoyu jiegou gaige yanjiu" (A Study of the Structural Reform of Secondary Education in Shanghai). *JYYJ* 8:25–34.

Educational Association of China. 1893. *Records of the First Triennial Meeting of the Education Association of China.* Shanghai: American Presbyterian Mission Press.

Educational Revolution Group of Shanghai Foreign Language Institute. 1972. "Some Experiences in Compiling Foreign Language Teaching Materials." *SCMP,* no. 733–34:86–95.

Eisner, Elliot, and Alan Peshkin, eds. 1990. *Qualitative Inquiry in Education: The Continuing Debate.* New York: Teachers College Press.

English. 1979. Beijing: Peoples Education Publishing House.

English Teacher's Book I. 1979. Beijing: Commercial Press.

Epstein, Irving. 1982. "An Analysis of the Chinese National Examination: The Politics of Curricular Change." *Peabody Journal of Education* 4:180–89.

Epstein, Irving, and John Hawkins. 1984. "Reevaluating Chinese Education." *Comparative Education Review* 28:503–13.

Esherick, Joseph W., and Jeffrey N. Wasserstrom. 1990. "Acting out Democracy: Political Theater and Modern China." *Journal of Asian Studies* 49:835–65.

Etherton, Alan R. B. 1974. *Teaching English to Chinese-Speaking Learners: A First Bibliography of Research and Studies.* Hong Kong: Chinese University of Hong Kong.

Fairbank, John K., ed. 1974. *The Missionary Experience in China and America.* Cambridge, Mass.: Harvard University Press.

Fairbank, John K., et al. 1975. *The I.G. in Peking: Letters of Robert Hart: Chinese Maritime Customs, 1868–1907.* Vol. 1. Cambridge, Mass.: Belknap Press.

Fang Keli. 1985. "The Categories of Ti and Yong in Chinese Philosophy." *Social Sciences in China* 6:115–29.

Fei Xiaotong. 1983. "Chinese Intellectuals Today and in History." *China Reconstructs* 4:8–11.

Fenn, William Purviance. 1976. *Christian Higher Education in Changing China 1880–1950.* Grand Rapids, Mich.: Eerdmans.

Fine, Michelle. *Framing Dropouts.* 1991. Albany: State University of New York Press.

Foreign Language Teaching Investigation Group of the Shanghai Municipal Education Bureau. 1972. "Elevate Understanding, Strengthen Leadership and Teach Foreign Languages Well." *SCMP,* no. 5111:95–99.

Foreign Language Teaching Investigation Group of the Shanghai Municipal Education Bureau. 1972. "Combine Foreign Language Teaching with Socialist Practice." *SCMP,* no. 5123:55–58.

Fox, Richard, ed. 1991. *Recapturing Anthropology: Working in the Present.* Santa Fe: School of American Research Press.

Fryer, John, and John C. Ferguson. 1893. "Educational Department Notes and Items." *Recorder* 24, no. 2:577–78.

Fu Ke. 1983. "Huigu zongjie, diaocha yanjiu, lizu gaige—guanyu woguo waiyu jiaoyu gaige de jidian shexiang" (Thoughts on China's Foreign Language Education Reforms). *Waiguoyu,* no. 5:1–6.

———. 1986. *Zhongguo waiyu jiaoyu shi* (History of China's Foreign Language Education). Shanghai: Shanghai Foreign Language Education Press.

Gao Naixin. 1983. "Xuexi waiyu de danwei shi juzi" (Foreign Languages Should be Studied at the Sentence Level). *RMJY,* no. 4:49.

Gao Yuan. 1981. "Guanyu gaozhong jieduan ban wenkeban de wenti" (The Problem of Conducting Liberal Arts Classes in Senior High Schools). *JYYJ,* no. 8:42–43.

———. 1984. "Six Measures to Ensure the Success of Key Middle Schools." *Chinese Education* 17, no. 2:57–60.

Gardner, Howard. 1989. *To Open Minds: Chinese Clues to the Dilemma of Contemporary Education.* New York: Basic Books.

Gasster, Michael. 1983. *China's Struggle to Modernize.* New York: Knopf.

Ge Qichao. 1982. "Genju nusheng xinli tedian zuzhi gaozhong wuli jiaoxue" (Organize the Teaching of Senior Middle School Physics According to the Special Psychological Characteristics of Girls). *SHJY*, no. 7–8:60.

Geertz, Clifford. 1983. *Local Knowledge: Further Essays in Interpretive Anthropology*. New York: Basic Books.

———. November 8, 1985. "The Uses of Diversity." The Tanner Lecture on Human Values presented at the University of Michigan, Ann Arbor.

Giroux, Henry A., and Peter McLaren, eds. 1989. *Critical Pedagogy, the State, and Cultural Struggle*. Albany: State University of New York Press.

Goldman, Merle. 1981. *China's Intellectuals: Advise and Dissent*. Cambridge, Mass.: Harvard University Press.

Goodlad, John. 1981. *A Place Called School*. New York: McGraw-Hill.

Grams, Nancy. 1969. "The Banner School Background of the Canton Tung Wen Kuan." *Papers on China*, no. 22. Cambridge, Mass.: Harvard University Press.

Grant, Gerald. 1988. *The World We Created at Hamilton High*. Cambridge, Mass.: Harvard University Press.

Graves, Rev. Bishop. 1893. "The Moral Influence of Christian Education in China." *Recorder* 24:323–31.

"A Great Debate on the Educational Front." 1977. *Peking Review*, 16 December:4–9.

Gregg, Alice H. 1946. *China and Educational Autonomy: The Changing Role of the Protestant Educational Missionary in China, 1807–1937*. Syracuse: Syracuse University Press.

Gu Maosheng. 1983. "Due xuexi chengji you, cha sheng de xinli fenxi" (Psychological Analysis of Excellent and Poor Students). *JYYJ*, no. 12:65.

Gu Mingyuan. 1982. "Lun zhongdeng jiaoyu de renwu he jiegou" (On the Purpose and Structure of Secondary School Education). *Beijing shifan daxue xuebao*, no. 5:1–11.

Gu Weiguo. 1989. "Qiantan zai chuzhong yingyu jiaoxue zhong ru he kefu xuesheng de nifan xinli" ("A Few Words on How to Counter Defiance in Junior Secondary School English"). *Zhong xiaoxue waiyu jiaoxue*, no. 2:5–6.

Guangming ribao [GMRB]. (Guangming Daily).

"Guanyu beijing waiguoyu xueyuan zhuanye shezhi jihua de baogao" (Report Concerning Plans for Establishing Specializations at Beijing Foreign Language Institute). 1983. In *Chronology*, p. 305. Beijing: Educational Studies Press.

"Guanyu chuanguo ewen zhuanke xuexiao di jueding" (Decision Concerning National Russian Specialized Schools). 1983. In *Chronology*, p. 48. Beijing: Educational Studies Press.

"Guanyu chuzhong bushe waiguoyu de shuoming de tongzhi" (An Explanation Concerning Not Establishing Foreign Language Classes in Junior Middle School). 1983. In *Chronology*, p. 102. Beijing: Educational Studies Press.

"Guanyu cong gaozhong yi nianji qishi de yingyu keben" (Concerning Beginning

English Texts for Senior Middle School Students). 1983. *RMJY*, no. 11:42–43.

"Guanyu dangqian waiguoyu xuexiao ji xiang gongzuo de yijian" (Some Opinions Concerning the Work of Foreign Language Schools). 1983. In *Chronology*, 357–58. Beijing: Educational Studies Press.

"Guanyu dangqian zhong xiaoxue jiaoyu jige wenti di tongzhi" (Concerning Several Problems of Elementary and Middle School Education). 1982. *RMJY*, no. 8:33.

"Guanyu fenpi fenqi banhao zhongdian zhongxue de jueding" (Decision to Successfully Run Key Middle Schools in Stages). 1983. In *Chronology*, p. 594. Beijing: Educational Studies Press.

"Guanyu jiaqiang zhongxue waiyu jiaoyu de yijian (wenjian zhaibian)" (Suggestions for Strengthening Secondary Foreign Language Instruction [draft excerpts]). 1982. *RMJY*, no. 10:48.

"Guanyu waiguoyu xuexiao chengding he tisheng jiaoshi zhiwu mingcheng de tongzhi" (Circular Concerning Determination of Job Title and Promotion of Teachers at Foreign Language Schools). 1984. In *Almanac*, p. 745. Shanghai: China Encyclopedia Publishing House.

"Guanyu waiyu jiaoyu qinian guize wenti de baogao" (Report Concerning the Problems of the Seven-Year Foreign Language Education Program). 1983. In *Chronology*, p. 355. Beijing: Educational Studies Press.

"Guanyu zai zhongxue jiaqiang he kaishe waiguoyu de tongzhi" (An Explanation Concerning Strengthening and Establishing Foreign Language Teaching in Middle Schools). 1983. In *Chronology*, p. 242. Beijing: Educational Studies Press.

"Guanyu zhongxue jige xueke jiaoxue yaoqiu de tongzhi" (Announcement Concerning Several Teaching Requirements). 1982. *RMJY*, no. 10:36–37.

"Guanyu zhuanfa shanghai putuoqu, xiangming zhongxue quanmian guanche jiaoyu fangzhen, jianqing xuesheng guozhong fudan di jingyan cailiao di tongzhi" (Announcement Concerning Transmitting Shanghai Putuo District Xiangming Middle School Experiences in Fully Implementing the Educational Policy of Reducing Student Work Load). 1982. *RMJY*, no. 4:9–10.

Gui Shichun. 1984. "Woguo ying yong yuyanxue yanjiu de guangkuo qianjing" (Applied Linguistics Research in China—a Perspective). *Waiguoyu*, no. 4:1–6.

Hampel, Robert L. 1986. *The Last Little Citadel: American High Schools Since 1940*. Boston: Houghton and Mifflin.

Hamrin, Carol Lee, and Timothy Creek, eds. 1986. *China's Establishment Intellectuals*. Armonk, N.Y.: Sharpe.

Hawkins, John N. 1983. *Education and Social Change in the PRC*. New York: Praeger.

Hawks, F. L. 1894. "A Plea for Reform in the Conduct of Dayschools." *Recorder* 25, no. 8:392.

Hayhoe, Ruth, ed. 1984. *Contemporary Chinese Education*. Armonk, N.Y.: Sharpe.

———. 1986. "Penetration or Mutuality? China's Educational Cooperation with Europe, Japan, and North America." *Comparative Education Review* 30, no. 4:532–59.

———. 1988. "Shanghai as a Mediator of the Educational Open Door." *Pacific Affairs* 61, no. 2:253–84.

———. 1989a. *China's Universities and the Open Door*. Armonk, N.Y.: Sharpe.

———. 1989b. "A Chinese Puzzle." *Comparative Education Review* 33:155–75.

Hayhoe, Ruth, and Marianne Bastid, eds. 1987. *China's Education and the Industrialized World: Studies in Cultural Transfer*. Armonk, N.Y.: Sharpe.

He Wenming. 1983. "Ruhe tigao xuesheng de yingyu tingshuo nengli" (How to Improve Student Speaking and Listening Abilities in English). *RMJY*, no. 11:35.

Henderson, Gail E., and Myron S. Cohen. 1984. *The Chinese Hospital: A Socialist Work Unit*. New Haven: Yale University Press.

Henze, Jurgen. 1984. "Higher Education: The Tension between Quality and Equality." In Ruth Hayhoe, ed., *Contemporary Chinese Education*, 93–153. Armonk, N.Y.: Sharpe.

———. 1987. "Educational Modernization as a Search for Higher Efficiency." In Ruth Hayhoe and Marianne Bastid, eds., *China's Education and the Industrialized World: Studies in Cultural Transfer*. Armonk, N.Y.: Sharpe.

"Higher Education: Problems of a Revolution." 1971. *Current Scene* 9:16–17.

Hirsch, E. D. 1987. *Cultural Literacy: What Every American Needs to Know*. Boston: Houghton Mifflin.

Ho, Ping-ti. 1967. *The Ladder of Success in Imperial China: Aspects of Social Mobility, 1368–1911*. New York: Columbia University Press.

Honig, Emily, and Gail Hershatter. 1988. *Personal Voices: Chinese Women in the 1980s*. Stanford: Stanford University Press.

House, Herbert. 1916. "English in Education in China." *Recorder* 47, no. 2:98–103.

Hu Chang-tu. 1962. *Chinese Education under Communism*. New York: Columbia University Press.

———. 1984. "The Historical Background: Examinations and Control in Pre-Modern China." *Comparative Education* 20:7–25.

Hu Menghao. 1985. "Gaige jiaoyu tizhi peiyang xinxing waiyu rencai" (Reform the Educational System, Train More Competent Personnel—SFLI's History, Present Condition, and New Developments). *Waiguoyu*, no. 1:4–9.

Hu Shi-ming and Eli Seifman. 1976. *Toward a New World Outlook: A Docu-*

mentary History of Education in the People's Republic of China, 1949–1976. New York: AMS Press.

Hu Xiaofeng, 1989. "Tansuo guilu, ti gao yingyu jiaoxue zhiliang" ("Explore the Laws of Teaching and Improve English Teaching"). *Secondary and Primary School Foreign Language Teaching,* no. 1:13–14.

Huang Jianhua. 1983. "Woguo qing shaonian xuesheng de daode renshi yanjiu baogao" (A Report on the Moral Understanding of China's Students). *JYYJ,* no. 12:50–59.

Huang Zhiqiang. 1983. "Women shi zeyang gaohao chuzhong yingyu jiaoxue de" (How We Teach Junior Middle School English Well). *SHJY,* no. 7–8:62–63.

Hunter, Neale. 1969. *Shanghai Journal: An Eyewitness Account of the Cultural Revolution.* Boston: Beacon Press.

Husen, Torsten. 1979. *The School in Question.* Oxford: Oxford University Press.

———. 1986. *The Learning Society Revisited.* New York: Pergamon Press.

Huters, Theodore D. 1985. "Hu Feng and the Critical Legacy of Lu Xun." In Leo Ou-fan Lee, ed., *Lu Xun and His Legacy.* Berkeley and Los Angeles: University of California Press.

Jackson, J. 1892. "Objectives, Methods, and Results of Higher Education in Mission Schools." *Recorder* 23, no. 12:556–63.

Jiang Chunfang. 1985. "Shangwai de jieri" (Greetings to the SFLI: It's Festival Day). *Waiguoyu,* no. 1:1–3.

Jiang Nanxiang. 1979. " 'Sanhao' shi women dang jianding bu yi di fangzhen" ('Three Merits' Is Our Party's Unshakable Policy). *RMJY,* no. 6:33.

Jiaohui xinbao, Volume 1 (Church News). 1973. Taiwan: Huawen Publishing.

"Jiaoyubu banhao waiguoyu xuexiao de jidian yijian (zhailu), 1979" (Excerpts of Suggestions by the Ministry of Education for Running Foreign Language Schools Well, 1979). 1984. In *Almanac,* 742–43. Shanghai: China Encyclopedia Publishing House.

"Jiaoyubu guanyu banhao waiguoyu xuexiao de tongzhi (zhailu), 1963" (Excerpts of Ministry of Education Circular Concerning Running Foreign Language Schools Well, 1963). 1984. In *Almanac,* p. 737. Shanghai: China Encyclopedia Publishing House.

"Jiaoyubu guanyu waiguoyu xuexiao chengding he tisheng jiaoshi" (Ministry of Education Circular Concerning Determination of Job Title and Promotion of Teachers at Foreign Language Schools). 1984. In *Almanac,* p. 745. Shanghai: China Encyclopedia Publishing House.

Jiaoyu Yanjiu [JYYJ] (Education Research).

"Jiejue xuexiao waiwen shi zi de yijian" (Thoughts Concerning Solving the Shortage of Foreign Language Teachers). 1984. In *Almanac,* p. 305. Shanghai: China Encyclopedia Publishing House.

Jin Feng and Shen Hewei. 1989. "Xiaoxuesheng chuangzao shiyong yingyu de jihui" ("Create Opportunities for Primary School Pupils to Use English"). *Zhong xiaoxue waiyu jiaoxue* 1, no. 1:7–8.

King, Edmund. 1984. "Chinese Educational Development in Comparative Perspective." *Comparative Education* 20, no. 1:165–81.

Knight, Sophia. 1967. *Window on Shanghai: Letters from China, 1965–67.* London: Andrea Deutsch.

Kong Yun. 1980. "Zhong li qing wen sixiang yao bude" (Emphasizing Sciences and Neglecting Humanities Is Unacceptable). *RMJY*, no. 8:41.

Kraus, Richard. 1981. *Class Conflict in Chinese Socialism.* New York: Columbia University Press.

Kuo Ping Wen. 1915. *The Chinese System of Public Education.* New York: Columbia University Teachers College Press.

Kupfer, C. F. 1893. "Dangers and Advantages of Day-school Programs". *Recorder* 24, no. 3:108–10.

Kwong, Julia. 1979. *Chinese Education in Transition: Prelude to the Cultural Revolution.* Montreal: McGill-Queen's University Press.

———. 1985. "Changing Political Culture and Changing Curriculum." *Comparative Education* 21, no. 2:197–208.

Lamontagne, Jacques. 1988. "Educational Development in China: Characteristics and Trends." Paper presented at the Comparative and International Education Society annual conference, Atlanta, Georgia.

Lan Chengdong and Zhang Zongru. 1984. "Aspirations and Inclinations of This Year's Senior High School Graduates." *Chinese Sociology and Anthropology* 16, no. 1–2 (Fall–Winter, 1983–84): 159–69.

Lather, Patti. 1991. *Getting Smart: Feminist Research and Pedagogy within the Postmodern.* New York: Routledge.

Latourette, Kenneth Scott. 1929. *A History of Christian Missions in China.* New York: Russell and Russell.

League of Nations. 1932. *The Reorganization of Education in China.* Geneva: League of Nations.

"Learning English." 1959. *China News Agency*, no. 264:6–7.

Lee Hong Yung. 1978. *The Politics of the Chinese Cultural Revolution: A Case Study.* Berkeley and Los Angeles: University of California Press.

Legge, James, trans. 1966. *The Four Books: Confucian Analects, the Great Learning, the Doctrine of the Mean, and the Works of Mencius, with Original Chinese Text, English Translation and Notes.* New York: Paragon.

Lehmann, Winfred P., ed.. 1975. *Language and Linguistics in the PRC.* Austin: University of Texas Press.

Levenson, Joseph R. 1968. *Confucian China and Its Modern Fate: A Trilogy.* Berkeley and Los Angeles: University of California Press.

Li Daoping. 1990. "Industrial Entrepreneurship: A Way out of Chinese Education's Quandary." *Chinese Education* 23, no. 2:52–55.

Li Hanhou. 1986. *Zou wo ziji de lu* (Going My Way). Beijing: Peoples Press.

Li Shaojun. 1990. "The Wave of Individualism." *Chinese Education* 23, no. 2:94.

Li Weirong. 1982. "Guanyu jiaodao zhuren de gongzuo." In *Shanghaishi zhong xiaoxue jiaoyu gongzuo jingyan xuanbian, 1980–1981* (A Collection of Shanghai Primary and Secondary Educational Work Experiences), p. 138. Shanghai: Shanghai Education Publishers.

Liang Qichao. 1959. *Intellectual Trends in the Ch'ing Period.* Cambridge, Mass.: Harvard University Press.

Lightfoot, Sara Lawrence. 1978. *Worlds Apart, Relationships between Families and Schools.* New York: Basic Books.

———. 1983. *The Good High School Portraits of Character and Culture.* New York: Basic Books.

Liu, Adam Yuen-ching. 1981. *The Hanlin Academy: Training Ground for the Ambitious.* Hamden, Conn.: Archon Books.

Liu Baohong. 1985. "Wei gaoxiao tousong gengduo hao di rencai" (Affiliated School: More Outstanding Students Cultured). *Waiguoyu*, no. 1:23–25.

Liu Qing. 1990. "From I Do Not Believe to I Have Nothing: A Study Note on the Culture of the New Generation." *Chinese Education* 23, no. 2:87–88.

Liu Tangjiang. 1980. "Shanghai 'gaokao zhuangyuan' di menjing" (The Key to Shanghai's Entrance Examination Number One Scholar). *RMJY*, no. 11:60–62.

Liu Xinwu. 1981. "The Teacher." In *Prize-winning Stories from China, 1978–1979,* 3–26. Beijing: Foreign Language Press.

Lofstedt, Jan-Ingvar. 1984. "Educational Planning and Administration in China." *Comparative Education* 20, no. 1:57–71.

———. 1987. "Practice and Work in Chinese Education, Why, How and How Much?" Paper presented at the annual meeting of the American Education Research Association, Washington, D.C.

Louie, Kam. 1984. "Salvaging Confucian Education." *Comparative Education* 20, no. 1:27–38.

Lu Dzai Djung. 1934. *A History of Democratic Education in Modern China.* Shanghai: Commercial Press.

Lu Xun. 1980. *Lu Xun Selected Works.* Vol. 1. Beijing: Foreign Languages Press.

Luo Yizun and Shen Jiaxian. 1983. "Qing shaonian xuesheng lixiang he xingqu de diaocha yanjiu" (Investigation of the Ideals and Interests of Students). *JYYJ*, no. 8.

Ma Boxiang. 1983. "Nu xuesheng de tedian he shehui xinxi de yinxiang" (The Special Characteristics of Female Students and the Influence of Society and the Media). *SHJY*, no. 7–8:20–21.

MacFarquhar, Roderick. 1974. *The Origins of the Cultural Revolution.* Vol. 1,

Contradictions Among the People, 1956–1957. New York: Columbia University Press.

Mao Zedong. 1971. *Selected Readings from the Works of Mao Tsetung.* Peking: Foreign Language Press.

"Mao zhuxi zixue yingyu" (How Chairman Mao Studied English on His Own). 30 December 1981. *Shanghai waiguoyu xueyuan bao.*

Marcus, George, and Michael M. J. Fischer. 1986. *Anthropology as Cultural Critique.* Chicago: University of Chicago Press.

Martin, W. A. P. 1896. *A Cycle of Cathay.* New York: Fleming H. Revell.

———. 1918. "The Tungwen College." In H. B. Morse, *The International Relations of the Chinese Empire,* 3:471–78. New York: Longman, Green.

Metz, Mary. 1986. *Different by Design.* New York: Routledge and Kegan Paul.

Masemann, Vandra Lea. 1986. "Critical Ethnography in the Study of Comparative Education." In Philip Altbach and Gail Kelly, eds., *New Approaches to Comparative Education,* 11–25. Chicago: University of Chicago Press.

"Mianqiang xuesheng guozhong zedan, quanmian tigao jiaoyu zhiliang" (Lessen the Students Excessive Responsibility, Raise Overall Educational Quality). 1982. *RMJY,* no. 5:32–34.

"Middle and Primary Schools Re-open Classes and Make Revolution." 1968. *Current Background,* no. 846.

Milton, David, and Nancy Milton. 1976. *The Wind Will Not Subside: Years in Revolutionary China, 1964–1969.* New York: Pantheon.

"The Ministry of Education Decides to Run a Number of Key Elementary and Secondary Schools Across the Country." 1984. *Chinese Education* 17, no. 2:18–20.

Miyazaki, Ichisada. 1976. *China's Examination Hell: The Civil Service Examinations of Imperial China.* New York: Weatherhill.

Mok, Poon-kun. 1951. *The History and Development of the Teaching of English in China.* New York: Columbia University Press.

Morse, Hosea Ballou. 1918. *The International Relations of the Chinese Empire,* Vol. 3, *The Period of Subjection 1894–1911.* New York: Longman, Green.

Mossberg, Barbara Clarke. 1990. "Point of View." *Chronicle of Higher Education,* 30 May:A44.

Munro, Donald. 1977. *The Concept of Man in Contemporary Society.* Ann Arbor: University of Michigan Press.

"Muster Strength to Run a Number of Key Middle Schools with Success." 1984. *Chinese Education* 17, no. 2:46–49.

National Governors' Association. 1989. *America in Transition: The International Frontier.* Washington, D.C.: National Governors' Association.

A Nation at Risk. 1983. Washington, D.C.: National Commission on Excellence in Education.

Ni Jiaju. 1985. "Jiji kaizhan chengren waiyu jiaoyu, wei sihua, duozuo gongxian" (On Foreign Language Education for the Adult). *Waiguoyu*, no. 1:14–17.

Noah, Harold, and John Middleton. 1988. *China's Vocational and Technical Training*. Washington, D.C.: World Bank.

Noyes, H. V. 1904. "Education in Mission Schools." *Recorder 35*, no. 1:573–78.

Paine, Lynn. 1990. "The Teacher as Virtuoso: A Chinese Model for Teaching." *Teachers College Record 92*, no. 1:49–81.

Peake, Cyrus H. 1932. *Nationalism and Education in China*. New York: Columbia University Press.

Peirce, Browyn Norton. 1989. "Toward a Pedagogy of Possibility in the Teaching of English Internationally." *TESOL Quarterly 23*, no. 3:401.

Peng Chun Chang. 1923. *Education for Modernization in China: A Search for Criteria of Curriculum Construction in View of the Transition in National Life, with Special Reference to Secondary Education*. New York: Columbia University Teachers College.

Pepper, Suzanne. 1978. "Education and Revolution: The 'Chinese Model' Revised." *Asian Survey 18*, no. 9:847–90.

———. 1980. "Chinese Education after Mao: Two Steps Forward, Two Steps Back and Begin Again?" *China Quarterly 81*:1–65.

———. 1982. "China's Universities: New Experiments in Socialist Democracy and Administrative Reform—A Research Report." *Modern China 8*, no. 2:147–204.

———. 1984. *China's Universities: Post-Mao Enrollment Policies and Their Impact on the Structure of Secondary Education*. Ann Arbor: University of Michigan Press.

———. 1986. "Deng Xiaoping's Political and Economic Reforms and the Chinese Student Protests." *UFSI Reports 30*:1–15.

Pischel, Enrica Collotti. 1977. "The Teacher." In Dick Wilson, ed., *Mao Tse-tung in the Scales of History*, 144–73. Cambridge: Cambridge University Press.

Powell, Arthur G., Eleanor Farrar, and David K. Cohen. 1985. *The Shopping Mall High School*. Boston: Houghton Mifflin.

"Premier Zhou En-lai's Report on the Work of the Government to the First Session of the Second National Peoples Congress." 1959. *Peking Review*, 21 April:8–27.

Price, R. F. 1970. *Education in Communist China*. London: Routledge and Kegan Paul.

———. 1971. "English Teaching in China (Changes in Teaching Methods, 1960–1966)." *English Language 26*, no. 1:71–83.

———. 1977. *Marx and Education in Russia and China*. London: Croom Helm.

———. 1981. "China: A Problem of Information?" *Comparative Education Review 25*, no. 1:85–92.

————. 1984. "Labour and Education." *Comparative Education* 20, no. 1:81–91.

Punch, Maurice. 1986. *The Politics and Ethics of Fieldwork*. Beverly Hills, Calif.: Sage Publications.

Qian Handong. 1988. "Xiandaihua jiaoyu xuyao xiandaihua sixiang" ("Modernized Education Requires Modernized Thinking"). *Shanghai Education* 11:14–15.

Qian Xingbo. 1990. "Impact of TOEFL and EPT on English Teaching in China." *Beijing Review* 33, no. 29:39–40.

Qian Xuesen. 1983. "Culturology—Study of the Creation of Socialist Spiritual Wealth." *Social Sciences in China* 4, no. 1:17–26.

"Quanrizhi liunianzhi zhonggdian zhongxue yingyu jiaoxue dagang" (Six-Year Full-Time Key Middle School English Teaching Outline). 1982. *Zhong xiaoxue yingyu jiaoxue yu yanjiu*, no. 3:1–8.

Quanrizhi zhongxue yinyu jiaoxue dagang (Full-time Secondary School English Language Teaching Outline). 1987. Beijing: Peoples Press.

Rawski, Evelyn. 1979. *Education and Popular Literacy in Ch'ing China*. Ann Arbor: University of Michigan Press.

————. 1985. "Elementary Education in the Mission Enterprise." In Suzanne Barnett and John K. Fairbank, eds., *Christianity in China: Early Protestant Missionary Writings*, 135–52. Cambridge, Mass.: Harvard University Press.

Records, China Centenary Missionary Conference. 1907. Shanghai: Methodist Publishing House.

The Reorganization of Education in China. 1932. New York: League of Nations.

Reform of China's Educational Structure—Decision of the CCP Central Committee. 1985. Beijing: Foreign Languages Press.

Reid, William. 1987. "Institutions and Practices: Professional Education Reports and the Language of Reform." *Educational Researcher* 16, no. 8:10–15.

Renmin jiaoyu [RMJY] (People's Education).

Renmin ribao [RMRB] (People's Daily).

"Renzhen baohu xuesheng shili" (Earnestly Protect Student Eyesight). 1982. *RMJY*, no. 5:20.

"Renzhen xuexi, qieshi guanche dang di shier da jingshen" (Study Conscientiously, Earnestly Carry Out the Spirit of the Twelfth Party Congress). 1982. *RMJY*, no. 9:3–4.

"Report from the National Work Conference on Secondary School Foreign Language Teaching." 1983. 27 May–3 June.

"Resolution on Questions in Party History since 1949." 1981. *Beijing Review* 24, no. 27 (6 July): 10–39.

Robinson, Jean C. 1986. "Decentralization, Money, and Power: The Case of People-run Schools in China." *Comparative Education Review* 3, no. 1:73–88.

Rohlen, Thomas. 1983. *Japan's High Schools*. Berkeley and Los Angeles: University of California Press.

Rosaldo, Renanto. 1989. *Culture and Truth: The Remaking of Social Analysis.* Boston: Beacon Press.

Rosen, Stanley. 1982. "Obstacles to Educational Reform in China." *Modern China* 8, no. 1:3–40.

———. 1983. "Restoring Keypoint Secondary Schools in Post-Mao China: The Politics of Competition and Educational Quality 1978–1983." Paper presented for the SSRC Conference on Policy Implementation in Post-Mao China, Ohio State University.

———. 1984. "New Directions in Secondary Education." In Ruth Hayhoe, ed., *Contemporary Chinese Education*, 65–92. Armonk, N.Y.: Sharpe.

Ross, Heidi. 1991. "The Crisis in Chinese Secondary Schooling." In Irving Epstein, ed., *Chinese Education: Problems, Policies, and Prospects*, 66–108. New York: Garland.

———. 1992. "Foreign Languages as a Barometer for Chinese Modernization." In Ruth Hayhoe, ed., *Education and Modernization: The Chinese Experience*, 239–54. New York: Pergamon Press.

Rozman, Gilbert, ed. 1981. *The Modernization of China*. New York: Free Press.

"Ruhe kefu xuesheng zai yingyu xuexizhong di liangji fenhua" (How to Lessen Ability Gaps Between English Language Students). 1983. *RMJY*, no. 3:36–37.

Saari, Jon L. 1990. *Legacies of Childhood: Growing Up Chinese in a Time of Crisis, 1890–1920*. Cambridge, Mass.: Council on East Asian Studies, Harvard University.

Samoff, Joel. 1991. "Socialist Education?" *Comparative Education Review* 35, no. 1:1–22.

Schlesinger, Arthur, Jr. 1974. "The Missionary Enterprise: Theories of Imperialism." In John K. Fairbank, ed., *The Missionary Experience in China and America*, 336–73. Cambridge, Mass.: Harvard University Press.

Schram, Stuart. 1974. *Mao Tse-tung Unrehearsed*. Hammondsworth: Penguin Books.

———. 1975. *Chairman Mao Talks to the People*. New York: Pantheon.

Schwartz, Benjamin. 1964. *In Search of Wealth and Power: Yen Fu and the West*. New York: Harper and Row.

Scovel, Janene. 1982. "Curriculum Stability and Change: English Foreign Language Programs in Modern China." Ph.D. diss., University of Pittsburgh.

Seven Contemporary Women Writers. 1982. Beijing: Panda Books.

Sewall, Gilbert T. 1983. *Necessary Lessons: Decline and Renewal in American Schools*. New York: Free Press.

Seybolt, Peter J. 1973. *Revolutionary Education in China*. New York: New York Arts and Sciences Press.

Shan Xianjian. 1989. "Gengxian waiyu jiaoxue guannian, tigao ketang jiaoxue zhiliang" ("Renew Conceptions of Foreign Language Teaching, Improve the Quality of Classroom Teaching"). *Zhong xiaoxue waiyu jiaoxue,* no. 2:1–5.

Shandong Province Youth League Committee. 1982. *Gongqingtuan ganbu gongzuo shouce* (Youth League Cadre Handbook). Shandong Province: Shandong Peoples Publishers.

Shang Yudu. 1983. "Shisi sui shaonian tedian ji 'ying qingchun' jiaoyu" (The Special Characteristics of Fourteen Year Olds and Education for Adolescents). In *Shanghaishi zhongxue jiaoyu gongzuo jingyan xuanbian, 1981–1982,* 95–97. Shanghai: Shanghai Education Publishers.

Shanghai Educational Examination Center. 1988. *Shanghaishi gaokao yingyu shiti pingxi, 1985–1987* (An Analysis of Questions on the Shanghai English Language College Entrance Examinations, 1985–1987). Shanghai: Shanghai Foreign Language Education Press.

Shanghai Educational Examination Center. 1989. *Shanghaishi gaozhong huikao* (The Shanghai Senior Secondary School Competency Examination). Shanghai: East China Normal University Press.

"Shanghai's Jiaotong University Established Special Relations with Sixteen Key Middle Schools." 1984. *Chinese Education* 17, no. 2:44–45.

Shanghai jiaoyu [SHJY]. Shanghai Education.

Shanghai Jingan District Wanan Secondary School. 1988. "Kongzhi jiaoxue guocheng tigao yingyu jiaoxue zhiliang" (Control the Process of Education and Improve English Teaching). *Shanghai Education,* no. 7–8:19–20, 10.

"Shanghai People's Government Promotes Thirty-six Comrades to Special Teachers, Confers the Title of Model Homeroom Teacher on Thirty-two Comrades including Wan Lin, and the Title of Model Principal to Tai Rende." 1980. *SHJY,* no. 3:2–3.

Shanghai shifan daxue xuebao (Shanghai Teachers College Journal).

"Shanghai Society of Foreign Languages Discusses Teaching of Foreign Languages and Translation." 1961. *SCMP,* no. 2494:15–16.

Shanghai waiguoyu xueyuan bao (Shanghai Foreign Language Institute News).

Shanghai zhong xiaoxue yingyu jiaoxue (Shanghai Primary and Secondary School English Teaching).

"Shanghaishi de zhongxin xiaoxue shi zemyang kaizhan gongzuo de" (How Shanghai Municipality's Central Primary Schools Have Developed). 1982. *RMJY,* no. 5:35–38.

Shanghaishi gaokao yingyu shiti pingxi, 1985–1987 (An Analysis of the Shanghai English Entrance Examination, 1985–1987). 1988. Shanghai: Shanghai Foreign Language Education Press.

Shanghaishi jiaoyu tongji, 1934–1935. (Shanghai Education Statistics, 1934–1935). 1935. Shanghai: Shanghai Publishing.

Shanghaishi nianjian (Shanghai Yearbook). 1946. Shanghai: Commercial Press.

"Shanghaishi xiaoxiandui gongzuo dagang" (Shanghai Municipality Young Pioneers Work Outline). 1983. *SHJY*, no. 11:40–42, 45.

Shanghaishi zhong xiaoxue jiaoyu gongzuo jingyan xuanbian, 1980–1981 (A Collection of Shanghai Primary and Secondary School Educational Work Experiences). 1982. Shanghai: Shanghai Education Publishers.

Shanghaishi zhongxue jiaoyu gongzuo jingyan xuanbian, 1981–1982 (A Collection of Shanghai Secondary School Educational Work Experiences, 1981–1982). 1983. Shanghai: Shanghai Education Publishers.

Shen Baoqing. 1986. "An Investigation in Some Questions Concerning the Current Teaching of Foreign Languages in Institutions of Higher Education." *Chinese Education* 19, no. 1:117–25.

Shirk, Susan. 1979. "Educational Reform and Political Backlash: Recent Change in Chinese Educational Policy." *Comparative Education Review* 23, no. 2: 183–217.

———. 1982. *Competitive Comrades: Career Incentives and Student Strategies in China.* Berkeley and Los Angeles: University of California Press.

Shturman, Dora. 1988. *The Soviet Secondary School.* New York: Routledge.

Shulman, Lee S. 1986. "Those Who Understand: A Conception of Teacher Knowledge." *American Educator* 10, no. 1:8–15, 43–44.

Silsby, J. A. 1903. "Educational Department." *Recorder* 34, no. 1:35.

———. 1904. "Educational Department." *Recorder* 35, no. 9:473–77.

Sirotnik, Kenneth. 1983. "What You See Is What You Get—Consistency, Persistency, and Mediocrity in Classrooms." *Harvard Education Review* 35, no. 1:16–31.

Sites, C. M. Lacey. 1904. "Educational Psychology of the Chinese: A Study in Pedagogy." *Recorder* 35, no. 5:245–54.

Sizer, Theodore R. 1984. *Horace's Compromise: The Dilemma of the American High School.* Boston: Houghton Mifflin.

"Studies of the Only Child." 1988. *Beijing Review,* 17–23 October: 31, 42, 112.

Song Chongjin. 1985. "Guanyu zhongxuesheng qingchunqi jiaoyu de diaocha" ("An Investigation of Secondary School Student Sex Education"). In *Jiaoyu Keyan Lunwenxuan,* 39–46. Shanghai: Changning District Education Bureau Office of Research.

Spence, Jonathan D. 1969. *To Change China: Western Advisers in China, 1620–1960.* Boston: Little, Brown.

———. 1990. *The Search for Modern China.* New York: Norton.

Spindler, George. 1982. *Doing the Ethnography of Schooling: Educational Anthropology in Action.* New York: Holt, Reinhart and Winston.

Spindler, George, and Louise Spindler. 1987. *Interpretive Ethnography of Education.* Hillsdale, N.J.: Lawrence Erlbaum Associates.

Starr, S. Frederick. 1979. "America's School: The Frontier of Language Learning." *ADFL Bulletin* 11, no. 1:38–42.

Strength through Wisdom: A Critique of U.S. Capability. 1979. Washington, D.C.: President's Commission on Foreign Language and International Studies.

Su Ching. 1985. *Qing ji tong wenguan ji qi shi sheng* (The Late-Qing Interpreter's College and its teachers and students). Taipei: Shih-wei.

Su Qishu. 1989. "Tigao xuesheng xuexi eyu jijixing de jidian tihui" (Practical Ways to Raise Student Motivation to Study Russian). *Zhong xiaoxue waiyu jiaoxue,* no. 6:8–9.

Sui, Helen, and Zelda Stern, eds. 1983. *Mao's Harvest: Voices from China's New Generation.* New York: Oxford University Press.

Sun Yingkang, et al. 1981. *Zhong xiao xuesheng xinli tedian yu jiaoyu* (Education and the Psychology of Primary and Secondary School Students). Henan Province: Henan Peoples Publishers.

Survey of the China Mainland Press. [SCMP]

Suttmeier, Richard. 1980. *Science, Technology, and China's Drive for Modernization.* Stanford: Hoover Institution Press.

"Syllabus of a Girl's Boarding School." 1903. *Recorder* 34, no. 4:195–97.

"Tan jinnian de yingyu shiti" (A Discussion of English Questions on the 1983 Entrance Examination). 1983. *RMJY,* no. 8:27–28.

Tang Caibao. 1983. "Jindai shanghai jiaoyu de xingqi he fazhan" (The Rise and Development of Shanghai's Education in Modern Times). *Shanghai shifan daxue xuebao,* no. 3:132–37.

"Teaching Students Practical Skills." 1988. *Beijing Review* 31, no. 30:40.

Teng, Ssu-yu, and John K. Fairbank. 1967. *China's Response to the West: A Documentary Survey, 1839–1923.* New York: Atheneum.

Thomson, James C., Jr. 1969. *While China Faced West: American Reformers in Nationalist China, 1928–1937.* Cambridge, Mass.: Harvard University Press.

"Tiyu you zuoye mei tian yi ke zhong" (Fifteen Minutes Daily Physical Education Homework). 1982. *SHJY,* no. 7–8:78.

Tobin, Joseph J., David Y. H. Wu, and Dana H. Davidson. 1989. *Preschool in Three Cultures: Japan, China, and the United States.* New Haven: Yale University Press.

Tong Nian, Yue Ruixiang, and Yang Xinyi. 1981. "Dangqian zhongxuesheng sixiang qingkuang de diaocha" (An Investigation of the Ideological Situation of Current Middle School Students). *JYYJ,* no. 4:36–40.

Touraine, Alain. 1991. "The Process of Democratization in Eastern European Countries." In *Rackham Reports.* Ann Arbor: The University of Michigan.

Tsang, Chiu-sam. 1933. *Nationalism in School Education in China.* Hong Kong: South China Morning Post.

Tu Huaicheng. 1982. "Zai gaokao pingjuan de rizi li" (When I was grading the Entrance Examination). *RMJY,* no. 11–12:64–66, 54–57.

Twiss, George Ransom. 1925. *Science and Education in China (A Survey of the*

Present Status and a Program for Progressive Improvement). Shanghai: Commercial Press.

Tyack, David. 1976. "Ways of Seeing." *Harvard Education Review* 46, no. 3: 355–89.

Unger, Jonathon. 1982. *Education under Mao: Class and Competition in Canton Schools, 1960–1980.* New York: Columbia University Press.

Waiguoyu (Foreign Languages).

Waiyu jiaoxue (Foreign Language Teaching).

"Waiyu jiaoyu qinian guize gangyao" (Outline for the Foreign Language Education Seven Year Program). 1984. In *Almanac,* p. 371. Shanghai: China Encyclopedia Publishing House.

Wakeman, Frederick. 1991. "Social Control and Civic Culture in Republican Shanghai." Paper delivered at the Shanghai Seminar, Institute of East Asian Studies, Berkeley.

Waller, Andrew G. 1977. "Chang Ch'un-ch'iao and Shanghai's January Revolution." *Michigan Papers in Chinese Studies,* no. 32. Ann Arbor: University of Michigan Center for Chinese Studies.

Wang Anyi. 1988. *A Lapse of Time.* San Francisco: China Books and Periodicals.

Wang Jianqing. 1981. *Zhili, rencai, yu jiaoxue* (Intelligence, Talent, and Education). Hefei: Anhui Peoples Publishers.

Wang Peidong. 1981. "Daxuesheng fazhan zhili yu peiyang nengli di wenti" (Problems of Developing the Intelligence and Training the Ability of College Students). *JYYJ,* no. 3:27.

Wang, Shih-Chieh. 1935. *Education in China.* Shanghai: China United Press.

Wang Zhenqiu. 1982. "Xiuding zhongxue eyu keben zhong de jige wenti" (Some Problems in Revising Secondary School Russian Language Textbooks). *RMJY,* no. 7: 52–54.

Wang Zongyan. 1982. "Guanyu zhongguo de yingyu jiaoxue he yanjiu" (Concerning English Teaching and Research in China: A Cursory Overview of Achievements in the Field Since 1949). *Language Learning and Communication* 1, no. 1:1–6.

Wei, Betty Peh-T'i. 1987. *Shanghai Crucible of Modern China.* New York: Oxford University Press.

Wenhui ribao [WHRB] (Wenhui Daily).

Wexler, Philip. 1987. *Social Analysis of Education: After the New Sociology.* New York: Routledge and Kegan Paul.

White, Gordon. 1976. *The Politics of Class and Class Origin: The Case of the Cultural Revolution.* Canberra: Australian National University.

———. 1981. *The Political Role of Teachers in Contemporary China.* Armonk, N.Y.: Sharpe.

"Why Is English Taught in Middle Schools?" 1961. *SCMP,* no. 2452:13–14.

Whyte, Martin King. 1974. *Small Groups and Political Rituals in China*. Berkeley and Los Angeles: University of California Press.

Widner, Eric. 1976. *The Russian Ecclesiastical Mission in Peking during the Eighteenth Century*. Cambridge, Mass.: Harvard University Press.

Willis, Paul. 1977. *Learning to Labor: How Working Class Kids Get Working Class Jobs*. Westmead: Saxon House.

Wilson, Dick. 1977. *Mao Tse-tung in the Scales of History*. Cambridge: Cambridge University Press.

Winn, Marie. 1983. *Children without Childhood*. New York: Pantheon.

Wison, Wilbur F. 1900. "Personal Experience Teaching English." *Recorder* 31, no. 11:573–78.

"Women tigao jiaoxue zhiliang de jiben jingyan" (Our Basic Experiences in Raising the Quality of Instruction). 1980. *RMJY*, no. 2:15.

"Women youle zhongxuesheng sixiang jiaoyu" (Our Middle School Students' Ideological Training). 1983. *SHJY*, no. 11:5.

Woodside, Alexander. 1983. "Some Mid-Qing Theorists of Popular Schools." *Modern China* 9, no. 1:3–36.

World Bank. 1981. *China: Socialist Economic Development. Annex G: Education Sector*. Washington, D.C.: World Bank.

———. 1985. *China: Issues and Prospects in Education. Annex I: Long-Term Development Issues and Options*. Washington, D.C.: World Bank.

Wright, Mary C. 1966. *The Last Stand of Chinese Conservatism: The T'ung-Chih Restoration, 1862–1874*. New York: Atheneum.

"Writers Discuss Cultural Pollution." 1983. *Beijing Review* 26, no. 50:10–11.

Wu Jing-yu. 1983. "Eclecticism: A Chinese Viewpoint." *Language Learning and Communication* 2, no. 3:287–93.

Wu Tao-ts'un. 1962. "On Careful Reading and Cursory Reading in Learning English." *SCMP*, no. 2779.

Wu Yuqian. 1982. "Zhongshi yingyu langdu xunlian" (Emphasize Reading Aloud in English). *SHJY*, no. 7–8:68.

Xinhua News Bulletin. New China News Agency, Hong Kong.

Xu Xun. 1983. "Gua jichu, gua chuzhong, tigao waiyu jiaoxue zhiliang" (Focus on Fundamentals in Junior Middle School and Improve the Quality of Foreign Language Teaching). *SHJY*, no. 7–8:64–65.

Xue Muqiao. 1981. *China's Socialist Economy*. Beijing: Foreign Language Press.

Yang Baolin. 1980. "Yingyu de beike he jiaoxue" (How to Prepare and Teach English). *SHJY*, no. 6:22–24.

Yang Dongping, 1990. "Set Up an Educational Program That Is Democratic, Centers around Man, and Is Alive." *Chinese Education* 23, no. 2:8.

Yang Jiang. 1982. *Cadre School Life, Six Chapters*. Hong Kong: Joint Publishing.

"Yanjiu nu zhong jiaoyu de tedian" (Research on the Special Characteristics of Middle School Girls' Education). 1983. In *Shanghaishi zhongxue jiaoyu gong-*

zuo jingyan xuanbian (A Collection of Shanghai Secondary School Educational Work Experiences). Shanghai: Shanghai Education Publishers.

Ye Chaoyang. 1983. "Jianjue shazhu 'huilu' feng" (Resolutely Put a Stop to the 'Twice-Baked' Tendency). *RMJY,* no. 6:25–26.

Ye Xiaoqing. 1983. "Chinese Traditional Culture and the Influx of Western Learning." *Social Sciences in China* 4, no. 4:39–68.

Yeh, Wen-hsin. 1990. *The Alienated Academy: Culture and Politics in Republican China, 1919–1937.* Cambridge, Mass.: Council on East Asian Studies, Harvard University.

Yen Renting. 1987. "Foreign Language Teaching in China: Problems and Perspectives." *Canadian and International Education* 16, no. 1:53.

"Yi jiaoxue wei zhongxin, de, zhi, ti quanmian fazhan" (Make Teaching the Priority for All-round Development). 1980. *RMJY,* no. 1:17–20.

Ying Juru. "You waiguo re de fancha" ("In Contrast to the Foreign Language Craze"). 1988. *Shanghai Education,* no. 11:28–29.

You Zhenglun. 1982. *Banzhuren gongzuo* (The Work of the Homeroom Teacher). Chengdu: Sichuan Peoples Publishers.

Young, Iris Marion. 1987. "Impartiality and the Civic Public: Some Implications of Feminist Critiques of Moral and Political Theory." In Seyla Benhabib and Drucilla Cornell, eds. *Feminism as Critique: On the Politics of Gender.* Minneapolis: University of Minnesota Press.

Yue Ping. 1983. "Preventing Ideological Pollution." *Beijing Review,* 21 November:26, 47, 22.

"Zai zhongxuesheng zhong pingxuan sanhao xuesheng de banfa" (Method for Selecting Three Merit Middle School Students). 1982. *RMJY,* no. 6:36–37.

Zeng Ji. 1981. "Zhongxue nan nu sheng de chayi yu jiaoyu" (Education and the Differences Between Middle School Female and Male Students). *JYYJ,* 12: 43–44.

Zhang Heru. 1983. "Guanyu zhong xiaoxue yuyan jiaoxue de jianjie wenti" (Problems Concerning Continuity in Primary and Secondary School Language Teaching). In *Shanghaishi jiaoyu gongzuo jingyan xuanbian, 1981–1982.* Shanghai: Shanghai Education Publishers.

Zhang Jianzhong and Zhou Jianying, et al. 1982. "Chuzhong yingyu jiaoxue shixian yanjiu" (Research in Experimental Junior Middle School English Teaching). *Zhong xiaoxue waiguoyu jiaoxue,* 2:6–10.

Zhang Luxian. 1980. "Guanche chuanmian fazhan fangzhen tigao jiaoyu zhiliang" (Carry Out the Policy of All-round Development, Improve Educational Quality). *RMJY,* no. 9–10:3–9.

Zhang Min. 1989. "Bangzhu xuesheng kefu xinli zhangai, xuehao waiyu de jidian zuofa" ("Study methods to Help Students Counter Their Psychological Obstacles"). *Zhong xiaoxue waiyu jiaoxue,* no. 2:7.

Zhang Weijun. 1983. "Fandu zai zhongxue yingyu jiaoxue zhong de diwei he zuoyong" (The Role and Position of Extensive Reading in English Language Teaching in Middle Schools). *Shanghai shifan daxue xuebao,* no. 4:144–46.

Zhang Wensong. 1983. "Cong shiji chufa, jiji shenzhong di gaige zhong xiaoxue jiaoyu" (Start with the facts and vigorously yet prudently reform primary and secondary school education). *SHJY,* no. 5:2–3.

Zhang Yourong. 1983. "Tushuguan gongzuo zhong de shu yu ren de bianzheng guanxi" (The Dialectical Relationship between Books and People in Library Work). In *Shanghaishi zhongxue jiaoyu gongzuo jingyan xuanbian, 1981–1982,* 119–22. Shanghai: Shanghai Education Publishers.

Zhang Yudu. 1982. "Banhao chuer xuesheng 'ying qing yun' jiaoyu" (Run Well Social Education for Junior Middle School Two Students). *SHJY,* no. 4:10–11.

———. 1983. "Shisi sui shaonian tedian ji 'ying qingchun' jiaoyu" (The Special Characteristics of Fourteen Year Olds and Education for Adolescents). In *Shanghaishi zhongxue jiaoyu gongzuo jingyan xuanbian, 1981–1982, 95–97.* Shanghai: Shanghai Education Publishers.

Zhang Zhidong. 1898. *Quan xue pian* (Exhortation to Study).

Zheng Dengyun. 1979. "Ping jingshi tongwen guan" (A Commentary on the Capital City Foreign Language Institute). *Shanghai shifan daxue xuebao,* no. 2:50–53.

Zhong xiaoxue waiyu jiaoxue (Secondary and Primary School Foreign Language Teaching).

Zhong xiaoxue yingyu jiaoxue yu yanjiu (Secondary and Primary School English Language Teaching and Research).

"Zhong zai kaocha jiben qiao" (Emphasize Basic Skills). 1980. *RMJY,* no. 8: 39–40.

Zhongguo gaodeng xuexiao jianjie (An Introduction to China's Tertiary Schools). 1982. Beijing: Educational Studies Press.

"Zhongguo gongchandang zhongyang weiyuanhui guanyu jianguo yilai dang de ruogan lishi wenti di jueyi" (Resolution on Questions in Party History Since 1949). 1984. In *Almanac,* 1–23. Shanghai: China Encyclopedia Publishing House.

Zhongguo jiaoyu bao (China Education News).

Zhongguo jiaoyu chengjiu 1949–1983 [Achievement] (Achievement of Education in China Statistics 1949–1983). 1984. Beijing: Peoples Education Press.

Zhongguo jiaoyu nianjian, 1949–1981 [Almanac] (China Education Almanac, 1949–1981). 1984. Shanghai: China Encyclopedia Publishing House.

Zhongguo jiaoyu xuehui and Zhongyang jiaoyu kexue yanjiusuo. 1984. *Sange mianxiang* (Facing Three Issues). Beijing: Educational Science Press.

Zhongguo qingnian (China Youth).

Zhongguo qingnian bao (China Youth News).

Zhonghua renmin gongheguo jiaoyu dashiji 1949–1982 [Chronology] (A Chronology of Education in the PRC 1949–1982). 1983. Beijing: Educational Studies Press.

"Zhongshi jiejue xuesheng zidan guozhong wenti" (Make Solving the Problem of Overburdened Students a Priority). 1984. In *Almanac*, p. 543. Shanghai: China Encyclopedia Publishing House.

Zhongxue xiaozhang jingyan tan (On the Experiences of Secondary School Principals). 1982. Shanghai: Shanghai Education Publishers.

Zhou Enlai. 1956. *Report on the Question of Intellectuals*. Peking: Foreign Language Press.

Zhou Jin. 1982. "Eclectic English Teaching Practiced." *China Daily*, 17 November:5.

Zhu Qixin. 1982. "Luelun zhong xiaoxue yingyu jiaoxue zhong jige guanxi de chuli wenti" (A Brief Discussion of a Few Problems of Management of Secondary and Primary School English Teaching). *Shanghai zhong xiaoxue yingyu jiaoxue*, no. 1:1–9.

Zhu Yulong. 1980. "Tantan zhong xiaoxue waiyu jiaoyu ji yuzhong xuanze" (Choosing Appropriate Foreign Languages for Primary and Secondary School Instruction). *SHJY*, no. 6:24.

Zhuo Renai. 1982. "Waiyu jiaoshi ye yao xue dian jiaoyuxue he xinlixue" (Foreign Language Teachers Should Also Study Education and Psychology). In *Shanghaishi zhong xiaoxue waiyu jiaoxue*, pp. 17–20, 42.

Zuijin sanshiwu nian zhi zhongguo jiaoyu (Education in China in the Last Thirty-five Years). 1931. Shanghai: Commercial Press.

Zunxun jiaoxue guilu tigao jiaoxue zhiliang (Follow Educational Laws to Improve Educational Quality). 1980. Beijing: Peoples Education Press.

"Zuo hao ying pi gaozhong biyesheng de sixiang zhengzhi gongzuo" (Carry Out Well Ideological and Political Work with This Year's High School Graduates). 1980. *RMJY*, no. 4:11.

Index

Ability: defined, 111–12; assessment of, 138–41, 162–63, 174; gender, 181–85. *See also* Talent

Administration. *See* Lu Xun Language School

Adolescence: boarding school life, 131–37, 144, 149; sexuality, 146–47; characteristics of, 151–52, 155, 199–200, 212; gender, 185; as symbol of nation, 199

Allen, Young, J., 25

Anti-Rightist Campaign, 45

Autonomy, 94–95

Chen Yi, 43, 46, 59

College attendance rates, 4n, 178, 206–7

Competition: among teachers, 87–89, 198; among homerooms, 148–49, 169; among science and humanities students, 191

Confucian education legacy: role and status of teachers, 72, 75; teaching practice, 107–8, 128

Creativity: and teaching, 9, 120–21, 125–27, 204; influence on moral education, 128, 190–91; as characteristic of "modernized thinking," 129

Critical ethnography, 6, 10–11, 13

Cultural Revolution: influence on foreign-language education, 37, 38, 56, 58–60; criticism of, 38–39, 54–55, 59, 74, 75, 103, 199; impact on teachers' views of education and politics, 60–63, 83, 102; influence on students, 64, 200; and gender, 184; mentioned, 55, 127, 155–56, 163, 179, 189, 194, 210

Culture: as dialogue, 5–6; as tool for making others, 14

Democracy: modernization defined as, 212–13; challenge of, 214–15

Deng Xiaoping: on "three directions," 8, 197; on key schools, 64–65

Efficiency: consequences for education, 184, 196–97; and commodity consciousness, 197, 203

Examinations, college entrance: foreign-language requirements, 38, 50, 98; reinstatement after Cultural Revolution, 60, 63; criticism of, 111, 113–14, 124–25, 176–77, 202; social function of, 123–24; gender, 184; reform of, 202–3; contents, 247–52

Foreign-language secondary schools: curriculum, 47–49, 51–53; establishment, 49–51, 217–20; administration, 51, 71; reinstatement after Cultural Revolution, 67, 221–26

"Four modernizations," 37–38, 64

Gender: personality and achievement, 136, 162, 164, 181–85; the "two jiao," 158; academic, occupational mobility, 179–82, 207–10

Government school foreign-language training: curriculum and teaching methods, 32–34; Nationalist Party foreign-language policy, 34–35

Great Leap Forward, 45, 49, 50

Homeroom collective, 142–44, 148. *See also* Adolescence

Humanities, 178–79. *See also* Competition

Hu Yaobang, 40, 151